Early Childhood Jewish Education

Also available from Bloomsbury

Does Religious Education Work?, James C. Conroy
A Hermeneutics of Religious Education, David Aldridge
Identity, Culture and Belonging, Tony Eaude
Children, Religion and the Ethics of Influence, John Tillson
Is Religious Education Possible?, Michael Hand
Islamic Education in Britain, Alison Scott-Baumann and
Sariya Cheruvallil-Contractor
A Theory of Catholic Education, Sean Whittle
Reimagining Liberal Education, Hanan Alexander

Early Childhood Jewish Education

Multicultural, Gender, and Constructivist Perspectives

Edited by
Sigal Achituv, Meir Muller,
Shelley T. Alexander, and
Hanan A. Alexander

BLOOMSBURY ACADEMIC
LONDON • NEW YORK • OXFORD • NEW DELHI • SYDNEY

BLOOMSBURY ACADEMIC
Bloomsbury Publishing Plc
50 Bedford Square, London, WC1B 3DP, UK
1385 Broadway, New York, NY 10018, USA
29 Earlsfort Terrace, Dublin 2, Ireland

BLOOMSBURY, BLOOMSBURY ACADEMIC and the Diana logo are
trademarks of Bloomsbury Publishing Plc

First published in Great Britain 2023
Paperback edition published 2024

Copyright © Sigal Achituv, Meir Muller, Shelley T. Alexander, and
Hanan A. Alexander, 2023

Sigal Achituv, Meir Muller, Shelley T. Alexander, and Hanan A. Alexander have
asserted their right under the Copyright, Designs and Patents Act, 1988, to be
identified as Editors of this work.

Cover image © tovfla / Getty Images

All rights reserved. No part of this publication may be reproduced or transmitted in
any form or by any means, electronic or mechanical, including photocopying,
recording, or any information storage or retrieval system, without prior
permission in writing from the publishers.

Bloomsbury Publishing Plc does not have any control over, or responsibility for, any
third-party websites referred to or in this book. All internet addresses given in this
book were correct at the time of going to press. The author and publisher regret any
inconvenience caused if addresses have changed or sites have ceased to exist, but
can accept no responsibility for any such changes.

A catalogue record for this book is available from the British Library.

Library of Congress Cataloging-in-Publication Data

Names: Achituv, Sigal, editor. | Muller, Meir, editor. | Alexander, Shelley
T., editor. | Alexander, Hanan A., 1953-editor.
Title: Early childhood Jewish education : multicultural, gender, and
constructivist perspectives / edited by Sigal Achituv, Meir Muller,
Shelley T. Alexander, and Hanan A. Alexander.
Description: London ; New York : Bloomsbury Academic, 2023. |
Includes bibliographical references and index.
Identifiers: LCCN 2022039540 (print) | LCCN 2022039541 (ebook) |
ISBN 9781350131057 (hardback) | ISBN 9781350227026 (paperback) |
ISBN 9781350131064 (adobe pdf) | ISBN 9781350131071 (epub)
Subjects: LCSH: Jewish religious education of preschool children. |
Early childhood education–Israel.
Classification: LCC BM103 .E27 2023 (print) |
LCC BM103 (ebook) | DDC 296.6/8083–dc23/eng/20221004
LC record available at https://lccn.loc.gov/2022039540
LC ebook record available at https://lccn.loc.gov/2022039541

ISBN: HB: 978-1-3501-3105-7
PB: 978-1-3502-2702-6
ePDF: 978-1-3501-3106-4
eBook: 978-1-3501-3107-1

Typeset by Newgen KnowledgeWorks Pvt. Ltd., Chennai, India

To find out more about our authors and books visit www.bloomsbury.com
and sign up for our newsletters.

To the memory of Chaya Rosenfeld Gorsetman (1947–2021), whose life embodied the Talmudic saying, "The world only exists because of the breath of young children" (Shabbat 119b). She was a valued member of and contributor to this collaborative project, who passed away before its completion. Chaya's professional life was dedicated to teaching and mentoring early childhood Jewish educators and the students they serve. Her memory inspires us to continue her legacy of moving our field forward in the areas of multiculturalism, gender awareness, and constructivism.

Contents

List of Figures	ix
List of Tables	x
Foreword	xi
Hanan A. Alexander	
Introduction: Capturing a Mosaic of the Field	1
Sigal Achituv, Meir Muller, and Shelley T. Alexander	

Part 1   Setting the Scene

1	The History and Current Status of Early Childhood Jewish Education in Israel	15
	David L. Brody, Shira Ackerman Simchovitch, and Shulamit Hoshen Manzura	
2	Early Childhood Jewish Education in the United States	29
	Ilene Vogelstein, Roberta Louis Goodman, and Shelley T. Alexander	
3	The Current State of Research and Writing about Early Childhood Jewish Education	45
	David L. Brody and Howard Deitcher	

Part 2   Three Contemporary Critical Lenses

4	From the Melting Pot, to the Salad Bowl, to the Seder Plate: Moving beyond Multiculturalism in Early Childhood Jewish Education	69
	Ilana Dvorin Friedman and Meir Muller	
5	Educating toward Gender Awareness, Feminism, and Cultural Sensitivity in Early Childhood Jewish Education Teacher Preparation	83
	Sharon Kaplan-Berkley and Haggith Gor Ziv	
6	Constructivism in Early Childhood Jewish Education	99
	Meir Muller, Sigal Achituv, and Chaya Gorsetman	

Part 3 Core Jewish Subjects through the Three Contemporary Critical Lenses

7   Teaching the Bible in Early Childhood Jewish Education   115
    Sigal Achituv
8   Strengthening Jewish-Israeli Identity and Promoting a Common
    Cultural Canon through Children's Literature: The Experience of
    Sifriyat Pijama   129
    Sylvia Kamowitz-Hareven
9   Holidays and Ceremonies in Israeli Early Childhood Jewish Education   147
    Shulamit Hoshen Manzura
10 Language-Conducive Strategies in Young Learners' Constructivist
    Hebrew Classrooms   161
    Margalit Kavenstock and Mila Schwartz
11 Enhancing Spiritual Awareness and Development in Early Childhood
    Jewish Settings   177
    Michael Shire and Deborah Schein

Part 4 Continuing the Work

12 Leadership in Early Childhood Jewish Education in the United States   193
    Lyndall Miller

Conclusion   207
    Sigal Achituv, Meir Muller, and Shelley T. Alexander

Glossary   211
Notes on Contributors   215
Index   219

Figures

3.1	Document by national context	51
8.1	Satisfaction with the program	138
8.2	Satisfaction with the books	139
8.3	Other book-related classroom activities	140
8.4	Perceived program impact—teachers	141
8.5	Perceived program impact—parents	141
8.6	Changes in home reading practices	142
10.1	Example of creating comics	170

Tables

1.1	Recommended Adult-to-Child Ratios and Number of Children per Individual EC Birth–3 Facility	22
3.1	Definitions of ECJE Database Genres	47
3.2	Definitions of ECJE Database Topics	47
3.3	Number of Documents in ECJE Database by Theme and Subtheme	49
4.1	Strategies and Examples of the Seder Plate Model	74
8.1	Sampling of Sifriyat Pijama Books	133
12.1	Comparison of Literature and Interview Leadership Capacities	202

Foreword
Hanan A. Alexander

The Jewish people is heir to an ancient way of life, but research in Jewish education—the transmission and transformation of that life across the generations—is a relatively young field of academic inquiry. It sits at the intersection of educational research and Jewish studies, and it overlaps with a number of adjacent scholarly disciplines, including religious education, religious studies, Israel studies, and more. Like other areas of educational research, it bridges a divide between scientific examination of relevant evidence, on the one hand, and a professional field of policy and practice, on the other, with an aim, among others, to improve the quality of how Jewish communities around the world transmit and transform their religious, cultural, national, linguistic, literary, and other heritages across the generations. It goes without saying that this process begins at the earliest stages of life when children are first initiated into the languages and customs of the families and communities into which they are born. Indeed, participation in Jewish preschool programs in Israel and across the world accounts for a significant portion of youngsters enrolled in any type of Jewish education whatsoever, formal or informal; and those who staff these programs constitute a vital subgroup of the worldwide guild of Jewish educators. Yet, as the emerging field of Jewish educational studies began to apply the methods and insights of modern educational scholarship to the demands of learning and teaching the Jewish heritage during the early decades of the past century, research in early Jewish education lagged woefully behind.

To address this lacuna, in 2010, the Center for Jewish and Democratic Education at the University of Haifa established a research group dealing with Jewish education in the early years in collaboration with the Van Leer Jerusalem Institute. Like other Van Leer research groups, the project was designed to bring together senior, midcareer, and beginning researchers in the field in order to highlight the most recent research on a topic of concern to the wider Jewish and general public in Israel and abroad. Known as the International Research Group on Jewish Education in the Early Years, it was clear from the outset that this initiative filled an important niche in the field. As word got out of the Center's intentions to establish such a group, key actors in Israel and the United States who were active in the field of early childhood Jewish education clamored to join; and twelve years down the line the group is still extraordinarily active and productive, sufficiently so to bring together this groundbreaking volume of research in early Jewish education.

The group had three primary goals. First, we wanted to convene a community of scholars with a primary interest in early Jewish education. This included doctoral students at all stages of their intellectual development, early and midcareer researchers with positions in institutions of higher learning or educational policy and practice, and leaders of programs for preparing early childhood Jewish educators. The number of such individuals is not large, and most were found in either Israel or the United States. It was, therefore, decided to focus on these two Jewish communities, which, in all events, are the largest in the world.

The second goal of the group was to redefine the field of early Jewish education in the minds of the community that we had convened as a field of *scholarship*, not only practice. Many of the participants served as leaders of early Jewish education programs. We needed to shift their attention from the immediate needs of educational policy and practice to more long-term questions about what it might mean to create a body of theoretical and empirical knowledge upon which to base that policy and practice. To accomplish this second goal, it was necessary to cultivate and refine the research skills and capacities of those who had joined the group.

This was our third goal. Although there is an established field of research in early childhood education, the fact that the scholarly focus on Jewish education in the early years is new made this third goal especially challenging. There were few senior scholars in the field to mentor a new generation of researchers. Many of those in the group constituted the first generation of researchers in the field. Hence, it was necessary to learn from one another and to grow together as a community of scholars. For this reason, among others, the group took on an extraordinarily collaborative tone. Rather than the sort of competition that is sometimes found among researchers in other academic disciplines, members of this group sought to support, learn from, and teach one another as they grew together to become the founding generation of scholars in this important subfield of Jewish educational research.

The group began by presenting their own work to one another and subjecting that work to commentary and critique. This led to a research workshop in Israel in 2011 that culminated in a special issue of the *Journal of Jewish Education* comprised primarily of the fruits of these deliberations. This was followed by a joint research project dealing with inclusion in early Jewish education, the findings of which were presented at a number of academic conferences and eventually published in a leading peer-reviewed journal of early childhood education. This book represents the products of the natural next stage of the group's development and, in turn, of research in early childhood Jewish education—a volume defining the current state of knowledge in the field.

This is an extraordinarily important accomplishment not only for research in early Jewish education but also for early education in a wide variety of contexts. The book should be of interest to scholars, policy makers, and practitioners in diverse fields of affiliation-oriented early education. In addition to Jewish education, this includes religious education in a variety of denominations and faiths; cultural, national, and ethnic education associated with numerous identities; language education both for communities that constitute a majority of the societies in which they reside and for those that constitute a minority; humanistic, democratic, and pluralistic education; and more.

This relevance to such a wide audience is tied to the fact that, in accordance with the makeup of the group, the book considers early childhood education from the perspectives of both Israeli and American Jewish experiences. Historically, Jewish identity has combined aspects associated with nationality, politics, and culture, on the one hand, with those related to religion, faith, and tradition, on the other. Although Jewish life in both Israel and the United States engages each of these dimensions of Jewish identity, the Israeli Jewish experience is grounded first in the power structures of a modern nation-state, whereas American Judaism is primarily conceived in terms of religion. Hence, the book considers challenges of early education in Israel's mandatory, state-funded system, which initiates into political and cultural as well as religious identity. It also considers early education in the loose network of voluntary and independently sponsored American programs, which focus primarily on religious affiliation.

These national, cultural, and religious affiliations are understood differently in each context. In Israel, where Jewish identity is tied to citizenship in a Jewish state as envisioned by the Zionist movement, there are many political ideologies—from left-leaning to right-leaning Zionism and even non- or anti-Zionism. Israeli religion, however, tends to be viewed from an Orthodox perspective. One either *is* or *is not* religious, where being "religious" entails a commitment to the observance of Orthodox interpretations of Jewish law. If one is not religious, then one is thought to be secular, which often implies that one embraces a cultural humanistic interpretation of Jewish identity. To be sure, there is a growing population of so-called traditional Jews in Israel, many of whom hail from Mizrachi (North Africa and Middle Eastern Jewish) backgrounds, whose attitude toward Jewish tradition is less dichotomous than that of their colleagues of Ashkenazi (Central and Eastern European Jewish) descent. That said, like their secular counterparts, traditional Jews are not strictly observant of Jewish law. However, the traditions that they do practice are thought to be Orthodox, albeit as interpreted by Mizrachi, not Ashkenazi, rabbis. In the American Jewish context, on the other hand, where political commitments relate mostly to issues shared with other Americans, Jew and non-Jew alike, religion is conceived from a denominational viewpoint, including Reform, Reconstructionist, and Conservative, in addition to Orthodox.

This book brings three key research themes to bear on early childhood Jewish education: multiculturalism, gender, and constructivism. Each of these themes challenges prevailing misconceptions about education in, from, or about a religious or cultural tradition, especially in the early years. First, whereas religious and cultural traditions are often presented as uniform or monolithic, the multicultural perspective understands them to be diverse and plural. Not only are there many cultures and traditions within one society, such as Israel or the United States, but there are also many varieties of customs and interpretations within particular faiths, nations, or ethnicities.

Second, Jewish religion and culture are often thought to have clearly defined and unalterable gender roles, in which the job of the early childhood educator is considered to be a female occupation. Viewing early Jewish education through the lens of gender allows us to reassess this assumption by reconceiving the roles of women and men not only in the education of young children but also within Jewish life more generally. This is an especially important task, given that gender roles are changing dramatically in today's world and will continue to do so in the years ahead.

Finally, if religions or cultures are thought to be uniform or monolithic, with clearly defined and inflexible gender roles, it is commonly believed that the task of education is to transmit those religions, cultures, and roles, unaltered, across the generations. According to this account, learners are expected to receive the heritage of their ancestors passively, as a form of what literary scholars have sometimes called "mimesis" or imitation. A constructivist perspective, on the other hand, suggests that genuine learning involves active participation on the part of youngsters, who co-construct the knowledge and experience that is handed down from the past in order to reshape it to meet the needs of new generations of affiliates.

I would be remiss if I did not acknowledge the dedication and professionalism of the editorial team of this volume without which it would not have seen the light of day: Chief Editor Dr. Sigal Achituv, Rabbi Dr. Meir Muller, Dr. Shelley Tornheim Alexander, and Professional Editor Michele Waldinger. In this connection, it is especially fitting to highlight the leadership of Shelley Alexander, who has coordinated the International Research Group on Jewish Education in the Early Years since its inception. After twenty-five years as a practitioner of early childhood Jewish education, she chose to dedicate the next stage of her professional life to advancing research in the field. Earning her doctorate in education from Gratz College with an in-depth study of the group, she led by example, both through her personal commitment to expanding her scholarly repertoire and through the spirit of collegiality that she cultivated. Having been fortunate enough to be married to Shelley for many years, I witnessed first-hand how she devoted endless hours to preparing for each of the group's meetings, communicating with its members, recording its deliberations, and advancing its various projects, including close collaboration with the authors and editorial team of this book, all with her characteristic kindness, caring, and modesty. It is also appropriate to acknowledge the commitment of every member in this unique community of scholars who have participated enthusiastically in all of the group's activities over many years, including authoring the chapters of this book. For the entire group, this has been a labor of love—for Judaism and the Jewish people and for children and their families.

It is with great pride that the Center for Jewish and Democratic Education at the University of Haifa has participated in preparing and publishing this volume. We sincerely hope that it will become the cornerstone of a growing body of knowledge in the field of early childhood Jewish education, dedicated to improving policy and practice in the field around the world. To continue advancing this significant scholarly agenda, in the immortal Aramaic words of the first-century rabbinic sage Hillel the Elder, "*zil g'mor*—go and study" (Babylonian Talmud, Tractate Shabbat, 31a).

Introduction: Capturing a Mosaic of the Field

Sigal Achituv, Meir Muller, and Shelley T. Alexander

Although early childhood Jewish programs have existed for more than a century—since 1898 in pre-state Israel and since the 1930s in the United States—the field of study of early childhood Jewish education (ECJE) has received scant attention by scholars. The groundbreaking book on Jewish education titled *The International Handbook of Jewish Education* (Miller, Grant, and Pomson 2011) provided a comprehensive overview of Jewish education with contributions from scholars of Jewish education worldwide. Yet little of its material included the perspective of early childhood education (ECE).

ECE "aims at the holistic development of a child's social, emotional, cognitive and physical needs in order to build a solid and broad foundation for lifelong learning and wellbeing" (UNICEF 2018). ECJE adds a focus on Jewish religious, spiritual, and cultural development. It seeks to integrate affective, cognitive, social, cultural, and physical development into a strong Jewish identity. It can also serve as a gateway for children and families' involvement in Jewish life and foster Jewish continuity. As scholars and researchers of ECJE, we believe that the field merits serious attention and that its practitioners, teacher educators, educational leaders, policy makers, and students can gain valuable guidance and insights from a research-based book dedicated solely to the discipline of ECJE.

Genesis of the Book

This book represents the ongoing fruits of collaboration of the historic International Research Group on Jewish Education in the Early Years, whose members, Israelis and Americans, have been working together since 2010 to address the lack of research in ECJE. The group was originally organized as a partnership between the Center for Jewish and Democratic Education at the University of Haifa and the Van Leer Jerusalem Institute and has continued since 2013 under the auspices of the University of Haifa. The members are researchers, administrators, teacher trainers, and policy makers with a wide range of academic backgrounds, Jewish experiences, and cultural orientations.

This unique community of learners provides a variety of opportunities for collaboration and networking, which have resulted in a 2011 research workshop attended by all group members, a published group article on teacher attitudes toward inclusion in the early childhood (EC) Jewish classroom (Alexander et al. 2016), numerous individual member academic articles, and multiple presentations at international conferences. Through the impetus of the group, the *Journal of Jewish Education*, the leading academic periodical in the field, agreed to dedicate a special edition to the topic of ECJE, of which 75 percent of the peer-reviewed articles were written by members of the group. In the editor's note to the edition, the journal observed that the International Research Group on Jewish Education in the Early Years was "helping to embed research in Jewish early years as a serious element within the field" (Miller 2013, 169).

This book is the next step in contributing to the field of ECJE by providing a volume of new, research-based work in the area. All members of the group wrote or cowrote chapters, and we three also served as editors of the volume. We chose to focus on the history, practice, and issues of ECJE in Israel and the United States because of the backgrounds of the members of the group and the fact that the two countries are currently the major population centers of the Jewish world. We also found that this focus allowed us to compare and contrast two very different cultural educational systems—one that is part of a public national framework, in which Jews comprise the majority of the country; and one that is privately based, in which Jews represent only about 2 percent of the population of the country (Dashefsky and Sheskin 2020; Pew Research Center 2021; Saxe et al. 2021). The research reflected in this book reveals common issues that both systems must face. Situated in democratic liberal countries, both are challenged with tackling the issues of a fast-paced, changing world while staying rooted in a traditional religio-cultural background and being subject to the complexities of educating on an appropriate cognitive, social, and affective developmental level of a young child. Based on the authors' expertise, some chapters focus solely on the Israeli or US context, while others cover both countries.

Perspective of the Book

In this volume, we sought to explore fundamental questions of the meaning and practice of ECJE in the context of some of today's most urgent societal and moral issues. As we continued our research following the publication of the *Journal of Jewish Education* special edition, we found that three contemporary critical pedagogical perspectives have become an essential part of the communal discourse regarding ECJE: multiculturalism, gender, and constructivism.

Multiculturalism

The issue of multiculturalism and how to educate children about difference has been a major concern in both the US and Israeli ECJE contexts. (Please note that the use of the term "multiculturalism" in this book refers to pedagogical practices relating to cultural and value pluralism and not to political ideology.) In the United States, the Jewish community has continually confronted the challenge of continuity and survival as a group that makes up a small fraction of the population, while (for all but the most insulated Jewish communities) wishing to meaningfully participate in the larger society. This has necessitated looking both externally and internally.

As Jews arrived in the United States, they were faced with the concern of integration into American life. An original goal in establishing Jewish preschools was to facilitate initiation into the country's public elementary school system and reinforce connections within the Jewish community (Vogelstein and Kaplan 2002). As multicultural education rose as a pedagogical model during the Civil Rights Movement, Jewish school leaders recognized the alignment of Jewish values with societal equality, shifting to a multicultural approach along with nurturing Jewish identity.

With increasingly large numbers of intermarried families and non-Jewish children participating in US early childhood Jewish programs, multiculturalism and inclusiveness within the Jewish community take on new meaning in the classroom. EC schools are often used as avenues for outreach, with family education as a core component (Kelner 2007). Questions of whether and how to include or honor other religious backgrounds of the students are an important concern for the US ECJE educator (Feeney, Freeman, and Muller 2012).

The Israeli educational discourse has also been dealing with the issue of multiculturalism for generations. In the early stages of statehood, the Ashkenazi-dominated Ministry of Education (Ashkenazi being from Central and Eastern European Jewry) focused on preparing the influx of children from non-Western countries for school achievement and initiating them into the Western-oriented society at large with little attempt to honor their background and culture (Snapir, Sitton, and Russo-Zimet 2012). Today the Ministry of Education guidelines advocate for affirming and respecting different cultural groups' values and practices. For instance, EC curricula are specifically designed with content areas allowing for the expression of different cultural values and practices (Aram and Ziv 2018), and efforts are made to create connections between the school, family, and community. The Ministry's Sifriyat Pijama (Pajama Library) Initiative (discussed at length in Chapter 8) sends high quality books to *ganim* (pre-elementary schools for ages three to six) to be taken home in an attempt to nurture individual family cultural identities, as well as collective Jewish-Israeli identities.

The polarization of contemporary Israeli society between the secular and the religious plays a role in this area. Just as the more liberal denominations in the United States are more open to educating for the "other" and multiculturalism, Israeli secular institutions are more receptive to opportunities for teaching about multiculturalism and providing for particularistic education of different cultural groups (Zimet and Gilat 2017). However, the sectoral structure of the school system mitigates against children's exposure to different religious and secular lifestyles (Brody 2018).

In Chapter 4, "From the Melting Pot, to the Salad Bowl, to the Seder Plate: Moving beyond Multiculturalism in Early Childhood Jewish Education," Ilana Dvorin Friedman and Meir Muller advocate for a form of culturally relevant pedagogy in which a community can respect its own cultural elements while honoring difference and dismantling injustice.

Understanding the theory and application of multicultural pedagogy can aid educators and policy makers in navigating issues of difference—both in preparing children from the earliest age to value other cultures and in developing their critical consciousness to eliminate bias toward minoritized cultures outside and within Judaism, all while preserving the Jewish distinctiveness that is such a large part of ECJE.

Gender

Gender plays a large role in ECJE, both because of the gendered history and practices of Judaism and because of the disproportionate participation of women as the vast majority of educators and policy makers in ECJE. Issues regarding gender play out in the educational domain in both the United States and Israel with the more traditional elements of the Jewish community being less open to questioning, reevaluating, and modifying their stance (Gorsetman and Sztokman 2013).

Discourses today pertaining to gender roles pose conflicts for the religious educator. For instance, Achituv (2019) argues that Israeli educators who teach Bible stories in religious EC programs often deal with contemporary issues of gender and feminism presenting conflicting values between their private beliefs and professional stance as representatives of established religious institutional norms.

Those interested in the field of ECJE must have a familiarity with and tools to deal with issues of gender disparity. In Chapter 5, "Educating toward Gender Awareness, Feminism, and Cultural Sensitivity in Early Childhood Jewish Education Teacher Preparation," Sharon Kaplan-Berkley and Haggith Gor Ziv discuss critical feminist pedagogy and how it acts as a lens to view, interpret, and humanize society and education. They discuss how they teach Jewish educators to perceive Judaism as a moral guide to inspire social change toward a gender-equal Jewish society. They advocate for culturally responsive teaching that cultivates multiple ways of thinking to help children develop positive individual identities.

Constructivism

As with any field of education, employing an appropriate pedagogical approach to learning is vital to ECJE. The authors in this book advocate for the constructivist model, which is the dominant pedagogical theory in contemporary education today. It is based on the idea that learners construct knowledge rather than passively taking in information. However, it can be seen to be at odds with religious education, which is widely viewed as the transferring of bodies of knowledge accepted to be the ultimate truth. Several chapters in this book argue against this view and provide examples of how ECJE can successfully employ a constructivist approach. They also describe areas that present challenges for doing so and suggest ways to cope with these challenges.

In Chapter 6, "Constructivism in Early Childhood Jewish Education," Meir Muller, Sigal Achituv, and Chaya Gorsetman outline the theories of constructivism and argue that religious customs, stories, doctrine, law, philosophy, and ways of being in the world can all be included in a constructivist classroom and that children being trusted to deduce information leads to a higher likelihood of their growing up to have an appreciation of and engagement with Judaism. They describe the challenges of teachers being unwilling to let children use art materials freely or exercising control over students to train them in performances for family members, and they provide examples of successes in facilitating conversations with children in Israeli ganim and having them put those values into practice in the local community. In Chapter 7, "Teaching the Bible in Early Childhood Jewish Education," Sigal Achituv discusses the challenge that telling Bible stories using a constructivist approach presents for religious Jewish educators in Israel. In Chapter 9, "Holidays and Ceremonies in Israeli Early Childhood Jewish Education," Shulamit Hoshen Manzura describes how a constructivist approach to teaching festivals can blend old and new traditions, while trying to examine deeper meanings. Chapter 10, "Language-Conducive Strategies in Young Learners' Constructivist Hebrew Classrooms," written by Margalit Kavenstock and Mila Schwartz, outlines core principles of constructivism and analyzes how four ECJE teachers of Hebrew as a second language in the United States apply constructivist language-conducive strategies in their classrooms.

Terminology Used in the Book

We consider "early childhood Jewish education (ECJE)" to be any formal instruction provided about Judaism or Jewish history and culture or in a Jewish setting to children prior to first grade. In the United States, that covers children from birth through kindergarten age, which is generally age five or six. ECE in the United States distinguishes between preschool, which is generally for ages two to four but may include children as young as infants, and kindergarten, which is generally for ages five to six and usually considered part of elementary school. Jewish education is voluntary and provided privately.

In Israel, what we call ECJE in this book covers children from birth until entry to first grade at age six or seven. Compulsory education begins at age three, when children begin to attend ganim, which include both preschool and kindergarten. Public education can be described as being provided in four "streams" or "tracks" in which parents can choose to enroll their children—"state" (secular Jewish education), "state-religious" (religious Jewish education), "independent" (*Haredi*—ultra-Orthodox—Jewish education), and "Arab." ECJE as discussed in this book includes the first three tracks.

Hebrew terms are frequently used in the chapters. The first time any Hebrew term is used in a chapter, its English translation is provided directly after it in parentheses. All Hebrew terms used in the book and their translations are also compiled in a glossary at the end of the book. Some of the terms relate to Jewish tradition and culture, while others are used in Israeli legislation and the early childhood profession.

Several chapters refer to "the Bible." All these references are to the Hebrew Bible.

Structure of the Book

The book is divided into four sections. The first section, entitled "Setting the Scene," includes descriptions of the field of ECJE in Israel and the United States, as well as a comprehensive review of the field's research literature from the year 2000 to the first half of 2020.

The first chapter, "The History and Current Status of Early Childhood Jewish Education in Israel," written by David L. Brody, Shira Ackerman Simchovitch, and Shulamit Hoshen Manzura, provides an overview of key characteristics of ECE systems in Israel, as well as a discussion of the Jewish aspects of ECE in the Israeli system. The chapter outlines the development of ECE in Israel, the scope and structure of the system, and the core mission and educational goals of the Early Childhood Division of the Ministry of Education and other bodies responsible for policymaking and pedagogic oversight. It also addresses teacher/caregiver training and professional development and the place of Jewish religion and cultural identity in the national ECE agenda.

The second chapter, "Early Childhood Jewish Education in the United States," written by Ilene Vogelstein, Roberta Louis Goodman, and Shelley T. Alexander, examines the history and major influential factors of ECJE in the United States. It begins with a historical perspective covering the initial mission of ECJE as a voluntary and private system, including the first steps in developing standards, curriculum, and educational approaches. The chapter offers information about providers, students, curriculum, and outreach to families. The topic of standards of the field considers curriculum resources, qualifications of providers, and the availability of data regarding the field.

The final chapter in this section, entitled "The Current State of Research and Writing about Early Childhood Jewish Education," by David L. Brody and Howard Deitcher, presents an overview of both research and professional writing about ECJE. It aims to provide a comprehensive and nuanced understanding about the various types of issues, questions, and key foci that have been researched from 2000 to the first half of 2020. The first categorization involved tagging the documents according to the genre of writing: research, practice, or policy. The second categorization divides the corpus of articles into three broad categories: structural underpinnings, curriculum content, and pedagogical considerations. The final analysis in the chapter treats the academic and professional context that gave rise to these studies.

The second section of the book, "Three Contemporary Critical Lenses," contains chapters that address the three theoretical lenses of this volume: multiculturalism, gender, and constructivism. They provide explanations of the critical theories and examples of their application.

Chapter 4, "From the Melting Pot, to the Salad Bowl, to the Seder Plate: Moving beyond Multiculturalism in Early Childhood Jewish Education," written by Ilana Dvorin Friedman and Meir Muller, deals with the pressing need within ECJE to interrogate biases and Eurocentric discourses that perpetuate inequities within classroom practices. The authors apply the metaphor of a "Seder Plate" (a special plate containing symbolic foods eaten or displayed at the Passover dinner known as a *seder*) to challenge the pedagogical models of the "melting pot" (assimilationist education) and the "salad bowl" (multicultural education) that devalue each child's culture. The Seder Plate model supports tenets of culturally relevant pedagogy and provides critical questions and strategies to implement this approach.

The fifth chapter, by Sharon Kaplan-Berkley and Haggith Gor Ziv, entitled "Educating toward Gender Awareness, Feminism, and Cultural Sensitivity in Early

Childhood Jewish Education Teacher Preparation," explores different approaches to preservice EC teacher education by addressing traditional gender issues, the development of social critical consciousness, and gender awareness in students. It presents a reflective educational approach by two Israeli teacher educators focused on the process of developing gender identity and inspiring social change toward a gender-equal Jewish society. It presents findings that indicate that secular and religious teachers in training programs deal with similar issues but through a different lens.

Concluding this section is Chapter 6, "Constructivism in Early Childhood Jewish Education," by Meir Muller, Sigal Achituv, and Chaya Gorsetman. The chapter begins with an explanation of constructivist theory and application with a special emphasis on Piaget's three types of knowledge. Within this framework the authors provide an overview of constructivism in religious education, including the tensions that exist when using constructivist theory in the teaching of religion and specifically in ECJE. The chapter concludes with recommendations to support Jewish and general religious educators using a constructivist pedagogy.

The third section of the book moves from background information and theory to application of the three critical perspectives in teaching particular ECJE subject matter. The section "Core Jewish Subjects through the Three Contemporary Critical Lenses" consists of five chapters, each examining a particular curricular subject in ECJE: the Bible, Jewish literature, Jewish holidays and ceremonies, the Hebrew language, and spirituality. The chapters cover ECJE in either Israel or the United States and discuss one of more of the three lenses.

The first subject to be examined is "Teaching the Bible in Early Childhood Jewish Education" (Chapter 7), written by Sigal Achituv. This chapter pertains to Israel and explores its subject through all three lenses. It describes different approaches to teaching the Bible and analyzes some of the challenges arising from it, particularly having to do with teachers' ideologies. It includes relevant references and examples from recent studies of Bible instructors and students in ECE departments at Israeli education colleges and of Israeli ECJE teachers. The chapter distinguishes how the teaching of the Bible is treated differently in the state and state-religious official Jewish educational streams.

Chapter 8, "Strengthening Jewish-Israeli Identity and Promoting a Common Cultural Canon through Children's Literature: The Experience of Sifriyat Pijama," by Sylvia Kamowitz-Hareven, shows how children's literature can serve as a vehicle for identity-building and cultural cohesion, highlighting the link between shared reading and values education and suggesting conceptual constructs for the mediation of common values within the plurality of contemporary Israel. Drawing upon the experience of Sifriyat Pijama, a program distributing free, age-appropriate books to families with young children, the chapter opens a discussion on the potential of a common Jewish-Israeli ethos among disparate strata of society. The book selection process seeks to identify quality books that promote meaningful conversations with young children surrounding multicultural, social justice, and gender issues.

The next subject, addressed in Chapter 9 written by Shulamit Hoshen Manzura, is "Holidays and Ceremonies in Israeli Early Childhood Jewish Education." It deals with the main characteristics of the educational practices in the teaching of Jewish holidays in Israeli ganim. The chapter offers insight into this subject through the prism of ceremony, which is often a peak event in preschools' activities toward or during the holidays, as observed in a variety of sociocultural contexts in the state, state-religious, and Haredi ganim. It discusses the roles of female students and teachers in these observances and the range of how autonomous ECJE educators consider themselves to be in teaching this subject, from those who believe there is a set, appropriate model that should be learned to those at the constructivist end of the scale, who seek to blend old and new traditions, while trying to examine deeper meanings.

The setting turns to the United States in Chapter 10, "Language-Conducive Strategies in Young Learners' Constructivist Hebrew Classrooms," by Margalit Kavenstock and Mila Schwartz. It seeks to analyze language-conducive strategies to create a constructivist learning environment for Hebrew as a second language in American EC settings. Teacher strategies are described as cultivating positive emotions toward Hebrew and increasing willingness to use it in a multimodal approach. The chapter concludes that systematic and specific professional training in teaching Hebrew as a second language is necessary in ECJE.

The final chapter of this section is "Enhancing Spiritual Awareness and Development in Early Childhood Jewish Settings," by Michael Shire and Deborah Schein. It deals with an understanding of spirituality in ECJE where children experience a rich, nonverbal inner life that, properly nurtured, can result in both spiritual awareness and development. The chapter explores how tapping into children's spiritual capacity through Torah Godly Play and spiritual moments helps to provide children time and space to explore their spiritual selves and prepare themselves for Jewish religious experiences. The chapter concludes with ideas and reflections for future research in spirituality for young Jewish children as a fundamental ingredient for human well-being.

The concluding section of the book is called "Continuing the Work." We have chosen a chapter, Chapter 12 by Lyndall Miller entitled "Leadership in Early Childhood Jewish Education in the United States," to illustrate how leadership capacities in the field of ECJE can be developed, something that is applicable to both the United States and Israel. Based on general research regarding leadership in ECE, this chapter suggests hypotheses about the essential capacities that ECE Jewish educators might need to create generative and inspired schools. Interviews with a number of major ECJE leaders, which leveraged both the general capacities and Jewish leadership tradition, explore the capacities most salient in this context. The chapter ends with implications for ECJE leadership professional development and suggestions for further research in leadership in ECJE.

Goals of the Book

Through the lenses of multiculturalism, gender, and constructivism, this book reflects on the challenges of transmitting Jewish heritage using developmentally appropriate pedagogy in the context of modern democratic values. The book's chapters use varied methodological approaches, including historical accounts, research studies (qualitative and quantitative), literature and theory reviews, and an autoethnographic study. They consider the multiple conceptual perspectives of the varied stakeholders in ECJE: school administrators, teachers, teacher educators, family members, students, policy makers, and Jewish organizational leaders. Thus, a diverse mosaic of insights is the backbone of this book.

We hope that the theories, viewpoints, and examples presented here will aid those involved in ECJE in addressing several issues: how to provide ECJE in a way that will best educate children to value Judaism while embracing difference and developing critical thinking; how to respond to the concerns of constituents who question the methods and approaches advocated here; how to teach educators to apply the best educational approaches to ECJE; and how to inspire administrators and leaders to promote and expand ECJE.

We also hope that the material presented here will inspire discussion, study, and future research. ECJE has always been a priority and obligation through the changing contexts and circumstances of the Jewish people over thousands of years. As authors and researchers, we continue this journey in anchoring the knowledge of the Jewish people's past heritage to contemporary times. Much in the field of ECJE, though, is still undeveloped, and we hope practitioners will continue a global dialogue and researchers will explore the many topics that remain to be investigated, including those suggested by the authors in this book. These include how to address special needs students in ECJE; a reorientation and renewed emphasis on the child as learner; explorations of how to improve Hebrew teaching pedagogic processes as a second language in ECJE; further research regarding teachers' perspectives and dilemmas regarding Bible teaching; questions of how to provide quality children's literature to be shared with family members; exploration of the application and merits of the practices advocated for here in other cultural contexts; development of standards and curriculum for the field of ECJE in the United States and the means to obtain demographic data that would aid in planning for its provision; introduction and implementation of Judaism in secular settings; research to understand how parents and educators might foster spiritual development and awareness in children and how ideas of God and religion become part of a young child's consciousness; programs that would allow for mentoring, professional development, and supportive communities for prospective leaders in the field of ECJE; and how to advocate for the field of ECJE and for social justice for those working in it.

The journey of this book has taken place while the world has been shaken by a global pandemic. It is our hope, as this book is being read, that the world is experiencing a period of healthy recovery. However, as Covid-19 continues to affect many aspects of ECJE, we also hope that this experience may add to our knowledge of how to best meet the needs of the youngest members of our community. Future researchers may find valuable lessons in exploring how remote learning has affected ECJE, how technology has been and can continue to be employed in teaching ECJE and communicating and staying in touch with stakeholders in the field, and how much a sense of community contributes to ECJE and how it can be maintained in challenging circumstances.

Acknowledgments

We wish to acknowledge and thank the many people and institutions that made this work possible. We are indebted to Hanan Alexander as the cofounder and senior academic of the International Research Group of Jewish Education in the Early Years, who has devoted both countless hours through the years and funding to ensure its continued existence, academic standards, and vitality. We are grateful to the Center for Jewish and Democratic Education at the University of Haifa for its continued support as a framework and home base for the International Research Group of Jewish Education in the Early Years and to the Ellie and Mark Lainer Family Foundation and the Jake and Janet Farber Family Foundation for generous funding through the years. Thanks are owed to the Van Leer Jerusalem Institute for its role in helping to establish and support the activities of the research group in its first three years and to Oranim College for Education for its generous funding of this book project. We wish to thank the publishing team at Bloomsbury, especially Anna Ellis and Mark Richardson, for guidance and recommendations to bring the book to the public. Without the tireless efforts and academic rigor of our distinguished colleague Michele Waldinger, the manuscript could not have attained its level of quality and clarity. Special thanks are due to all the authors who collaborated in this venture and the many educators who have dedicated their professional lives to ECJE and the children they serve, whose experiences are captured in this book.

References

Achituv, S. 2019. " 'It Bothers Me, but I Will Not Bring It into the Kindergarten': Gender Perception Conflicts of Religious Kindergarten Teachers as Reflected in Their Work." *Religious Education* 114 (4): 1–13. https://doi.org/10.1080/00344087.2019.1600108.

Alexander, S. T., D. L. Brody, M. Muller, H. G. Ziv, S. Achituv, C. R. Gorsetman, J. Harris, C. Tal, R. Goodman, D. Schein, and I. Vogelstein. 2016. "Voices of American and Israeli Early Childhood Educators on Inclusion." *International Journal of Early Childhood Special Education* 8 (1): 16–38.

Aram, D., and M. Ziv. 2018. "Early Childhood Education in Israel: History, Policy, and Practice." In *Handbook of International Perspectives on Early Childhood Education*, edited by J. L. Roopnarine, J. E. Johnson, S. F. Quinn, and M. M. Patte, 101–14. London: Routledge. https://doi.org/10.4324/9781315562193.

Brody, D. 2018. "Constructing Early Childhood Curriculum and Assessing Young Children in Israel's Mosaic of Culture." In *International Handbook of Early Childhood Education,* edited by M. Fleer and B. van Oers, 1191–1210. Dordrecht: Springer Netherlands. https://doi.org/10.1007/978-94-024-0927-7_61.

Dashefsky, A., and I. M. Sheskin, eds. 2020. *American Jewish Year Book 2019.* New York: Springer.

Feeney, S., N. K. Freeman, and M. Muller. 2012. "Differing Faiths in a Faith Based Program." *Young Children* 67 (3): 70–1.

Gorsetman, C. R., and E. M. Sztokman, 2013. *Educating in the Divine Image: Gender Issues in Orthodox Jewish Day Schools*. Waltham, MA: Brandeis University Press.

Kelner, S. 2007. "Who Is Being Taught? Early Childhood's Adult-Centered Approach." In *Family Matters: Jewish Education in an Age of Choice*, edited by J. Wertheimer, 59–79. Waltham, MA: Brandeis. http://hdl.handle.net/10192/26633.

Miller, H. 2013. "Foundations for Lifelong Jewish Engagement." *Journal of Jewish Education* 79 (3): 168–73.

Miller, H., L. Grant, and A. Pomson. 2011. *International Handbook of Jewish Education*, vol. 5. Dordrecht: Springer Science & Business Media.

Pew Research Center. 2021. "Jewish Americans in 2020." May 11, 2021. https://www.pewforum.org/2021/05/11/jewish-americans-in-2020/.

Saxe, L., D. Parmer, E. Tighe, R. M. de Kramer, D. Kallista, D. Nussbaum, X. Seabrum, and J. Mandell. 2021. "American Jewish Population Estimates 2020 Summary & Highlights." American Jewish Population Project. Brandeis Steinhardt Social Research Institute. https://ajpp.brandeis.edu/documents/2020/JewishPopulationDataBrief2020.pdf.

Snapir, M., S. Sitton, and G. Russo-Zimet. 2012. *The Israeli Kindergarten in the 20th Century*. [In Hebrew.] Beer Sheva, Israel: Ben Gurion Research Institute for the Study of Israel and Zionism and Ben Gurion University.

UNICEF. 2018. "Early Childhood Education: Every Child Deserves Access to Quality Early Childhood Education." Accessed January 2, 2022. https://www.unicef.org/education/early-childhood-education.

Vogelstein, I., and D. Kaplan. 2002. *Untapped Potential: The Status of Jewish Early Childhood Education in America*. Baltimore, MD: JECE Partnership.

Zimet, G. R., and I. Gilat. 2017. "Impact of Culture Context on Perceptions of Arab and Jewish Early Childhood Education Students Regarding Early Childhood Education and Care." *Journal of Research in Childhood Education* 31 (2): 281–94.

Part One

Setting the Scene

1

The History and Current Status of Early Childhood Jewish Education in Israel

David L. Brody, Shira Ackerman Simchovitch, and Shulamit Hoshen Manzura

A distinguishing feature of early childhood Jewish education (ECJE) in Israel is that it revolves around the Jewish calendar. National holidays and school vacations follow the Jewish festival cycle, which permeates the environment and the public space in a way that occurs only in Israel. The rhythms and seasons of Israel are in sync with the festivals, and the spoken language is Hebrew. All these factors, taken together, allow Jewish education to take place in a more organic fashion than anywhere else on the globe, with the environment of the child providing naturally occurring invitations to learning. For example, prior to a holiday, supermarkets, malls, and shops market products related to that holiday and the media broadcasts holiday-themed programming.

This chapter outlines how the system of early childhood education (ECE) in Israel and, within it, the Jewish educational component came to be and how it operates now. While the term "early childhood Jewish education" and its acronym "ECJE" are used throughout this book, the Israeli case differs from that of the United States. In Israel, the national educational system purports to educate all children in the country, most of whom are Jewish. Thus, a more precise rendition of the term "ECJE" for Israel would be "ECE for Jewish children." Nonetheless, we will use the term "ECJE" here when appropriate in order to align our references to this Israeli component with the term used for such education in the United States.

The first part of this chapter covers the history of ECE in Israel since its start in the Yishuv (pre-state Israel) at the end of the nineteenth century and continues through its development since the establishment of the State of Israel in 1948, including societal, political, philosophical, religious, and pedagogical influences, as well as the laws that have come to govern it. The second part of the chapter details the current state of ECJE in Israel, outlining the scope and structure of the system—the types of programs and categories of ECJE, the facilities and demographics of ECE programs, its educators (including qualifications and training), and its curriculum (with an explanation of the place of Jewish religion and cultural identity).

There are some Hebrew terms used in ECJE in Israel that differ from those of its American counterpart. While the US early childhood (EC) context distinguishes between preschool for ages three to four and kindergarten for ages five to six, the term *gan* (plural *ganim*) in Hebrew denotes all ECE programs for three- to six-year-olds. The term *ganenet* (plural *gananot*) refers to a teacher in a gan in Israel. This chapter will conclude with a discussion of points of connection between ECJE programs in Israel and in the United States.

ECJE in the Yishuv

The Hebrew kindergarten movement in Israel was founded in 1898 by European philanthropists in the spirit of Friedrich Fröbel and Johann Heinrich Pestalozzi (Read 2018). Until that time, the cheder (all-boys Jewish school where only religious studies are taught) model was dominant; it continues to this day in the Haredi (ultra-Orthodox) sector.

The first EC classroom opened in Rishon Lezion and was called gan—"children's garden" in Hebrew. This is a translation of the German term "kindergarten," coined by Fröbel. The term "gan" is used to describe a framework for the education of young children and includes both preschool and kindergarten, which are often distinct in other countries (Aram and Ziv 2018). Fröbel and Pestalozzi paved the way for the establishment of the first kindergartens in Europe at the end of the nineteenth century, and their influence was felt in the Yishuv (Read 2018). The pedagogy of the European kindergarten movement emphasized learning through activity for both girls and boys rather than the cheder's male-only frontal instruction and emphasis on memorization of sacred texts.

In the early part of the twentieth century, with the founding of the first kibbutzim (collective agricultural settlements), an additional model of progressive ECE was created. This led to a feminist revolution in the Yishuv by opening the gates to employ women as teachers (Aram and Ziv 2018). The educational leaders of the Yishuv also followed European developments in their adaptation of the concept of childhood as a distinct period worthy of age-appropriate pedagogy (Dekel and Kark 2019). From that time on, Israel's ECE system has been influenced by, and is open to, different progressive trends in educational thought and practice (Aram and Ziv 2018).

From its inception, ECE in the Yishuv functioned in Hebrew (except for a small minority of Haredi programs in Yiddish). Conversation in Hebrew in the educational system served as an essential factor in the revival of the Hebrew language for spoken and written use in daily life. Thus, ECE played a crucial role in the development of an emerging Hebrew culture and a unified Israeli national identity. The Zionist (belief in the establishment of a Jewish state in the land of Israel) movement arose amid the nationalist reawakening in Europe, and the nationalist fervor of the Yishuv leaders influenced the use of ganim as a socializing institution (Orr 2007). In the fifty years following the establishment of the first gan, until the enactment of the 1949 Israel Compulsory Education Law, ganim in the spirit of Pestalozzi, Fröbel, and Montessori became a major cultural agent of the Zionist movement (Dayan 2016; Shchori-Rubin 2015).

Miriam Snapir, Shosh Sitton, and Gila Russo-Zimet's *The Israeli Kindergarten in the 20th Century* (2012), published only in Hebrew, has a rich description of the historical, philosophical, and pedagogical trends that influenced the historical development of ECJE in Israel. It describes the focus of the burgeoning EC programs as becoming twofold—teaching the nascent Hebrew language as the new mother tongue and inculcating ceremonies and rituals connected to the Jewish national homeland, what they term the development of "the Hebrew child" (44–5).

European intellectual and political developments influenced ECE in the Yishuv during this time. Educators in ganim were influenced by the Enlightenment ethos of creating "the new Jew," with an emphasis on Judaism as a culture rather than a religion, a trend that has been identified as central to Israeli secular culture (Tal 2013). This new Zionist culture relied on traditional sources such as the Bible and holidays as a basis for the new identity. The absence of appropriate teaching materials led the EC pioneers of this period to recruit Hebrew poets and authors, such as Haim Nachman Bialik and Levine Kipnis, to write stories, books, poems, and songs for inculcating the Hebrew language and Zionist culture in young children (Snapir, Sitton, and Russo-Zimet 2012, 69–72). Holidays were a significant theme in this new Hebrew children's literature, creating a folklore around the holiday cycle and weekly Shabbat (Sabbath) ritual in the gan (see Chapter 9 in this book for a discussion of the current celebration of festivals and Shabbat in ECJE in Israel and Chapter 8 for a discussion of current children's literature in Israel).

During the second and third decades of the twentieth century, Fröbellian notions of learning through play gave way to the humanistic philosophy of Montessori and Dewey (Lombard and Jasik 1983). Following this theory of activity-based learning, the gananot of the Yishuv abandoned their rigid organization focused on Hebrew-language learning and embraced a more humanistic curriculum. Music education took on a central role through musical games and Hebrew songs, intended to further the children's sensorimotor development as well their Hebrew-language skills (Snapir, Sitton, and Russo-Zimet 2012, 60–1).

Snapir, Sitton, and Russo-Zimet (2012) identify the next influence to reach the shores of Palestine from Europe as that of Freud in the 1930s. As Freud's psychodynamic theories gained popularity among educators at all levels, those responsible for ECE in Israel introduced this conceptual framework to the gananot as well (Aram and Ziv 2018). Gananot were prompted to tune into the emotional side of the child: to encourage free choice within the play milieu and to provide group learning experiences appropriate to the child's developmental level (which included teaching holidays and national elements through stories and other means geared toward the child's emotional and cognitive needs) (Snapir, Sitton, and Russo-Zimet 2012, 62–3).

The low point of ECJE in the Yishuv began in 1933 and lasted for sixteen years. At that time, financial responsibility for the educational system shifted from the World Zionist Organization to the leadership of the Yishuv. Due to extreme financial difficulties, Yishuv leaders defunded preschool education, considering it a luxury. The British Mandate exacerbated the situation when, in 1940, it ruled that the education of five- to six-year-olds was to be placed in the hands of local municipalities, excluding the education of younger children altogether. ECE activities were left to the Union of Gananot, which included meetings and summer training, focusing on previously determined foundational elements, such as Montessori, hygiene, and the Hebrew language (Iram 1993).

ECE and ECJE in the State of Israel

ECE found its rightful place in the nation's educational system only with the founding of the state. In 1949, a year after statehood, the Israel Compulsory Education Act, 1949, was passed by the first Knesset (Israeli parliament) for free—and compulsory—education from five years of age (one year prior to the start of elementary school) for all children in Israel. (The law was not fully implemented until 1953 with the State Education Law, discussed later in this section.)

This was the first time in modern Jewish history that ECJE was provided for all Jewish children in one country. While the program was largely secular, particular elements of tradition were included and later became canonized as essential elements of the curriculum. Thus, holidays, Bible stories, and Shabbat celebration became the core of the curriculum for both secular and religious ganim. This aligns with the Basic Laws of Israel, created later in 1955, which state, "The government will strive to heighten the Jewish consciousness in elementary, secondary, and higher education; to deepen the roots of young people in our nations' past and our historical heritage; and to strengthen their attachment to world Jewry" (Proceedings of the Knesset 1955, 230).

The first three years after the founding of the state saw an influx of immigrants from Europe, Asia, and Africa tripling the Jewish population in this short period (Hacohen 2003). The ideal of the "Hebrew child" was replaced with the ethos of "the Israeli child," and once again the EC teachers were called upon to socialize young children through language and culture. During this critical time in the state's history, the developmental theories of Geselle found popularity among EC educators. The emphasis on natural progression in all realms of development allowed freedom of activity for the child to develop at her own pace and in her own path. Freud's psychodynamic theory also remained popular.

Many of the leaders of ECE in this period came from kibbutzim. Miriam Roth, from the secular kibbutz Sha'ar Hagolan, wrote the first Hebrew book on preschool pedagogy and penned many classics of Israeli children's literature. Malka Haas, from the religious kibbutz Sde Eliyahu, pioneered research in children's art as self-expression and championed "the junkyard," the imaginative playground that characterized kibbutz ganim (Haas and Gavish 2008). Gideon Levine (1989), from the secular kibbutz Lehavot Habashan, initiated the *gan zorem* (flowing kindergarten), based on free choice and free play, an approach that greatly influenced ECE throughout the country. The pedagogic trends introduced by kibbutz educators continued to impact ECE in the country for many decades, emphasizing the connection between the Jewish festival cycle and the land.

The State Education Law in 1953 signaled a shift from partisan control of public education (based on worker ideologies and political parties) and specified a three-track sectorial system for the education of Jewish children: state, state-religious, and independent (Haredi). In addition, a track for Arab Israelis, which included Muslim and Christian communities, was created (Brody 2018). Despite this multitrack plan, guidance for teachers portrayed a neutral model, one of preparing a stimulating environment with broad autonomy for the teacher to plan her own curriculum based on the needs of the children as she understood them. Together with this, each track created its own teacher-training institutions (two-year seminaries), thus, initiating a sectorial system both in training and in schooling. While the national infrastructure required no particular religious content, it was taken for granted that holidays were to be celebrated according to the population makeup of each gan and its sectorial affiliation (Snapir, Sitton, and Russo-Zimet 2012, 107–12).

During this period, EC educators continued to draw on the early Zionist traditions of reenvisioning traditional holidays through a Zionist lens. For example, Hanukkah became the story of military heroism (Zion and Spectre 2000) and Tu B'shvat (Jewish Arbor Day) an event focused on planting trees to reforest the land (Pintel-Ginsberg 2006).

Throughout the first decade of the founding of the state, there was a bitter debate among EC leaders, academics, and the Ministry of Education regarding the appropriate way to deal with the masses of children from non-Western countries (Berkovich and Avigur-Eshel 2019). These children were found to lag behind their Western peers in school achievement; thus, the onus of preparing them for school fell on the gananot. They were labeled en masse as *te'unei tipuach* (in need of nurturing). The home cultures of the te'unei tipuach were largely disregarded, and no attempt was made to honor ethnic customs and mother tongues that differed from the Western focus of the curriculum planners. Policy makers who opposed this deficit view based their pedagogical approach on the tenets of progressive education, as espoused by Dewey, and they proposed allowing children to play in a stimulating environment in order to meet their educational needs. While this approach did not encourage recognition and acceptance of the children's home culture, it did follow what was considered progressive educational practices. However, once the students entered elementary school, they were treated as a "deficit" population and confronted with a very different academic/structured approach, which delineated a planned program, small group work, and a set curriculum (Snapir, Sitton, and Russo-Zimet 2012, 121–4). Unrelated to this deficit paradigm, the Ministry of Education supported a curriculum based on the Jewish holiday cycle, for both the religious and the secular schools, aimed at the broad spectrum of populations that constituted the newly founded state.

In the 1950s and 1960s, the EC curriculum focused on preparing children for first grade, rather than supporting their development (Snapir, Sitton, and Russo-Zimet 2012, 145–53). An approach called "the intensive system" was instituted with formal methods for teaching language and concepts and downplaying the tenets of progressive education, which had been broadly accepted earlier.

In 1968, the School Supervision Law specified conditions for the licensing of schools in Israel, regulating how schools were opened and operated. The intent was to ensure that all schools, including those that were not part of the public education system, would meet certain basic requirements.

The next two decades (the 1970s and 1980s) saw the rise in curriculum-building based on disciplinary foci, albeit grounded in constructivist psychological theory. The theoretical basis for these endeavors was found in the work of Piaget (Huitt and Hummel 2003) and Bruner (Olson 2014) on the psychological side, and Schwab (1983) on the curriculum vector. The Ministry of Education established a pedagogic center for curriculum development, and the EC aspect was dealt with "in house" through an office of pre-elementary education. Particular foci were science, math, language, the Bible, and social-emotional development. This style of top-down curriculum contradicts its Piagetian grounding; nonetheless, it remained in vogue through the 1990s as a plethora of programs was developed and presented to the gananot with a range of expectations for implementation, depending on the style of the regional state supervisor. Resistance to this approach emerged from Gideon Levine, of the Oranim Kibbutz College. He promoted a humanistic, progressive style based on a holistic understanding of the developing child (Snapir, Sitton, and Russo-Zimet 2012, 178–210).

Recognizing the importance of ECE, the Israel Compulsory Education Act, 1949, was originally written with the intention of expanding to include free, compulsory education from three years of age. Only in 1984 was mandatory education from age three legislated, although it was put into effect gradually due to economic constraints, causing families to have to pay for the schooling of three- and four-year-olds. The Special Education Law of 1988 provided for special education for individuals between the ages of three and twenty-one.

In the 1990s, there was a push for Jewish content in the school curriculum at all levels. The Shenhar Commission published a report in 1994 providing the basis for bolstering Jewish topics such as literature, values, and Jewish practice in the M schools (Dror 1999), and this led to a national syllabus. This effort found a voice in the EC curriculum with the Tochnit Misgeret (Framework program), which detailed a general curriculum framework, including the scope and sequence of Bible and holiday teaching required in ganim (Lombard 1995). Although the force of this document has waned in the twenty-first century, giving way to other curriculum reforms in the ganim (Dori 2018), the Bible, holidays, and some elements of Jewish tradition are addressed in secular ganim, as detailed in the following section.

While the ganim had at times become more structured, achievement-oriented, and geared toward "academic" success, in their attempt to deal with the influx and integration of diverse immigrant backgrounds, the pendulum swung back toward constructivism with the Ministry of Education's 2010 official guidelines for EC educators rooted in the theoretical approaches of Vygotsky and Bronfenbrenner, as well as constructivist pedagogy (Aram and Ziv 2018). In 2014, the Israel Compulsory Education Act, 1949, was fully enacted, making almost all ECE for children from age three universal, public, and free. This expansion of EC services had serious implications for national standard-setting across the educational scene, including infrastructure, teacher training, curriculum, and professional development. In July 2017, a law that established an EC council to operate within the Ministry of Education was passed. In July 2021, the government decided to transfer the responsibility and authority of supervision of day care centers for infants up to the age of three from the Ministry of Labor, Welfare and Social Services to the Ministry of Education. On January 5, 2022, a day care center reform was implemented by the Ministry of Education, which included changes in standards (e.g., doubling the supervision standards; appointing an early childhood supervisor in each local authority; training, guidance, and accompaniment for the therapeutic-educational staffs in the day care centers; and an additional budget for building 180 new day care centers).

The Current Status of ECE in Israel

Types of Pre-elementary School Programs and Categories within Israel's Educational System

The current Israeli ECE system is complex, but it can be looked at first and foremost as divided into programs for children from birth to age three and programs for children ages three through six. Available data (Rabinovitz 2019) report that approximately 60 percent of Israeli children ages birth through three are enrolled in ECE programs, which until the present time had been under the aegis of the Ministry of Industry and Welfare. It should be noted that many frameworks are private and unsupervised by the Ministry of Welfare or authorized organizations. In addition to serving as a major avenue for cultural transmission, ECE is a response to other societal issues. The need for childcare and the development of EC programs was in part a result of the economic need to include women in the workforce (Zimet and Gilat 2017).

As stated previously, the Israeli pre-elementary state system for children starts at age three and ends upon entry to first grade at age six or seven, in the state, state-religious, independent (Haredi), and Arab tracks. These designations of programs largely indicate to what extent they are supervised and/or funded by the state. Additional categorizations unrelated to the level of state involvement include schools that adhere to a particular educational philosophy (e.g., Montessori, kibbutzim, democratic, bilingual, TALI, and Waldorf) and have a special pedagogical focus or a particular religious orientation.

Special mention of the Haredi ECE sector should be made here, as it services 30 percent of all Jewish pre-elementary school children (ages three through six), according to Horowitz (2016). There is also a segment of the ECE frameworks for Haredi boys in a class of institutions that are recognized by the state but not subject to state supervision, making that sector an even larger portion of Israel's preschool population. Most Haredi ECE programs for girls are recognized but not part of the state school system. They include large networks such as Beit Yaakov (a worldwide system of Haredi schools for girls), Sephardi (Jews who trace their roots back to the Iberian Peninsula, North Africa, and the Middle East), and Maayan HaChinuch Hatorani (established under the leadership of Rabbi Ovadia Yosef).

As a result of initiatives and ongoing pressure, in 2014, the Ministry of Education established Haredi state education as another official stream rather than being labeled "independent," although only a minority of Haredi schools choose to belong to this category. Haredi education from birth to age six includes educational frameworks in which children's families identify with different Haredi groups. The educational goals among Haredi EC educators and the curriculum foster preservation of community beliefs and patterns that are implemented through a behaviorist approach, focusing on content anchored in Jewish law. One unique aspect of this approach is the emphasis on reading instruction for boys from age three.

Facilities and Demographics of ECE Programs

The programs for children aged birth through three are either home-based, in single-group facilities, or in centers with two to eight or more classes headed by a coordinator or director and supervised by the Ministry of Labor and Welfare. These supervised centers care for only 23 percent of children birth through age three (Weissblei 2013) out of 60 percent of total children cared for in ECE programs. The state recommends adult-to-child ratios in these programs and maximum number of children per individual facility (see Table 1.1), although there is often a gap between these recommendations and reality (Rosenthal 2009).

ECE classes for children ages three through six come under the supervision of the Ministry of Education and can contain up to thirty-five children. The 2014 legislation lowering the age of compulsory education to three led to the decision that classes for three-year-olds of thirty children or more would require an additional adult aide in the classroom. Government facilities for this age group (three through six) are maintained in separate structures, usually two per building, and situated within neighborhoods. They are typically independent of elementary schools, both physically and administratively.

Children from birth through age three generally attend programs six days a week for five to eight hours a day from their first encounter with a childcare facility, with no part-time options. Socioeconomic standing often determines the kind of program a child will attend, with respect to the adult-to-child ratio, enrichment or specialty programs, the size and quality of the physical facility, and level of training of the caregivers. The daily schedule in Israeli ECE programs through age six includes many of the same components that can be found in other countries, such as whole- and small-group activities, unstructured play time, and outdoor play, and the physical facility usually includes the same type of play and exploration areas (e.g., a socio-dramatic play area, library corner, and art area).

Table 1.1 Recommended Adult-to-Child Ratios and Number of Children per Individual EC Birth–3 Facility

Age of Child (in months)	Recommended Adult-to-Child Ratio	Maximum Number of Children per Facility
3–15	1:3	12
16–24	1:5	18
25–36	1:6	21

Sociocultural Context of ECE in Israel

While educational programs and curriculum are crucial, the sociocultural context significantly influences young children's growth and identity. Israel is a small country marked by cultural diversity and shaped by massive waves of Jewish immigration from more than seventy countries around the world. It has a mix of Jewish and Arab populations and is characterized by many languages, with traditional family patterns existing alongside modern lifestyles. It is a nation influenced by Western culture along with a Middle Eastern heritage, including values and practices ranging from highly Orthodox religious perspectives to secular ways of life. The ethos of Israeli society regarding children and their families is expressed in a belief that "the greatest joy in life is to watch children growing up" (Lavee and Katz 2003, 203). As geography mandates that extended family in Israel will never be more than eight hours away by car, most children regularly experience multigenerational family celebrations. Extended family members are also often involved in the care of young children. There is a strong collective sense of responsibility for children in Israel, and so neighbors and close friends also play a prominent role in childrearing. Because of the rigid sectorial organization of Israeli society and education, young Israelis are less likely to meet and play with children from sectors other than their own.

The EC Educator in Israel

As in many places around the world, the EC educator in state schools in Israel is usually female, although a very small but growing number of male teachers are now seen in the field (Brody 2014). In boys' education in the Haredi sector, many of the teachers are male. Teachers in the Jewish sectors are almost always Jewish. An exception is found in the bilingual Hebrew/Arabic classes, whose staff includes both Jewish and Arab teachers. In state-religious programs, the teachers typically identify as religious, while in the secular programs, they are primarily secular, with a few religious faculty.

As in other areas, there is a sharp divide in the training requirements between programs for children birth through age three and those for children ages three through six. Many caregivers of children birth through age three receive little if any formal training or professional development. Teachers of children ages three through six receive their certification in teachers' colleges in four-year programs that grant teaching certification and a bachelor's degree in education. In the past decades, there has been a trend among kindergarten teachers to obtain a master's degree in education. Assistants are often untrained, although there are now increasingly more pre- and in-service programs for this population (Teuval and Guberman 2010).

In state-run programs, the ganenet is the manager of the gan and is responsible for every aspect of running her class, including work plans, scheduling, assessment, direction of staff, communication with parents, community administrative issues, managing the budget, and more. The work is based on the policies and guidelines set by the Ministry of Education.

The regulations for the certification of teachers contain guidelines for a core curriculum and include education studies, disciplinary studies (with required hours of Judaic content such as Bible studies and the Jewish festival cycle), pedagogy, and practicum. The required number of study hours of Judaic content is approximately three per week in each year of study. In religious teacher-training colleges, the required number of hours of Judaic content is the same, although the substance is different. Teachers' colleges also certify educators for EC programs that include children with special needs.

Salaries for teachers in state-run programs are paid twelve months a year in accordance with the national teachers' salary scale, which includes benefits. Each ganenet is awarded a sabbatical every seventh year. During that year, she can choose a course of study according to her wishes and needs. Those working with children from birth through age three are paid on a lower salary scale and earn considerably less than the ganenet with academic training.

Teachers of children aged three to six are required to participate in sixty hours a year of nationally coordinated professional development programs. Professional development hours are accumulated, and participation earns points that increase one's salary and allow for advancement from one level to another on the national scale. Professional development in a wide range of topics is offered to teachers, including Jewish topics or specific disciplines or approaches through their application to Judaic content.

Prior to their formal academic training, the EC educator in the Jewish sector in Israel has typically gone through the education system, where a substantial number of hours were spent on mandatory Judaic content, and participated in fact or vicariously in many holiday celebrations. Echoes of sacred texts underlie daily speech, and many other facets of Israeli life draw from Jewish sources. This being the case, it is important to note that not all teachers have a deep understanding of Judaism, and a sense of alienation toward Jewish religiosity and Jewish sources is sometimes expressed. The Jewish life experience of teachers in the religious sectors provides them a fluency of Jewish religious knowledge and practice that may not be shared by their secular peers.

Jewish Curricular Content in Israeli ECE

There are seven core content areas developed by professional interdisciplinary teams in the Ministry of Education that define the curricular contours of ECE in Israel. These core areas include language and literacy, mathematics, science and technology, the arts, physical education, and biblical heritage (Ministry of Education 2010). The curricula in these content areas are based on three perspectives: developmental, responsiveness to individual and familial differences, and communal-cultural. These curricula are directed at all children, including state, state-religious, and Arab streams, and appear in both Hebrew and Arabic. Furthermore, the documents call for a balance between guided, structured learning activities (primarily in small groups), experiences that the children initiate with adult assistance, and free-play activities without adult intervention. These components are expressed in the ministry's concept of "gan of the future" (Turgeman, Aldroki-Pinus, and Gerald 2019). Highlighted are student well-being and agency, using four anchors that comprise the foundation for quality learning experiences: self-expression, initiative and creative production, community activity, and wider life learning.

As mentioned earlier, a great deal of time is spent on the Jewish festival cycle from the earliest age (including infants) and across all Jewish sectors in the system. No obligatory curriculum exists, and each educator crafts learning opportunities based on aspects of the festival that are appropriate for different ages. In state programs, this subject matter is taught through a national, historical, cultural lens with no requirement to include blessings, religious or ritual observance, or mitzvah language (language referring to directives found in the written and oral Torah [the holy scroll containing the Five Books of Moses]). In state-religious programs, this subject matter is taught through a national, historical, cultural lens but with an additional layer of instruction that includes religious practice, belief, prayers, and blessings. However, Shabbat is included in all programs through the same lens. Bible stories are also part of the state-mandated curriculum for children ages three through six, with differences in the selection of stories, quantity of stories, and frequency with which they are told recommended for children in state or state-religious classes. It is also important to mention that in the process of attaining literacy in the Hebrew language, children are exposed to the roots of the language found in ancient texts.

Although the system is highly centralized, what goes on in classrooms is a much more autonomous affair. There is wide variation in how "Jewish" the Jewish studies are in any individual program. What educators do in their classrooms with Judaic content is impacted by many variables, including geography, ethnic makeup of a community, and levels of knowledge and experience among educators.

Several initiatives in Judaic content are worthy of mention here. TALI, which is an acronym for enhanced Judaic studies, is an organization that works in collaboration with the Ministry of Education providing professional development and materials to several hundred EC educators in the state system across the country. These programs identify as TALI ganim but are part of the recognized state (i.e., secular) EC system. Sifriyat Pijama (Pajama Library), the Israeli sister program of the North American program PJ Library*, has distributed over ten million Jewish values–themed books through the EC system (Chapter 8 in this book is devoted to the work of Sifriyat Pijama). Several other organizations have created materials and professional development programs to expand and enrich the Judaic knowledge and pedagogy of EC professionals nationwide. Another recent trend is to educate religious and nonreligious children together in an integrated framework.

Final Thoughts

ECJE in Israel and the United States share a common mission of transmitting Judaism and strengthening Jewish life of children and their families. Educators have an opportunity to learn from each other about supporting the individual child, working with families, designing curriculum, addressing the needs of children with learning differences, educating teachers, and providing compelling explorations of Judaism and Jewish life. Conversely and significantly, dialogue, engagement, and collaboration can lead to personal growth on the part of the educator, as assumptions about Jewish life are challenged and different ways of thinking and experiencing Judaism unfold.

For those involved in ECJE in the United States, closer connections with Israel educators could involve:

- experiencing the variety of Jewish lifestyles;
- exploring the richness of Jewish history, culture, religion, and peoplehood in Israel; and
- deepening their knowledge of Judaism, particularly of Israel and Hebrew.

Chapter 2 will detail the history and status of ECJE in the United States and conclude with the valuable insights that those involved with ECE in Israel could gain from ECJE in the United States.

References

Aram, D., and M. Ziv. 2018. "Early Childhood Education in Israel: History, Policy, and Practice." In *Handbook of International Perspectives on Early Childhood Education*, edited by J. L. Roopnarine, J. E. Johnson, S. F. Quinn, and M. M. Patte, 101–14. London: Routledge. https://doi.org/10.4324/9781315562193.

Berkovich, I., and A. Avigur-Eshel. 2019. "Out with the Old, in with the New: Three Ages of Israeli Public Education Policies." In *Digital Protest and Activism in Public Education: Reactions to Neoliberal Restructuring in Israel*, 11–31. Bingley, UK: Emerald.

Brody, D. 2014. *Men Who Teach Young Children: An International Perspective*. London: IOE.

Brody, D. 2018. "Constructing Early Childhood Curriculum and Assessing Young Children in Israel's Mosaic of Culture." In *International Handbook of Early Childhood Education*, edited by M. Fleer and B. van Oers, 1191–1210. Dordrecht: Springer Netherlands. https://doi.org/10.1007/978-94-024-0927-7_61.

Dayan, Y. 2016. "The Invention of Kindergarten from Fredrich Froebel (1782–1852) to the Hebrew Kindergarten." [In Hebrew.] *B'maagalei Chinuch, Mechkar, Iyun V'yetzira* 6:124–34.

Dekel, N., and R. Kark. 2019. "Universal Values in Childhood Concepts and Education in the 'New Yishuv,' 1882–1914." *Israel Affairs* 25 (1): 85–101. https://doi.org/10.1080/13537121.2019.1561178.

Dori, N. 2018. "Values Education in Religious Kindergartens." [In Hebrew.] *Da'at* 15:2–19.

Dror, Y. 1999. "Years of Committees to Reinforce Jewish Studies and Jewish Consciousness in Israel's Non-religious Sector: Conclusions from Historical Curricular Research." In *Abiding Challenges: Research Perspectives in Jewish Education*, edited by Y. Rich and M. Rosenak, 161–88. Bnei Brak: Freund and Bar-Ilan University.

Haas, M., and T. Gavish. 2008. *Touching Reality: On the Co-construction of Knowledge and Identity in the Junkyard Playgrounds of Israel*. Washington, DC: Association for Childhood Education International.

Hacohen, D. 2003. *Immigrants in Turmoil: Mass Immigration to Israel and Its Repercussions in the 1950s and After*. Syracuse, NY: Syracuse University Press.

Horowitz, N. 2016. "Haredi Society—Situation Report 2016." Haredi Institute for Public Affairs. https://machon.org.il/en/publication/haredi-society-situation-report-2016/.

Huitt, W., and J. Hummel. 2003. "Piaget's Theory of Cognitive Development." *Educational Psychology Interactive* 3 (2): 1–5.

Iram, Y. 1993. "Preschool Provision and the Development of Education in Eretz Israel (Palestine), 1898–1948." *Journal of Educational Administration and History* 25 (2): 161–71.

Lavee, Y., and R. Katz. 2003. "The Family in Israel: Between Tradition and Modernity." *Marriage & Family Review* 35 (1–2): 193–217.

Levine, G. 1989. *Pedagogy of the Flexible Gan*. [In Hebrew.] Haifa: Ach.

Lombard, A. 1995. *Program Framework for the Gan*. [In Hebrew.] Jerusalem: Ministry of Education.

Lombard, A. D., and L. S. Jasik. 1983. "The Education of Young Children in Israel." In *Comparative Early Childhood Education*, edited by R. G. Lall and B. M. Lall, 19–31. Springfield, IL: Thomas.

Ministry of Education. 2010. *Educational Activities in the Kindergarten, Guidelines for the Educational Staff*. [In Hebrew.] Pedagogical Administration, Division of Pre-school Education, Israel Ministry of Education.

Olson, D. R. 2014. *Jerome Bruner: The Cognitive Revolution in Educational Theory*. London: Bloomsbury.

Orr, E. 2007. "Identity Representations within Israeli Society." In *Social Representations and Identity*, edited by G. Moloney and I. Walker, 43–60. New York: Palgrave Macmillan.

Pintel-Ginsberg, I. 2006. "Narrating the Past? New Year of the Trees? Celebrations in Modern Israel." *Israel Studies* 11 (1): 174–93. https://doi.org/10.2979/isr.2006.11.1.174.

Proceedings of the Knesset. November 2, 1955, 230. [In Hebrew.]

Rabinovitz, M. 2019. *Frameworks for Young Children*. [In Hebrew.] Jerusalem: Knesset Research and Information Center.

Read, J. 2018. "Taking Froebel Abroad. Transnational Travel by Froebelian Teachers in the 1910s and 2010s: India and South Africa." *Early Years* 38 (2): 156–70.

Rosenthal, M. K. 2009. *Standards for Running Educational Frameworks for Toddlers: Report of the Advisory Committee Headed by Prof. Rosenthal*. [In Hebrew.] Jerusalem: Ministry of Industry, Trade and Employment, Day Care and Early Childhood Care Division.

Schwab, J. J. 1983. "The Practical 4: Something for Curriculum Professors to Do." *Curriculum Inquiry* 13 (3): 239–65.

Shchori-Rubin, Z. 2015. "The Story of the Kindergarten in the Land of Israel." [In Hebrew.] *Katedra* 153:170–5.

Snapir, M., S. Sitton, and G. Russo-Zimet. 2012. *The Israeli Kindergarten in the 20th Century*. [In Hebrew.] Beer Sheva, Israel: Ben Gurion Research Institute for the Study of Israel and Zionism and Ben Gurion University.

Tal, C. 2013. "What Do We Mean by Jewish Education in Professional Development for Early Childhood Education?" *Journal of Jewish Education* 79 (3): 335–59. https://doi.org/10.1080/15244113.2013.816119.

Teuval, E., and A. Guberman. 2010. *Kindergarten Assistant Training Course—Evaluation Research Findings*. [In Hebrew.] Jerusalem: David Yellin College.

Turgeman, M., D. Aldroki-Pinus, and M. Gerald. 2019. "The Gan of the Future, to Be Me, to Belong and to Discover the World." [In Hebrew.] *Da Gan* 12:8–19.

Weissblei, E. 2013. *National Education Councils—A Comparative Review. Submitted to the Education, Culture and Sports Committee*. Jerusalem: Knesset, Research and Information Center.

Zimet, G. R., and I. Gilat. 2017. "Impact of Culture Context on Perceptions of Arab and Jewish Early Childhood Education Students Regarding Early Childhood Education and Care." *Journal of Research in Childhood Education* 31 (2): 281–94.

Zion, N., and B. Spectre. 2000. *A Different Light: The Big Book of Hanukkah*. New York: Devora.

2

Early Childhood Jewish Education in the United States

Ilene Vogelstein, Roberta Louis Goodman, and Shelley T. Alexander

In the United States, the Jewish community has continually confronted the challenge of continuity and survival as a group that, as of 2020, is only approximately 2 percent of the US population (Saxe et al. 2021; Pew Research Center 2021; Dashefsky and Sheskin 2020). Unlike in Israel, early childhood Jewish education (ECJE) is voluntary and private, which presents additional challenges. It is typically affiliated with a particular denomination (e.g., Reform, Conservative, or Orthodox) or an institution of religious or communal significance. Early childhood education (ECE) as a whole in the United States also uses different terminology, applies to different ages, and is governed differently than in Israel: It distinguishes between preschool (generally for ages two to four but some preschools accept children as young as infants) and kindergarten (generally for ages five to six and usually considered part of elementary school) and is governed by a complex mix of federal, state, and local (county, city, and school district) laws and requirements.

This chapter will cover the history of ECJE in the United States, how it is provided now, and the current standards of the field. The first section on history covers the initial mission of ECJE in the United States and the first steps in developing standards, curriculum, and educational approaches for the field. The second section on how ECJE is provided discusses it being voluntary and private; the issue of competition among programs; and information about providers, students, curriculum, and outreach to families. The third section on standards of the field considers curriculum resources, qualifications of providers, and the availability of data regarding the field. The chapter concludes with a discussion of points of connection between ECJE programs in the United States and Israel.

History of ECJE in the United States

Mission

As Jews arrived in the United States, they were faced with the concern of integration into American life. Jewish early childhood (EC) programs first emerged in the United

States in the 1930s (Rotenberg 1977). The goal in establishing Jewish preschools was in principle dual-faceted: to facilitate initiation into American culture (and prepare the children for public elementary school) and to reinforce connections within the Jewish community. The programs were primarily part-time and created opportunities for young Jewish children to gather and interact with each other (Vogelstein and Kaplan 2002).

Over the decades, there were several women, considered to be the matriarchs of ECJE in the United States, serving as directors of EC departments of Jewish community organizations and founding programs and teaching ECJE in educational institutions. Among them were Marvell Ginsburg, Miriam Feinberg, Rena Rotenberg, Cheryl Meskin, Floreva Cohen, Rivka Behar, Esther Elfenbaum, and Ruth Feldman. They also wrote articles for their constituents on ways to integrate Jewish education into their programs (Meskin 2005) and books for Jewish EC programs, such as *Torah Talk* (Chubara, Feinberg, and Rotenberg 1989).

The professional expertise of these directors led to the expansion of Jewish content in ECJE. Their educational philosophy was formed largely in response to trends in the field of ECE that they learned at National Association for the Education of Young Children (NAEYC) conferences. In 1979, a group of Jewish EC educators met at the annual NAEYC conference and offered a Shabbat (Sabbath) and Havdalah (ritual ceremony concluding the Sabbath) experience for Jewish educators attending the conference. The group grew from a handful to hundreds and became an official network group at NAEYC that expanded Shabbat programming into a preconference day for exploring best practices and workshops on Jewish topics. The network remained active for more than twenty years. In 1990, the Commission on Jewish Education in North America was established to "revitalize Jewish education," including researching the state of Jewish educators in the United States and establishing an inventory of best practices (discussed in the next section on "Standards for the Field").

In a 2019 interview with chapter coauthor Ilene Vogelstein, Lyndall Miller explained that the primary factors that came to influence ECJE were the intention of the directors and the vision and mission of the programs. The multiple visions and educational philosophies of the programs formed the basis of the Jewish content in the programs. For some, ECJE was about providing experiences that created awe and wonder around Jewish life and rituals. For others, it was about inspiring pride in children and their families about being Jewish and developing a disposition to continue to participate in Jewish life (Kelner 2007). And, yet, for others, it was about providing an environment that supported inquiry, authenticity, and joy (Ben-Avie et al. 2011).

Standards for the Field

One result of the Commission on Jewish Education in North America's 1990 blueprint plan as stated in its catalytic report *A Time to Act* (Mandel Associated Foundations 1990) was to document examples of outstanding educational practice in Jewish education in the United States. Utilizing best practice principles in the general field of education, coupled with best practices in ECJE, a cohort of Jewish EC professionals (of whom many were the matriarchs of ECJE) created guidelines for ECJE. A compilation containing short descriptions of schools meeting those guidelines was published as *Early Childhood Jewish Education: The Best Practices Project in Jewish Education* (Holtz 1996).

The implementation of *A Time to Act*, through the Council for Initiatives in Jewish Education (CIJE), led to foundational studies regarding Jewish educational personnel in EC programs, which then served as the catalyst for additional research, specifically in the field of ECJE, such as Vogelstein and Kaplan (2002), Beck (2002), and Rosen (2005), as well as numerous articles on the subject, including those of Vogelstein (2008) and Muller (2013). It also fueled the establishment of organizations such as the Coalition for the Advancement of Jewish Education (CAJE) EC department in 2002, the Jewish Early Childhood Education Initiative (JECEI) in 2011(http://www.jecei.org/), the Jewish Early Childhood Education Leadership Institute (JECELI) in 2012 (http://jeceli.org/), and BUILDing Jewish ECE in 2014. It further led to the development of instruments defining excellence in the field: *Defining Excellence in Early Childhood Jewish Education* (Krug and Schade 2004), *Vision for Conservative Early Childhood Programs: A Journey Guide* (Handelman 2009), and "Standards of Excellence for Jewish Community Centers and Synagogues with Early Childhood Education Centers" (Rose Community Foundation 2017; Miller 2017).

Curriculum

The initial determinant of the extent of Jewish education present in Jewish EC programs was often based on denominational affiliation. For example, programs that adhered to religious observance and practice focused on content such as *parshat hashavuah* (the weekly Torah [the holy scroll containing the Five Books of Moses] reading), holiday rituals, and prayer. Programs that had no Jewish denominational affiliation, such as Jewish Community Center (JCC) EC programs, generally included less Jewish content. Their focus was largely on holiday crafts and/or Jewish values (Feldman 2002).

For most programs, whether synagogue-affiliated or not, the curriculum was oriented around the Jewish calendar. For instance, in the week before a Jewish holiday, children would customarily make items associated with the holiday—honey pots for Rosh Hashanah (Jewish New Year), *hanukkiot* (ritual candelabra) for Hanukkah, and Israeli flags for *Yom Ha'atzmaut* (Israel Independence Day). Most classrooms had a Shabbat bulletin board and a weekly Shabbat experience with candle lighting and children participating in the blessings.

Educational Approaches

The formation of the North American Reggio Emilia Alliance (https://www.reggiochildren.it/en/reggio-emilia-approach/) in 2002 significantly impacted ECJE. For instance, JECEI embraced a Reggio-inspired constructivist approach as a foundation (Ben-Avie et al. 2011).

Programs that ascribed to the Reggio educational approach shifted from being directive- and theme-based to implementing a constructivist educational philosophy (see Chapter 6 of this book for a thorough discussion of constructivism). Many of these programs initially struggled with how to incorporate Jewish content into an emergent curriculum. However, the constructivist approach led to more authentic and sustained Jewish experiences replacing teacher-centered simplistic holiday craft activities (Muller, Gorsetman, and Alexander 2018).

The Reggio philosophy also further highlighted the understanding that the core of ECE centered around building and sustaining relationships. Reggio-inspired ECJE programs recognized the importance of an emotional as well as a cognitive connection to Judaism (Ben-Avie et al. 2011). Jewish experiences became child-driven and sustained for long periods of time. For example, instead of the teacher simply reading a book about the holiday of Sukkot (one of the three biblical holidays celebrated by building huts) and the children visiting the synagogue's sukkah (a hut built for usage during the holiday of Sukkot) to hang paper chains, classrooms were transformed into construction sites. Children debated what material they should use to build and decorate their sukkah. Sensory tables became the desert as children reenacted the biblical experience of living in the wilderness. Food was harvested from the class garden, and lulavim (Sukkot ritual fronds) were made from natural materials.

How ECJE Is Currently Provided

ECE is voluntary in the United States in part because it generally covers the age before compulsory education is required by federal or state authorities. Compulsory education laws in the United States require that children receive schooling for a certain period of time. The age requirements are generally set by the individual states. There are certain exceptions, such as homeschooling, but virtually all states have mandates for when children must begin school—typically by the age of six or seven. Some states mandate full- or part-day kindergarten, but pre-kindergarten (also referred to as pre-K) is voluntary in most states.

Jewish education has been private in the United States because federal, and often additionally state, law prohibits public funds paying for religious education. A brief background of what is commonly referred to as "separation of church and state" is provided in this section, followed by a mention of recent court decisions that may lead to changes in that status (at least to some extent) in the future. We then discuss the issues of competition among programs that result from ECJE being voluntary and private and conclude the section with the topics of providers, students, curriculum, and family outreach.

Separation of Church and State

The First Amendment to the US Constitution requires a separation between government and religion—the Establishment Clause states that "Congress shall make no law respecting an establishment of religion." Quoting Thomas Jefferson, the US Supreme Court has stated that the Establishment Clause was intended to accomplish this end by erecting a "wall of separation between Church and State" (*Everson v. Board of Educ. of Ewing*, 330 US 1, 15–16 [1947]). Therefore, religious education is not provided and funded by the public.

However, that sentence regarding religion in the First Amendment continues on to add, "or prohibiting the free exercise thereof" (the Free Exercise Clause). The First Amendment, thus, guarantees both freedom from and freedom of religion, in language that is unclear and difficult to interpret, which has led to hotly contested debates among legal authorities, political officials, and religious and nonreligious groups about its application. (Some individual states also have prohibitions on use of state funds for religious education.) This has led to a patchwork of laws and challenges regarding how much religion is allowed in public schools (particularly regarding issues such as school prayer and public vouchers for payment of religious school tuition).

American Jews have been among those most concerned about the separation of religion and state, with the ever-present question of Jewish continuity at stake. Throughout most of the twentieth century, they overwhelmingly supported a high wall of strict separation of church and state, as protection against possible religious discrimination and persecution and "as the only defense against a Christian-dominated state" (Sarna 2002, 63). In recent decades, though, there have been escalating concerns that the wall of separation has risen into a barrier that threatens to exile religion—including Judaism—from American lives completely. Increasing numbers of Jews, fearing Jewish losses from assimilation and secularization, have broken ranks and begun to urge government accommodation to religion (Cohen 2002, 43; Dalin 2002, 306). Among those are proponents of the use of vouchers for Jewish day schools and other Jewish education.

The recent conservative tilt in the US Supreme Court has led to decisions in which the Free Exercise Clause increasingly takes precedence over the Establishment Clause. The Court ruled on June 30, 2020, that states must allow religious schools to participate in programs that provide scholarships with tax-exempt money to students attending private schools (without deciding whether public money could be spent on religious instruction), a decision that opened the door to more public funding of religious education (*Espinoza v. Montana Department of Revenue*, 591 US __, 140 S. Ct. 2246 [2020]). On December 8, 2021, the court heard the case of a state's exclusion of religious schools from its policy of private school tuition assistance for students in towns without a public school, considering the constitutionality of the use of public money to attend schools that provide religious instruction (*Carson v. Makin*, Docket 20-1088). The Union of Orthodox Congregations of America (Orthodox Union), the nation's largest Orthodox Jewish umbrella organization; the Jewish Coalition for Religious Liberty; and the National Jewish Commission on Law and Public Affairs, joined by Agudath Israel of America and other groups, filed amicus curiae (friend of the court) briefs urging the court to reverse the appellate decision and allow parents to use state tuition assistance payments at religious schools. The Anti-Defamation League, the Central Conference of American Rabbis, the Jewish Social Policy Action

Network, the Men of Reform Judaism, the National Council of Jewish Women, the Reconstructionist Rabbinical Association, the Union for Reform Judaism, and the Women of Reform Judaism joined in an amicus brief filed by twenty-three religious and civil rights organizations urging the court to affirm the decision and disallow public funding of religious education. There has not been a decision by the court as of the writing of this chapter.

Competition among Programs

Jewish ECE options compete with private general/secular/or full-day care centers and programs; other faith-based programs; and, in some cases, free public pre-K education. Jewish EC schools compete with one another, especially in more densely Jewish populated areas. In metropolitan areas, parents often have choices among ECJE programs, based on many factors, as the schools vary in their Jewish ideology, educational approach, days and hours open, ages of children served, location, and cost. Even in places with small Jewish populations under two thousand, various opportunities for ECJE may be available.

Schools have a vision of what they hope to accomplish. For some, this vision is expressed tacitly or implicitly, discernible in what they do. The descriptions of the school found in different forms of communication is designed to attract new students and provide insights into what the school is attempting to do. Many schools have a mission or vision statement articulating explicitly their purpose and outcomes. In some cases, various stakeholders—directors, parents, teachers, clergy/heads of institutions, lay leaders, and/or community leaders—are involved in a process leading to the development of a mission or vision statement. In other cases, the director might craft the statements on her own.

A school's quality most affects those concerned about ECJE schools functioning as a way of deepening the Jewish experience and informing attitudes and behaviors of children and parents. Ben-Avie et al. (2011) found a connection between parents' perceptions of quality and their willingness to engage in Jewish life.

> The key factor is the level of excellence of Jewish ECE programs' underlying "operating system." It is worth considering that the parents who rate that their children's JECE programs operate at a superb level are more open to enhancing their lives with Jewish connections. Thus, for many parents the promotion of a children's Jewish identity is not an important criterion when choosing a JECE program. However, if they perceive and experience the JECE programs as excellent and well-run, they will become more engaged in Jewish actions after they enroll their children as a "side effect." (750)

However, there are factors other than quality that influence the choice of ECJE. A study of Jewish parents in Greater Boston found that "parents consider hours, location, and cost first. Other factors enter into the decision-making process only after a particular preschool meets parents' requirements with respect to these considerations" (Rosen and Schwartz 2015, 55). For these parents, the Jewish environment and learning were secondary, an added benefit for the families.

A current federal proposal for combined federal and state funding of voluntary universal pre-K for three- and four-year-olds, contained in the Build Back Better Act, H.R. 5376, 117th Cong. (2021–2), could have substantial impact on existing ECJE. As is evident in some states, if courts continue in the trend of allowing public funding of some or all religious aspects of schooling and universal pre-K is provided, Jewish preschool programs nationally could find a solution to their funding problems. The issue of competition with public programs as to cost could be lessened, although there could be increased issues of competition arising with a proliferation of preschool programs. (There could be a benefit to ECJE programs, though, if parents who wanted their children to have a Jewish education but had not intended to begin it at such an early age decided to enroll their children in Jewish preschools to keep up with children in the universal program.)

Assuming there would still be questions regarding the amount of Jewish content allowed in schools funded under the universal program, there could be a split among American Jews as to support for ECJE as part of universal pre-K. Orthodox educators objected to the limitations of how much religious instruction could be included in a universal pre-K program in New York, even after it made concessions specifically to accommodate them (Nathin-Kazis 2014).

Providers

Institutions

ECJE programs are overwhelmingly situated in or with host institutions: larger organizations with an EC program as one component. These include Jewish day schools, Jewish Community Centers, synagogues, and *Chabad* (a Chassidic community with the majority of residence in Israel and the United States). There are a few schools providing ECJE that are independent or self-incorporated (Schaap 2004). Some Jewish programs are even offered in the educator's home.

Teachers

There are two main challenges regarding teachers in ECJE programs: finding personnel with both Jewish studies' knowledge and credentials in ECE and paying teachers and directors living wages.

To be a teacher in many private EC settings for ages birth to five, one only needs a high-school education (Vogelstein 2008) and usually some basic continuing education courses. In some states, this means taking classes with no accountability—no required readings, papers, or tests; rather, just spending time in class. However, to teach in a public elementary school, including pre-K (four-year-olds) and kindergarten (five-year-olds), a teacher generally must have at least a bachelor's degree in education (or in some states or localities, a bachelor's degree in any subject along with a teaching certificate).

Many ECJE teachers lack background in Jewish education and/or Jewish content. Pittsburgh JECEI/Bonim Beyachad conducted an unpublished 2016 survey of ECJE schools and personnel in metropolitan Pittsburgh, in which chapter coauthor Roberta Louis Goodman participated, and found that 42 percent of ECJE educators in that area did not identify as Jewish or lacked Jewish educational experience; a number of the teachers expressed that they felt they knew enough to teach about Jewish holidays but lacked knowledge beyond that, such as Jewish values and texts.

Salaries are the biggest challenge to finding qualified educators. To keep tuition low to compete with ECE (and childcare) alternatives, ECJE providers typically keep salaries of their ECJE teachers low—often not much more than minimum wage. The fact that the vast majority of this underpaid profession of ECJE educators is female has been noted by women's advocacy groups. Even in Jewish day schools, ECJE teachers are not necessarily paid on the same salary scale as teachers of kindergarten and elementary grades in secular schools, and many do not receive health benefits whether they are full- or part-time employees.

An important benefit that may be offered, though, is reduced tuition for teachers' children in the ECJE program, if it is connected with a day school or congregation, although only some teachers are eligible for this benefit. Another benefit valued by some teachers is paid time off for Jewish holidays.

If universal pre-K becomes a reality, there could be further competition for teachers eligible for the higher pay that is likely be offered in that program. This could lead to higher salaries being offered for ECJE positions (which might be affordable for the institutions if ECJE programs become eligible for public vouchers and are not so pressured to keep their costs to a minimum in order to keep their tuition low). Alternatively, it could lead to qualified ECJE educators being lured to higher-paying jobs in universal pre-K programs, further exacerbating the challenge of finding quality ECJE educators.

Students

Because ECJE in the United States is private, voluntary, and provided through different institutions, documenting the age and number of ECJE students is difficult. A few organizations and researchers in recent years have attempted to establish demographic information regarding ECJE students, although numbers are difficult to compare in that they apply to different ages, programs, and geographical areas.

Age of Students

Families enroll their children in ECJE at different ages, some as young as infancy. The increase of households with two full-time working parents and single-parent households creates a demand for more programs for children under the age of three (Linden 2016). The shortage of Jewish full-day childcare programs, especially for infants, is a concern (Kolben 2011; Vogelstein 2008); one challenge to the system is that some ECJE centers are open only part-day. Parents are known to put their unborn babies on waiting lists for infant care as soon as they find out they are pregnant.

Families' need to be connected to the Jewish community can also affect the age at which they enroll their children in ECJE. A 2001/2002 study of parents who had sent their children to Jewish preschools in Baltimore, Denver, and Chicago found that families that just had their first child tend to feel very isolated and would benefit from a supportive program (Beck 2002). A more recent study in Chicago also observed that families with children under the age of two were particularly receptive to ECJE programming efforts as they had a greater desire to be connected to the Jewish community (Rosen 2013). A 2015 study of EC decisions among Jewish parents in Greater Boston (Rosen and Schwartz 2015) suggested that families in which the oldest child is under three are less likely to feel connected to the community.

Enrollment Numbers

The Avi Chai Foundation, a philanthropic organization supporting Jewish education and Jewish life, conducted five national censuses of Jewish day schools at five-year intervals beginning with the 1998–9 school year. The final census, conducted in 2018–19 (Besser 2020), presented data provided by 906 Jewish day schools, stated to be every known Jewish day school at that time. It reported 18,999 children enrolled in programs for four-year-olds. It stated that a significant number of children in this age group were not included in the data, though, because the census excluded institutions that operated exclusively at the preschool level. Thus, it also did not report any enrollment numbers for children from infancy through age three.

The JCC Association of North America (JCCA) and the Union of Reform Judaism (URJ), in a 2019 press release announcing their partnership to address challenges facing the field of ECJE (URJ 2019), reported that their work impacted 65,000 children from 50,000 families and 10,000 educators across 475 EC centers in the United States and Canada. (These numbers did not indicate the ages of the children, how many children and families identified as Jewish, or how the numbers were distributed between the United States and Canada.)

Schaap (2004) estimated there were 122,541 children in ECJE in 2000, a doubling of enrollment from the early 1980s. Ilene Vogelstein estimated in 2008 that there were 78,000 children (mostly three- and four-year-olds) enrolled in ECJE programs affiliated with congregations (56,000), JCCs (13,000), and independent schools (9,000). She noted that the 2003–4 Avi Chai census reported 32,000 four- and five-year-olds in Jewish day schools (Schick 2005) and that the 1999–2000 Avi Chai census reported 7,000 children under the age of four attending Jewish day school EC programs (Schick 2000). With anecdotal information suggesting the number of children in congregational and home-based programs, Vogelstein estimated the total number of Jewish children in 2008 in any kind of Jewish EC program as between 130,000 and 140,000—less than a quarter of the potential population. Although ECJE programs are not limited to children being raised Jewish, today there is some evidence of ECJE programs shutting down due to the decline in the Jewish population in certain geographic areas; for example, the northern suburbs of Chicago saw the loss of five ECJE schools in the past five years.

Curriculum

ECJE schools are generally autonomous institutions, which translates into diversity. Schools make their own choices as to what content and pedagogy to implement. Even in cases of affiliation with a national movement or organization, schools are largely left to make their own choices and set their own direction. Curriculum is an area in which schools have the liberty to create their own.

Schools are influenced by educational trends in the larger American ECE arena. Popular approaches, in no particular order, include constructivist, Montessori, Reggio-inspired, play-based, developmentally appropriate, and positivistic. Schools can follow one or a combination of these approaches. Montessori is the one with the most training requirements and restrictions imposed in order for it to be able to be aligned with this type of school. Even when a school explicitly claims one or more of these approaches, much is dependent on the school culture and training and skills of the teachers.

Schools vary in the degree to which curriculum is teacher- or student-initiated. On one end of the spectrum, the director and teachers set the curriculum. On the other end, curriculum is emergent or negotiated, an interplay between teacher and learner, where it responds to children's interests and arises from their interactions with one another. The content schools share is teaching Jewish holidays, including Shabbat, Jewish values, Israel, food blessings, and some Hebrew. Certain schools teach Torah primarily through parshat hashavuah. The depth and breadth of all these subjects and the visibility of Jewish learning and living varies greatly among the schools. The messages and interpretations vary as well.

The Friday celebration of Shabbat is a highlight in schools, one that is shared frequently with parents, grandparents, caretakers, and siblings. Blessings and singing are central to this experience. They are festive, filled with each school's rituals.

Values can be presented through a Hebrew word, stories, and actions. Some programs are carried out for others, such as collecting food to teach and do tzedakah (a righteous or charitable act) or a mitzvah (directive found in the written and oral Torah) related to feeding the hungry. Others focus on the children's behavior, such as adding *gemilut chasidim* (acts of kindness) or displays when teachers ask children to share their interactions with classmates or family members during the week and write them down.

Other examples of commonly shared curricular content are different kinds of blessings and markers of Jewish peoplehood. For instance, reciting a blessing before eating a snack or lunch is commonplace regardless of the school's affiliation. Some Israel experiences are standard around Yom Ha'atzmaut, with the "pretend trip to Israel" being a favorite of ECJE teachers (Applebaum and Zakai 2020). The challenge for many schools is to, as the title of a popular Jewish EC handbook written for teachers suggests, make *Jewish Everyday* (Handelman 2000)—in other words, to integrate Judaism into the classroom throughout the day. In some schools, the daily environment and learning experiences are filled with Jewish symbols, books, songs, blessings, themes, play areas, and Hebrew. In others, the Jewish experience seems to come to the forefront primarily when the Jewish "holiday boxes" of objects and activities appear at different times during the year.

Family Outreach

Efforts are emerging to reach and engage families with young children beyond enrolling them in an ECJE program. Synagogues with or without formal ECJE programs are known to open their doors to anyone in the community, without requiring participants to be members, in order to attend services designed for young children on Shabbat (Tot Shabbat) and holidays, especially the High Holy Days, and for other experiences designed to build relationships and connect them to the organized Jewish community. A staff member or volunteers often serve as ambassadors, helping to create a network for families, introducing them to other families with children of similar ages, and guiding them to resources. Typical types of synagogue-sponsored programs include parenting classes, play groups, and Shabbat enrichment classes at secular EC schools. The hope is that these families will remain connected to the Jewish community, even affiliating with synagogues, JCCs, or other Jewish institutions.

PJ Library®, a program created by the Harold Grinspoon Foundation, provides Jewish books for parents and grandparents to read to young children. Through partnerships with Jewish organizations throughout North America, PJ Library® has encouraged programming outside of the home to bring together families, some in open or public spaces (e.g., museums or botanical gardens). (See Chapter 8 of this book for a discussion of the Israeli sister program, Sifryat Pijama, Pajama Library.)

Some families attend parent/child classes as an entry point into ECJE programs. Schools vary in how "family-centric," rather than "child-centric," they are. Being family oriented includes offering parenting classes, Jewish learning opportunities for parents, family holiday experiences, and social activities for parents and/or families. Providing guidance and support to parents on parenting and childrearing and assisting parents in identifying Jewish experiences now and in the future to further their Jewish "journey" are other ways educators are family-centric.

Standards of the Field

In this open, private system where schools operate independently, schools must meet federal, state, and local licensing requirements where applicable, but there is no central authority to impose standards as to the Jewish education component of ECJE. As discussed previously, early efforts developed research and instruments to define best practices. However, these were not all successful.

Various organizations have made ongoing efforts to define and promote standards of quality for ECJE. JECEI, sponsored by the Steinhardt Foundation, was a national effort aiming to inform schools throughout the range of host institutions (JCCs, synagogues of different denominations, and day schools). It ended its consulting with schools in 2011 but today remains a website (http://www.jecei.org/) that provides research, curricula, tools, and materials for use by organizations wishing to adopt its approach to ECJE. JCCA's EC department built on JECEI's efforts and developed the Sheva Center (https://jcca.org/what-we-do/sheva/), a partnership with JCCs to promote leadership development and raise the quality of their ECJE programs. An example of a local effort is that of Pittsburgh JECEI/Bonim Beyachad, which created a self-study process (https://jfedpgh.org/JECEI) that ECJE schools can undertake. The previously described national joint effort by URJ and JCCA announced in 2019 (URJ 2019) has yet to be implemented.

Curriculum

There is no Jewish group or authority to impose uniform curriculum standards on ECJE programs, and there are no content areas that are required to be covered for a program to be considered ECJE. Some local Jewish organizations provide sample curricular resources for sale or for free to ECJE providers. For example, the Jewish Education Center of Cleveland has a curriculum available for purchase called "Fingerprints: Discovering Jewish Life," which combines principles of ECE and quality Jewish education for full-time ECJE, focusing on Jewish holidays. It also sells comprehensive guides for teachers in part-time ECJE schools, one for pre-K and another for kindergarten. During the pandemic, it began to offer a free one-year curriculum online for kindergarten through sixth grade (Haier 2021). Some local Jewish Federations provide free curriculum resources on their websites. JCCA's Sheva Center creates curriculum materials in its program working with six lab communities within JCCs.

Qualifications of Providers

Schools

Most ECJE schools adhere to a variety of government secular requirements for licensure focusing on the health and well-being of children and teachers related to teacher-to-child ratio, health standards, and administrative practices; however, some choose to take an exemption of licensing, which requires less adherence to government regulation. Others pursue state quality efforts that examine curricular practices and educational opportunities—toys, materials, teacher/child interaction—and some even seek national accreditation. A few Jewish communities have produced quality expectations, and some national efforts have attempted to define what "Jewish" looks like in terms of excellence in ECE.

Teachers and Administrators

The lack of general availability of degree- or credential-bearing programs for ECJE teachers and directors has been a challenge. Long-standing degree or credential programs for ECJE teachers exist in Orthodox and Chabad seminaries, as well as at Yeshiva University and Hebrew College. And JECELI has attempted to address the shortage of trained ECJE directors, in part through local mentorship and fellowship programs (Jewish Federation 2019). It is only recently, though, that community and institutional efforts have been made to find creative paths to university credentials in ECJE. In 2019, the Jewish United Fund partnered with the Erikson Institute to create a twenty-month online Master of Science in EC Education to be piloted in Chicago (Erikson Institute 2019). And in 2020, American Jewish University launched a first of its kind online Bachelor of Arts completion degree in ECE (American Jewish University 2020) to add to their already existing MAEd in ECE.

Availability of Data

Policy makers, planners, philanthropists, and professional and lay leaders are hindered in making decisions about where to invest resources to optimize the ECJE experience and provide outreach because demographic data about the potential student population is hard to come by. There are two main reasons for this. First, there is no central organization responsible for collecting this data. The US Census Bureau does not collect data on religious affiliation in its demographic surveys or decennial census, and there is no central Jewish authority in the United States to collect authoritative data. Second, in the United States the questions of who is a Jew and whom ECJE should serve are difficult ones. Individuals can identify as Jews in many different ways, and providers of ECJE make their own decisions about whom they wish to serve, with many providers not limiting their services only to children or families who have a member who identifies as Jewish.

There are some organizations that conduct national Jewish population studies, although the studies are costly and results vary widely due to the different criteria used. The American Jewish Year Book has provided an annual record of statistics on the American Jewish population since 1899. Its 2019 survey (Dashefsky and Sheskin 2020) estimates that the American Jewish population is 6.97 million. The Pew Research Center (2021), an independently funded fact tank, conducted its most recent national Jewish population study in 2020. It provided information both about what it means to be Jewish in America—identifying through the Jewish religion; considering oneself Jewish culturally, ethnically, or by family background; having a Jewish parent; or being raised Jewish—and about how many people in America identify as Jewish in some way. The survey found that approximately 1.8 million children were being raised Jewish *in some way* (approximately 1.2 million being raised exclusively Jewish by religion, 400,000 being raised as Jewish but not by religion, and 200,000 being raised both as Jewish by religion *and* in another religion). The Steinhardt Social Research Institute at Brandeis University prepared an analysis in 2021 of the population estimates from the 2020 American Jewish Population Project, one of the largest programs of independent research in this area, which reported a population of Jewish children in America of 1,583,000 (defined as a child who lives in a household with at least one adult who identifies as Jewish by religion or who self-identifies as Jewish, has at least one Jewish parent, and does not belong to any other religious group) (Saxe et al. 2021). The analysis compared the estimates from these three major sources and noted how the disparity in the numbers highlights the challenges associated with assessing the size and characteristics of the US Jewish population.

In addition to the discrepancies between the studies, none provide all of the data that would be helpful in planning for ECJE nationally, such as the ages of children with parents who identify as Jewish or the number and ages of children enrolled in

ECE programs, Jewish or otherwise. The studies also do not provide local, metro-area-based data, even basic population numbers of families with young children and their ages, which are crucial to know because planning and funding occurs locally. There are some studies done by local Jewish community groups, but they are sporadic.

Final Thoughts

As stated in Chapter 1 on ECJE in Israel, the United States and Israel share a common mission of transmitting Judaism and strengthening Jewish life of children and their families. Educators in the two countries have an opportunity to learn from each other about supporting the individual child, working with families, designing curriculum, educating teachers, and providing compelling explorations of Judaism and Jewish life. Despite the diverse and complex dynamics of providing ECJE in the United States, those involved with ECJE in Israel could gain valuable insight about:

1. living in and appreciating a pluralistic, multicultural setting both within Judaism, with its varieties of expression, and among different religions and cultures (e.g., Arab and migrant segments of Israeli society);
2. diversifying the ways content is approached, underlying, and supporting the different ways Judaism is expressed, interpreted, and lived; and
3. structuring school finances to allow for a better student-to-teacher ratio enabling smaller class size and individualized programs.

References

American Jewish University. 2020. "American Jewish University Unveils Bachelor of Arts in Early Childhood Education." June 16, 2020. https://www.aju.edu/newsroom/press/American-Jewish-University-Unveils-Bachelor-of-Arts-in-Early-Childhood-Education.

Applebaum, L., and S. Zakai. 2020. "'I'm Going to Israel and All I Need to Pack Is My Imagination': Pretend Trips to Israel in Jewish Early Childhood Education." *Journal of Jewish Education* 86 (1): 94–119. https://doi.org/10.1080/15244113.2019.1696659.

Beck, P. 2002. "Jewish Preschools as Gateways to Jewish Life: A Survey of Jewish Preschool Parents in Three Cities." *Contact: The Journal of the Steinhardt Foundation for Jewish Life* 5 (1): 6–7. https://www.bjpa.org/search-results/publication/5288.

Ben-Avie, M., I. Vogelstein, R. L. Goodman, E. Schaap, and P. Bidol-Padva. 2011. "Early Childhood Education." In *International Handbook of Jewish Education*, edited by H. Miller, L. D. Grant, and A. Pomson, 749–65. New York: Springer.

Besser, M. 2020. *A Census of Jewish Day Schools in the United States 2018–2019*. New York: Avi Chai Foundation.

Chubara, Y., M. Feinberg, and R. Rotenberg. 1989. *Torah Talk: An Early Childhood Teaching Guide*. Denver, CO: Alternatives in Religious Education.

Cohen, N. W. 2002. "An Overview of American Jewish Defense." In *Jews and the American Public Square: Debating Religion and Republic*, edited by A. Mittleman, J. D. Sarna, and R. Licht, 13–46. Lanham, MD: Rowman & Littlefield.

Dalin, D. G. 2002. "Jewish Critics of Strict Separationism." In *Jews and the American Public Square: Debating Religion and Republic*, edited by A. Mittleman, J. D. Sarna, and R. Licht, 291–310. Lanham, MD: Rowman & Littlefield.

Dashefsky, A., and I. M. Sheskin, eds. 2020. *American Jewish Year Book 2019*. New York: Springer.

Erikson Institute. 2019. "New Training Opportunity for Early Childhood Education Leaders Announced." Erikson Institute. February 8, 2019. https://www.erikson.edu/news/new-training-opportunity-for-early-childhood-education-leaders-announced/#:~:text=The%20Jewish%20United%20Fund%20%28JUF%29%20and%20Erikson%20Institute,practice%20and%20experience%20while%20they%20complete%20the%20degree.

Feldman, R. 2002. *An Ethical Start*. New York: JCC Association.

Haier, M. 2021. "La-Bri'ut: The JECC's Free Jewish Learning Curriculum Reaches Thousands of Students." Covenant Foundation. Accessed November 11, 2021. https://covenantfn.org/articles/to-our-health-and-wellness-the-la-briut-curriculum-of-the-jewish-education-center-of-cleveland/.

Handelman, M. S. 2000. *Jewish Everyday: The Complete Handbook for Early Childhood Teachers*. Denver, CO: ARE.

Handelman, M. S. 2009. *Vision for Conservative Early Childhood Programs: A Journey Guide*. New York: United Synagogue of Conservative Judaism.

Holtz, B. W. 1996. *Early Childhood Jewish Education: The Best Practices Project in Jewish Education*. Council for Initiatives in Jewish Education. Accessed August 17, 2020. https://files.eric.ed.gov/fulltext/ED428839.pdf.

Jewish Federation. 2019. "LA Invests Creatively in Jewish Early Childhood through Federation's JECELI-LA." The Jewish Federation of Greater Los Angeles. March 28, 2019. https://www.jewishla.org/l-a-invests-creatively-in-jewish-early-childhood-through-federations-jeceli-la/.

Kelner, S. 2007. "Who Is Being Taught? Early Childhood's Adult-Centered Approach." In *Family Matters: Jewish Education in an Age of Choice*, edited by J. Wertheimer, 59–79. Waltham, MA: Brandeis. http://hdl.handle.net/10192/26633.

Kolben, D. 2011. "Jewish Day Care Is Missing Link." *Forward*. December 28, 2011. https://forward.com/articles/148654/jewish-day-care-is-missing-link/.

Krug, C., and L. Schade. 2004. *Defining Excellence in Early Childhood Jewish Education*. Medford, MA: Center for Applied Child Development, Eliot-Pearson Department of Child Development, Tufts University.

Linden, W. 2016. "Jewish Early Engagement Forum (JEEF): A Conversation with Founder Rachel Raz." *Jewish Boston*. June 3, 2016. https://www.jewishboston.com/jewish-early-engagement-forum-jeef/.

Mandel Associated Foundations. 1990. *A Time to Act*. Lanham, MD: University Press of America. https://www.bjpa.org/content/upload/bjpa/c__w/Time%20to%20act.pdf.

Meskin, C. 2005. *Jewish Values for Growing Exceptional Jewish Children*, vol. 3. New York: CAJE (Coalition for the Advancement of Jewish Education).

Miller, L. F. 2017. "An Opportunity Not to Be Missed: Marketing Jewish Early Childhood Education to Parents." *Gleanings* 4 (2): 11.

Muller, M. 2013. "Constructivism and Jewish Early Childhood Education." *Journal of Jewish Education* 79 (3): 315–34. https://doi.org/10.1080/15244113.2013.816116.

Muller, M., C. Gorsetman, and S. T. Alexander. 2018. "Struggles and Successes in Constructivist Jewish Early Childhood Classrooms." *Journal of Jewish Education* 84 (3): 284–311. https://doi.org/10.1080/15244113.2018.1478533.

Nathin-Kazis, J. 2014. "Why Would Yeshivas Reject Pre-K Program Designed for Them?" *Forward*. June 12, 2014. https://forward.com/news/200006/why-would-yeshivas-reject-pre-k-program-designed-f/.

Pew Research Center. 2021. "Jewish Americans in 2020." May 11, 2021. https://www.pewforum.org/2021/05/11/jewish-americans-in-2020/.

Rose Community Foundation. 2017. "Standards of Excellence for Jewish Community Centers and Synagogues with Early Childhood Education Centers." Rose Community Foundation. April 21, 2017. https://rcfdenver.org/blog/standards-excellence-jewish-community-centers-synagogues-early-childhood-education-centers/.

Rosen, M. I. 2005. "Beginning at the Beginning: What Should the Jewish Community Be Doing for New Jewish Parents?" Paper presented at the International Conference on Jewish Education, Florida International University, Miami, FL, January 12, 2005. https://bir.brandeis.edu/bitstream/handle/10192/22959/Beginning%20at%20the%20Beginning.pdf?sequence=1&isAllowed=y.

Rosen, M. I. 2013. "Looking for Connections: A Study of Jewish Families with Young Children in Chicago." Summary report prepared for the Jewish United Fund/Jewish Federation of Metropolitan Chicago, March 2013. Accessed November 2, 2021. https://www.bjpa.org/content/upload/bjpa/c__c/Looking%20for%20Connections%20-%202013%20Chicago%20Report.pdf.

Rosen, M. I., and H. Schwartz. 2015. *How Jews Choose: A Study of Early Childhood Decisions among Jewish Parents in Greater Boston. A Research Study Report of Combined Jewish Philanthropies*. Boston, MA: Combined Jewish Philanthropies.

Rotenberg, R. 1977. "A Survey History of Jewish Early Childhood Education." MA diss., Baltimore Hebrew University.

Sarna, J. D. 2002. "Church-State Dilemmas of American Jews." In *Jews and the American Public Square: Debating Religion and Republic*, edited by A. Mittleman, J. D. Sarna, and R. Licht, 47–68. Lanham, MD: Rowman & Littlefield.

Saxe, L., D. Parmer, E. Tighe, R. M. de Kramer, D. Kallista, D. Nussbaum, X. Seabrum, and J. Mandell. 2021. *American Jewish Population Estimates 2020 Summary & Highlights*. American Jewish Population Project. Brandeis Steinhardt Social Research Institute. https://ajpp.brandeis.edu/documents/2020/JewishPopulationDataBrief2020.pdf.

Schaap, E. 2004. *Early Childhood Jewish Education and Profiles of Its Educators*. CAJE. June 24, 2004. file:///C:/Users/19165/Downloads/policyarchive_file_17896.pdf.

Schick, M. 2000. *Census of Jewish Day Schools in the United States*. New York: Avi Chai Foundation.

Schick, M. 2005. *Census of U.S. Day Schools 2003–04*. New York: Avi Chai Foundation.

URJ (Union for Reform Judaism). 2019. "JCC Association of North America and the Union for Reform Judaism Launch Unprecedented Partnership to Strengthen Field of Jewish Early Childhood Education." Union for Reform Judaism. December 19, 2019. Accessed July 22, 2021. https://urj.org/press-room/jcc-association-north-america-and-union-reform-judaism-launch-unprecedented-partnership.

Vogelstein, I. 2008. "Early Childhood Jewish Education: 'If Not Now, When?'" In *What We Now Know about Jewish Education: Perspectives on Research for Practice*, edited by R. L. Goodman, P. A. Flexner, and L. D. Bloomberg, 373–85. Lewisville, NC: Torah Aura Productions.

Vogelstein, I., and D. Kaplan. 2002. *Untapped Potential: The Status of Jewish Early Childhood Education in America*. Baltimore, MD: JECE Partnership.

3

The Current State of Research and Writing about Early Childhood Jewish Education

David L. Brody and Howard Deitcher

Children have always been considered the most important social group in Jewish society for perpetuating the study of the Torah (the holy scroll containing the Five Books of Moses) and Jewish life. This concept is firmly rooted in the following Talmudic (the body of Jewish civil and ceremonial law and legend) dictum:

> Rabbi Judah said: "Come and see how beloved are children by the Holy One blessed be He. The Sanhedrin was exiled, but the *Shechina* [the Divine Presence] did not go into exile with them. The priestly watches were exiled, but the Shechina did not go into exile with them. When however, children were exiled, the Shechina went into exile with them." (Lam. Rabbah 1:32)

This chapter attempts to gain a comprehensive and nuanced understanding of the various types of issues, questions, and key foci that have enabled early childhood Jewish education (ECJE) over the past two decades to fulfill this Talmudic commitment. To do so, we performed a study with the aim to construct a conceptual framework of the corpus of written documents related to ECJE. Throughout this study, we discovered a wealth of written material that deepened our understanding and appreciation for the complex nature of ECJE and the multiple modes of addressing these issues. The need to collect, categorize, and identify issues that have been addressed is critical, as it allows us to take stock of what writings have shaped and impacted ECJE to date and, concurrently, shine light on some of the gaps in research and analysis that deserve further attention.

To gain an overview of the range of critical issues confronting ECJE, we examined the literature through three lenses: What are the key structural underpinnings that researchers and practitioners of ECJE address in their writing? What are the curricular topics that have been studied to date, in which contexts have they been studied, and why have they been studied? What pedagogical considerations are most prominent in transmitting foundational ideas, concepts, practices, and values in ECJE?

In any project of this nature, limitations need to be set. First, we focused on evaluations, policy papers, and research studies that were conducted in North America, Israel, and other diaspora communities. While ECJE in the diaspora is typically affiliated with an institution of religious or communal significance, in Israel the case is different. Israeli society has taken on the task of educating its youngest members through a values-driven system of public education that is divided into sectors (Brody 2018). Thus, an appropriate definition of ECJE in Israel includes both the history and practice of the public education system in the country, particularly in areas that reflect Jewish cultural, religious, and national values. Therefore the documents selected for Israeli ECJE include many aspects of the public education system dealing with policy, curriculum, and pedagogic considerations. (These parameters of ECJE in Israel and the United States are discussed comprehensively in Chapters 1 and 2 of this book.) Second, we selected materials that inform the ECJE field of practice, excluding descriptions of particular programs and activities and teacher guides that lacked analysis and reflection that could directly address the macro issues under examination. Third, ECJE is a dynamic and evolving field of study, and we acknowledge that certain materials may not have been included. We encourage other researchers to move this agenda forward. Finally, we report here only the publication and its basic content, not the major findings or other essential aspects of its content. Our aim is to describe the range and density of writing and research on the various themes we have identified. At the end of the chapter, we will suggest lacunas in this corpus and areas in need of further attention, both on the discursive and the research level.

Methodology

Obtaining a comprehensive corpus of research and reflective writing about ECJE entailed searching several education databases, including Ebsco Education Source, Proquest, ERIC, Google Scholar, the Hebrew University Library Search Engine, the University of Haifa Library Search Engine, and Dissertation Abstracts. We used the following search terms: early childhood (EC), kindergarten, preschool, young children, and Jewish. We limited the search to articles, books, reports, and unpublished theses from the year 2000 to the first half of 2020. We also turned to scholars, policy makers, educators, and community leaders in the field in both the United States and Israel, requesting that they refer us to published documents related to ECJE, including research, reflective writing, and institutional reports. We searched for documents in English or Hebrew only. This initial search yielded 150 documents.

Criteria for including documents in the corpus consisted of several factors. The document had to relate to Jewish education for children ages zero to eight. Jewish education as broadly defined in this book's Introduction had to be addressed. The publications were limited to scholarly journals, master's theses and doctoral dissertations published or unpublished, professional magazines and journals, and institutional reports. Documents from the popular press and newspapers were excluded. This winnowing process resulted in a corpus of ninety-six documents, which were uploaded to a shared library within Mendeley (reference manager software) for easy access and the creation of a tagged database. When available, the full text of the documents was uploaded. We read the abstracts of all documents, and where abstracts were not available, we scanned the entire document in order to identify topics addressed.

Table 3.1 Definitions of ECJE Database Genres

Genre	Definition
Research	Systematic investigation of a topic, including research question, empirical qualitative and quantitative data collection, and analysis; includes program research published by an institution or agency for evaluation and policy purposes and not found in peer-reviewed journal
Practice	Description of practice in a single classroom or center, curriculum description, and program description
Policy	Policy document or policy recommendation; may appear within a document labeled as research or practice

Each document was tagged according to the genre of writing: research, practice, or policy. The definitions of these categories are given in Table 3.1.

Following this genre categorization, we generated a lengthy list of topics, which was then reduced by aggregating similar foci into twenty somewhat broader categories that included all of the topics identified. These categories were then sorted into three major groups: structural underpinnings, curriculum content, and pedagogical considerations. Structural underpinnings include macro issues that describe and determine the forms and quality of ECJE. Curriculum content includes specific content areas that constitute the basis of the ECJE curriculum. Pedagogical considerations include descriptions, presentations, and analyses of various factors related to the learner, the teaching process, and approaches to teaching and learning. If a document fit more than one category, it was assigned all appropriate tags. It was then addressed in this study according to all of its descriptors. This typology is presented in Table 3.2.

Table 3.2 Definitions of ECJE Database Topics

Topic	Definition (What Document Addresses)
Structural underpinnings	
ECJE in general	Importance, functions, benefits of ECJE; overview of ECJE systems
Teachers	Recruitment, retention, and identity of ECJE teachers
Professional development and leadership	Programs and policies related to preservice and in-service learning and development of ECJE educators and leaders
Evaluation	Standards and evaluation of ECJE programs and children's performance
Curriculum content	
Bible and literature	Teaching of Bible and rabbinic stories, books, literature, use of language arts
Hebrew	Teaching and use of Hebrew language in ECJE
Jewish calendar	Teaching of holidays, Shabbat (Sabbath), and other events such as the Holocaust

(continued)

Table 3.2 Definitions of ECJE Database Topics (Continued)

Topic	Definition (What Document Addresses)
Israel	Teaching about Israel
Spirituality and values	Prayer, rituals, wonder, ethics and morals, Jewish values, citizenship
Identity	Strengthening Jewish identity
Arts	Dance, music, plastic arts
Pedagogical considerations	
Pedagogy	Pedagogical methods, theory, and approaches in ECJE
Parents/family	Parents' roles in ECJE, parents' attitudes, family education
Teacher attitudes/beliefs	How teachers think about their ECJE work, about specific content areas, and about pedagogies
Children's attitudes	Children's attitudes toward topics within ECJE
Children's behavior/cognition/development	Play, construction of knowledge, applied theories of child development in ECJE
Gender	Treatment of gender in ECJE programs
Special needs	Inclusion, special education, learning disabilities within ECJE
Media	Use and evaluation of media in ECJE

One additional categorization was used to identify the geographical context of the document. Each item was classified as dealing with ECJE in Israel, the United States, the UK, or another diaspora nation.

Analysis

Using the Mendeley platform, we analyzed the corpus according to the genre, according to the three broad content categories, and according to geographical context. In order to avoid bias and achieve reliability in the categorization process, each author independently tagged 30 percent of the documents in the corpus. The tagging was compared and adjustments in the definitions made in order to achieve agreement. Following this procedure, each author independently tagged another 35 percent of the documents in the corpus. This analysis led to a deep understanding of the nature of research and reflective writing in ECJE over the past twenty years.

Findings

Descriptive Statistics of the Corpus

The entire corpus was analyzed according to various criteria in order to understand its characteristics as a body of writings about ECJE. In the first criterion, the genre of the writing, *research* included systematic studies using empirical tools, with reported findings; *policy* included reports, reflective writing, and descriptions with policy recommendations; and *practice* included program descriptions without policy recommendations, research questions, or a systematic methodology of examining the programs highlighted. An overwhelming portion of the corpus was identified as research (68 percent), while policy accounted for 14 percent and practice for 18 percent. A possible explanation for this finding lies in the methods used to identify documents for the corpus. Primary academic search engines were used; thus, a high number of research articles were found. Many of the practice and policy documents were identified through consultation with experts and professionals in the field, yielding a lower number.

The second criterion used for characterizing the corpus was thematic, with themes generated both by a deductive and by an inductive method—by defining themes from general knowledge about ECJE and by inducing broad categories from the many themes found in the materials themselves. The first theme, structural underpinnings, included documents dealing with organizational issues that impact ECJE. The second theme, curriculum content, included documents addressing the various components of the ECJE curriculum. The third theme, pedagogical considerations, dealt with a variety of topics that conceptualize the pedagogy of ECJE. Structural underpinnings and curriculum content each accounted for roughly a quarter of the writings, while pedagogical considerations accounted for roughly half of the corpus. This distribution might be explained by the nature of pedagogical considerations, which are very broad and encompassing, while the other two themes are more specific as shown in Table 3.2.

While these three thematic categories define the corpus by addressing the content of the writing, their subthemes more precisely identify the many foci found in the corpus. Thus, we identified the subthemes and number of documents in each. Each document warranted multiple codings; thus, the total of items coded is far greater than the total number of items in the corpus (see Table 3.3).

Table 3.3 Number of Documents in ECJE Database by Theme and Subtheme

Themes and Subthemes	Number of Documents
Structural underpinnings	38
ECJE in general	12
Teachers	7
Professional development	11
Evaluation	8
Curriculum content	43
Bible and literature	7
Hebrew	3
Jewish calendar	7
Israel	6
Spirituality and values	10

(*continued*)

Table 3.3 Number of Documents in ECJE Database by Theme and Subtheme (Continued)

Themes and Subthemes	Number of Documents
Identity	7
Arts	3
Pedagogical considerations	78
Pedagogy	13
Parents/family	20
Teacher attitudes/beliefs	15
Children's attitudes	11
Children's behavior/cognition/development	6
Gender	8
Special needs	3
Media	2

Within structural underpinnings, there were 38 documents. The most frequent subthemes were the field of ECJE in general (12/38) and the combined subthemes about teachers and professional development (teachers, 7/38; professional development, 11/38). Evaluation of programs accounted for only 8 out of 38 documents.

Within curriculum content, there was a pronounced emphasis on spirituality and values (10/43), followed by Bible and literature (7/43); the Jewish calendar, which included holidays (7/43); Israel (6/43); identity (7/43); and the arts and Hebrew with only 3 documents each. Writings on teaching the Hebrew language in Israel were not included in the corpus because they were not considered to be within the value parameters of ECJE. This stands in contrast to documents addressing teaching Hebrew in the diaspora, because there the promotion of the Hebrew language is grounded in a value set that touches both on Zionism and on religious practice. It should be noted that these numbers represent what researchers and writers have chosen to address, not the relative importance of the various content areas in the curriculum.

Within pedagogical considerations, the most frequent subtheme was parents and family (20/78), both as a target of ECJE and about their involvement, generally thought to benefit the young child's education. This was followed by teacher attitudes and beliefs (15/78), and pedagogy (13/78), which includes a wide range of topics. There were several documents about children's attitudes (11/78), less about gender issues (8/78) and children's behavior, cognition, and development (6/78), and even fewer about special needs (3/78) and media (2/78).

A final categorization of the corpus involved examining the national context of the documents (see Figure 3.1). They were divided almost equally between Israel (44 percent) and the United States (49 percent), with a very small number addressing ECJE in the context of both Israel and the United States (4 percent) or in other diaspora contexts (4 percent), including the UK, Germany, and South Africa.

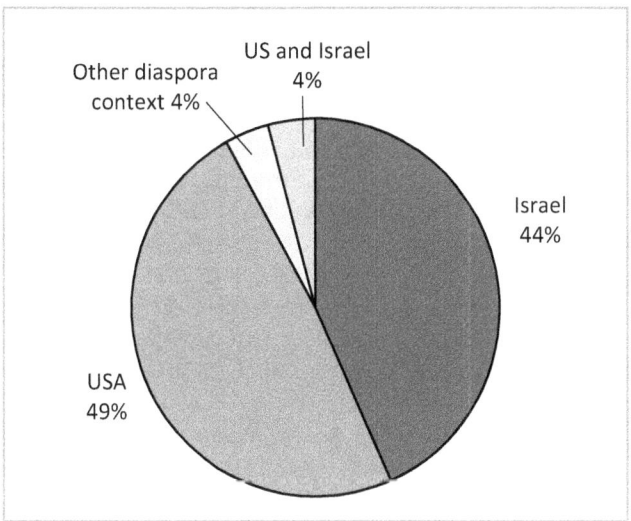

Figure 3.1 Document by national context, by % (N=113).

Thematic Analysis of the Documents

Structural Underpinnings

The phenomenon of ECJE has developed over time according to the needs of the communities that spawned and supported its growth. As an institution in Weberian terms (Lachmann 2007), ECJE could only develop through professional leadership both in the educational and wider communal contexts. Documenting these developments, scholars and practitioners have written articles that attempt to capture these innovations. Those documents are addressed in our first subtheme under the theme of structural underpinnings—ECJE in general. Beyond these broad overviews, other writings have honed in on three areas of endeavor that are critical to the success of the entire project: teachers, professional development, and program evaluation. The documents that address each of these underpinnings are reviewed in subsequent sections.

ECJE in General

This category yielded material ranging from book chapters to professional magazine and opinion pieces. Two items address the Israeli context, and eight address the US context. Both Aram and Ziv (2018) and Brody (2018) penned chapters in international handbooks of early childhood education (ECE) by different publishers. Aram and Ziv's chapter provides a historical overview, organization, and curriculum descriptions of Israeli ECE, while Brody's chapter analyzes the sectoral nature of Israeli ECE. Likewise, in the US context, two book chapters written three years apart each focus on different aspects of ECJE. Vogelstein (2008) stressed the need for quality, surveys, and institutional initiatives and delineated policy considerations. Ben Avie et al. (2011) explored the crises facing US ECJE, including issues of quality and staffing. Two survey reports reveal the reality of ECJE at the turn of the twentieth century. Vogelstein and Kaplan (2002) analyzed a survey of center directors, and Beck (2002) examined ECJE in three different cities.

In addition, two journalistic approaches that present collections of brief articles for the general public on a variety of issues related to ECJE were found. The older of the two is an issue of *Contact*, from the Jewish Life Network, including articles on the importance of ECJE, parents, programs for infants and toddlers, Jewish Community Centers (JCCs), curriculum issues, and independent schools (Valley 2002). More recently, the Davidson School of Jewish Education published a magazine, *Gleanings*, with a collection of articles by ECJE experts on a variety of topics regarding family, leadership, and professional development (Young 2017). With a spotlight on ECJE for infants and toddlers, Wertlieb and Rosen (2008) reported on a survey of Jewish programs across the United States and addressed the needs of young Jewish parents. Pickenson-Feldman and Goldsmith (2002) surveyed ECJE in JCCs. Grinspoon (2002) penned an op-ed piece describing ways to build independent ECJE centers that are not formally affiliated with any denomination or movement. Finally, an opinion piece published by the Jewish Early Childhood Education Initiative (JECEI) outlines arguments supporting the importance of ECJE (JECEI 2011).

The Israeli material was written by scholars of EC educators for an international audience interested in an analytic description of ECE in the country. On the other hand, the US material was written largely by informed practitioners who addressed critical issues about the quality and availability of ECJE programs.

Teachers

The quality of ECJE is largely dependent on the teachers. While Israeli researchers have examined teachers from the perspective of their inner worlds, US writers have largely focused on the culture of employment in centers that provide ECJE. Both Brody and Baum (2007) and Golden and Mayseless (2008) examined how Israeli EC educators dealt with incidents of terror, while Brody (2009) investigated their handling of teaching about the Holocaust. US researchers Feeney, Freeman, and Muller (2012) looked at the dilemma based on religious conflicts in the Jewish preschool setting resulting from the queries of non-Jewish students. Using a different lens, Goodman has reported on the culture of employment in ECJE in specific settings (Goodman and Schaap 2008; Goodman, Bidol-Padva, and Schaap 2006), while Lasday, Spack, and Schaap (2007) analyzed a Coalition for the Advancement of Jewish Education (CAJE) initiative to improve the culture of employment in preschool settings.

Professional Development

Professional development of ECJE teachers and directors is thought to be a crucial strategy for achieving high-quality programming. Three articles were identified that deal with this issue in the Israeli context, seven in the US context, and one in the context of both countries. Tal (2013) investigated perceptions of Israeli stakeholders regarding how ECJE should be learned and taught. Specific professional development endeavors were examined by Hod-Shemer and Wertheim (2011) regarding an EC citizenship program, and an article by Brody and Friedman (2012) involved a community of practice model. In the United States, Vogelstein and Kaplan (2002) wrote about professional development in Baltimore, Maryland; Meskin (2001) wrote about New York City; and Lasday, Spack, and Schaap (2007) wrote about Dade County, Florida. Grant and Robins (2001) compared the impact of a two-year Judaic enrichment program in two Conservative synagogue preschools.

In a broader perspective, Vogelstein (2008) described countrywide professional development standards. Similarly, a national initiative for excellence that includes a professional development component was elaborated by Bidol-Padva and Goodman (2011). The use of outside experts in professional development was examined in a case study of one school (Brody and Gorsetman 2013).

Evaluation

Evaluation is a systematic effort to determine if a program is performing as per standards (Scheerens et al. 2003). The term also applies to children's performance in meeting program goals. Two articles about evaluation in Israel are focused on the child. Brody (2018) described how children are assessed in Israel's *ganim* (pre-elementary schools for children ages three to six), while Israelashvili (2017) researched the effect of the child's and evaluator's culture on child assessment outcomes. A third evaluation focused on the content and impact of Sifriyat Pijama (Pajama Library) in Israeli ECE (see Chapter 8 in this book for a discussion of this program). This 2013/2014 study was informed by a series of interviews and meetings with the program's staff, as well as teacher feedback on the content and impact of the program (RAMA n.d.).

The US articles relate to three different tools developed to evaluate program quality. The first was written by Krug and Schade (2004), scholars from Tufts University's Eliot-Pearson Department of Child Study and Human Development, to develop quality indicators for ECJE. A second tool was developed by JECEI to measure the extent to which schools achieved the standards of performance that the organization set for participating schools through specific indicators (Bidol-Padva and Goodman 2011). ECJE policy makers in Colorado developed their own standards of excellence as recently described by Wassom (2018). No publications were found in which these tools were used to measure program outcomes. A series of studies found on the PJ Library® website examined the impact of PJ Library® (see Chapter 8 in this book for information on this program) on families, and these studies were based on empirical evidence. They are conducted every three years and examine how this project shapes the Jewish identity of parents, children, and families. The most recent survey was published in 2016 and compares results from the previous studies. Interestingly, the documents related to evaluation consist largely of evaluation tools, while the PJ Library® empirical studies provide an empirical perspective to the field.

Curriculum Content

A significant number of materials address content issues, as this category occupies a formative role in ECJE. The range of topics is expansive and thereby reflects the possibilities, opportunities, and challenges faced by the field. Our survey covered seven content-building blocks: Bible and literature, Hebrew, the Jewish calendar, Israel, spirituality and values, identity, and the arts.

Bible and Literature

We identified seven articles that relate to Bible stories and children's literature. Three of them discuss areas of content and pedagogy: one focuses on representations of "the other" in Israeli Haredi (ultra-Orthodox) education (Manzura 2005), a second presents pedagogical guidelines for US ECJE (Handelman 2000), and a third integrates both US and Israeli settings (Deitcher 2013). Three articles examine teacher identity in the telling of Bible stories (Achituv 2013, 2019; Achituv and Manzura 2016), and one article is on the parents' role in Jewish storytelling (Alexander 2013). Although the range of articles in this category is diverse, their cumulative number is limited. (The PJ Library® and Sifriyat Pijama projects in North America and Israel involve children's literature, but the documents we found regarding those programs involved evaluation and were included under that category.)

Hebrew

Surprisingly, we found only three documents that address the role of the Hebrew language in ECJE. Two articles evaluate a Hebrew immersion program (Robins 2005, 2006), and one focuses on pedagogical issues in teaching Hebrew in US settings (Handelman 2000).

Jewish Calendar

The Jewish calendar has always served as an essential resource for ECJE. Much of the Jewish content in EC programs revolves around holiday stories, symbols, and traditions, which make the Jewish calendar a central area of focus. Seven articles were coded in the calendar rubric, of which five address particular issues in Israeli ECJE, one addresses a specifically US issue, and one is more general. Five of the seven entries focus on pedagogical challenges in teaching young children topics related to the Jewish calendar. Bogetich (2018) mined the rich possibilities of storytelling as a pedagogy for teaching Jewish holidays. Gor Ziv (2016) adopted a critical feminist pedagogy in teaching Jewish holidays in Israeli national ganim. Handelman (2000) offered teachers a series of pedagogical considerations and suggestions for teaching young children about the power and impact of the Jewish holidays in Israeli state-religious ganim. Yaffe and Rapoport (2013) investigated how secular Israeli teachers deal with Shabbat in their ganim. And Brody (2009) analyzed various pedagogical strategies that an Israeli *gan* (singular of ganim and pre-elementary schools for children ages three to six) teacher adopts in addressing emotionally laden issues on Holocaust Remembrance Day. Hass, Manzura, and Gavish (2007) argued for the adoption of proactive pedagogy that is firmly rooted in the social and cultural norms of the relevant community. A single article on teacher attitudes was conducted by Avraham Hai (2010), in which attitudes and perceptions of nonreligious Israeli teachers were examined regarding the *Kabbalat Shabbat* (the ceremony or prayers welcoming the Jewish Sabbath) ceremony in EC settings.

Israel

Six articles were found that research the field of Israel education, five in US settings and one (Ben-Nun 2008) that discusses teaching Zionism and Yom Ha'atzmaut (Israel Independence Day) in Israeli ganim. In attempting to delve deeper into the underlying challenges, two of the pieces examine teacher attitudes toward Israel education (Applebaum and Zakai 2020; Ben-Nun 2008), and two explore pedagogical complexities in teaching Zionism in the US context (Handelman 2000; Young 2017). Finally, two record young children's ideas, attitudes, and questions about the role of Israel in their lives and implications for practice (Zakai 2015; Zakai and Cohen 2016).

Spirituality and Values

We identified ten articles that address issues of spirituality in ECJE. Three of these explore the world of children's beliefs and how they evolve over time (Brody 2007; Deitcher 2014; Diesendruck and Haber 2009). Four examine issues of pedagogy in spiritual education (Deitcher 2014; Handelman 2000, 2009; Wachs 2002). Two studies focus on teachers' beliefs and how they shape their teaching spirituality (Feeney, Freeman, and Muller 2012; Schein 2013). Finally, Bilu (2003) conducted an anthropological study about a ritual for Haredi young boys and its effect on their spirituality.

Identity

Seven studies were found that focus on issues related to identity formation in ECJE, three in the Israeli context and four in the US Jewish community. These studies adopt a range of diverse research approaches. Two articles investigate family identity—one examines the impact of *Shalom Sesame* (the Israeli version of *Sesame Street*) on attitudes, practices, and values (Fisch et al. 2013), and one surveys various ways that ECE shaped family identity in various ECJE settings (Young 2017). Four articles explore pedagogy of teaching identity—one focuses on robotics (Libman 2011); two examine teaching Jewish ideas, values, and practices in Israeli ECE (Hass, Manzura, and Gavish 2007; Drori 2018); and the fourth explores issues of pedagogy and cultural identity (Kennedy 2006). Finally, one article traces teachers' identity as a result of their teaching civics in Israeli ECE (Hod-Shemer and Wertheim 2011).

Arts

The research of arts in ECJE covers three areas that shed light on larger educational issues. Zer-Zion (2019) employed a historical lens to trace the role of theater in gaining a deeper understanding about the social, educational, and national goals of pre-state Israeli ECE. Gluschankof (2008) analyzed social/cultural themes in Israeli EC music, and Geiger (2016) compared the repertoire of current songs in Israeli ganim as practiced in two geographical areas.

Pedagogical Considerations

A great deal of attention has been paid in the literature to pedagogical considerations, both theoretically and practically. We will begin this discussion with those writings about pedagogy itself in ECJE and then proceed to specific areas that relate directly to pedagogy: parents and family; teacher attitudes and beliefs; children's attitudes; children's behavior, cognition, and development; gender; special needs; and media.

Pedagogy

Thirteen items were identified that dealt with either specific or multiple pedagogies. Snapir, Sitton, and Russo-Zimet (2012) penned a comprehensive history of ECE in Israel, which includes pedagogies in vogue at different points throughout the past century. While focusing on childhood in general and not specifically on young children, Dekel and Kark (2019) analyzed the influence of modern European pedagogies on Zionist (belief in the development and protection of Israel) educators in the Yishuv (pre-Israeli state) and their innovative views of childhood. Brody's (2018) chapter on Israeli ECE addresses those aspects of pedagogy that underpin approaches to curriculum and child assessment. From the US perspective, Handelman (2009) articulated the pedagogies that define ECJE for the Conservative movement, and Kennedy (2006) delineated the intersections of pedagogy and cultural identity in ECJE. Adaptations in pedagogies by ultra-Orthodox teachers are explored in Haller, Golden, and Tavecchio's (2018) study. Particular pedagogies are addressed in several articles: Korczak's pedagogies (Efron 2008), constructivism (Muller 2013; Muller, Gorsetman, and Alexander 2018), homeschooling (Lewis 2017), and feminism (Gor Ziv 2016). Golden (2006) used an anthropological perspective to shed light on pedagogy in practice in Israeli ganim with a focus on social order and on political violence as perceived by children in a Jewish-Palestinian gan (Golden 2009).

Parents and Family

ECE in general is integrally bound up with families, and family education is thought by many to be a major goal of ECJE (Kelner 2007). Pomson and Schnoor (2018) examined how ECJE affects family life. It is no surprise, then, that parents and family are a central aspect of writings about ECJE pedagogy and that twenty additional documents were identified in this category. The topic with the most publications in this category is research about parental attitudes and choices about educational frameworks for their children. Two surveys were conducted by specific communities to learn how Jewish parents make their choice of a preschool for their children, including a study on the Boston community (Rosen and Schwartz 2015) and a similar earlier study on Baltimore, Denver, and Chicago (Beck 2002). Scholarly interest in Jewish parental choice of preschool education comes to the fore in Manning's (2013) study of unaffiliated parents' choices of religious training for their young children, Bekerman and Tatar's (2009) examination of Jewish and Palestinian Israelis' parental choice to enroll their children in a bicultural program, and Harel's (2010) research on pluralism as a consideration in preschool choices. Another parental educational choice is homeschooling, a phenomenon that has attracted some Jewish parents of young children (Lewis 2017). Related to this choice is parental use of television for enhancing their children's cultural identity, which was researched by Spezia (2012) in her master's dissertation.

Another area of interest in writing and research about families and ECJE is parent/family involvement, outreach, and education, and several research studies were found on the topic. Alexander (2013) focused on parents' reading of bedtime stories to their children. A close look at ECJE programs from the perspective of family involvement was found in a comparison of two ECJE programs with the JECEI network, each of which was based on a model of family engagement (Comer and Ben-Avie 2010). Vogelstein (2008) wrote about the impact of ECJE on family life using empirical data. The PJ Library® (2017) project set family education as a major goal, as evaluated in their report. A more theoretical approach is Kelner's (2007) analysis of ECJE programs, in which he considered parents as the target of such programs. Seven brief, non-research-based articles related to family involvement are in the collection *Gleanings* (Young 2017). Finally, we found three articles about Jewish parental involvement in infant/toddler education (Hendler 2002; Rosen 2006; Wertlieb and Rosen 2008).

The effect of culture on the young child was examined from an anthropological perspective in Bilu's (2003) treatise on *milah* (circumcision) and male identity and Segall et al.'s (2015) analysis of transmission of ethnic essentialism by parents. A historical lens was brought to bear on the Jewish family in antiquity by Tropper (2006).

Teacher Attitudes and Beliefs

Fifteen articles were found that address a range of topics on the attitudes and beliefs of ECJE teachers. Ten studies were conducted in Israeli settings and five in the US Jewish community. One of the most striking features in this category is the high number of studies that employed narrative research as the principal means to gain a deeper and more nuanced understanding about teachers' attitudes. Feeney and Freeman (2012) adopted a narrative research approach as they attempted to identify teachers' response patterns to children's religious beliefs. Four other studies (Brody 2009; Ben-Nun 2008; Avraham Hai 2010; Drori 2018) use narrative research to shed light on teachers' beliefs about teaching and celebrating various Jewish holidays. Finally, two researchers, Achituv and Manzura, investigated educators' attitudes in Israel's national religious schools. Achituv (2012) examined the effects of their ethical and cultural identity as well as their gender identity (Achituv 2019) on telling Bible stories to young children, while Manzura (2007) studied how gender bias shapes the core identity of the children. Yafeh (2007) and Manzura (2010) investigated how beliefs of Israeli ultra-Orthodox teachers reinforce gender regimes in that society, while Dvorin Friedman (2018) studied the effect of teacher beliefs in Orthodox schools in the United States in terms of the implications for gender consciousness.

Golden and Mayseless (2008) conducted an ethnographic study in which they traced how an Israeli kindergarten teacher's attitude shaped a learning environment that was inherently unpredictable. In a different ethnographic study, Brody and Baum (2007) uncovered two models of resilience that Israeli EC teachers adopted in dealing with their children's fears and anxiety during the 2000–1 school year, a particularly stressful period. Bidol-Pavda, Rapchik-Levin, and Schapp (2006) surveyed attitudes of EC educators working in Jewish schools in Florida and suggested a series of strategies to raise their stature and culture of employment. Finally, Bidol-Padva and Goodman (2011) studied attitudes of EC educators in Jewish schools by focusing on their interactions with parents' groups and children's attitudes, cognition, and behaviors.

Children's Attitudes

A total of eleven articles were identified as focusing on young children's attitudes and beliefs. Three of these studies dealt with ethnicity, measuring Jewish-Israeli children's attitudes toward their own and toward Arab ethnicity. Diesendruck and Haber (2009) examined children's beliefs about the heritability of ethnicity, while Diesendruck et al. (2013) further studied the transmission of ethnic essentialism from parents to children. Another study on the attitudes of Israeli children toward Arabs through figure drawings was conducted by Teichman (2001). Feelings of US Jewish children toward Israel was the topic of a study by Zakai and Cohen (2016), while Zakai (2015) conducted similar research a year earlier. Zakai also researched US Jewish children's feelings about the war between Israel and Hamas (Zakai 2019). The political socialization of Jewish-Israeli children was studied by Nasie, Diamond, and Bar-Tal (2016). The teleological categories of secular and religious Jewish-Israeli children were compared in order to understand how a belief in God affected these constructions (Diesendruck and Haber 2009). Finally, we found a study exploring how the creation of robots in a kindergarten strengthened children's Jewish identity (Bers, Matas, and Libman 2013).

Children's Behavior, Cognition, and Development

Another aspect of the child's perspective is their behavior, cognition, and development. Six research studies were found dealing with these factors. Muller's (2010) epistemological study of children's construction of knowledge in Jewish education is a pioneering window on children's cognition. His later study of constructivism focuses on this particular conceptualization of cognition (Muller 2013). Gluschankof (2008) expanded the research on children's cognition by looking closely at the cultural context as it influences the musical expression of young Israeli children. Contextualizing the culture of the kindergarten classroom, Golden and Mayseless (2008) researched how teachers' construction of the social environment influenced children's coping with political and social unpredictability in Israel. Researching the Orthodox community in London, Lindsey et al. (2003) examined emotional and behavioral disorders of Jewish preschoolers as reported by parents. Schein (2013) explored young children's spiritual development as an outgrowth of their environment.

Gender

The articles we found dealing with gender were based on empirical research, with one exception. Gender is a specific pedagogical focus in Gor Ziv's (2016) article that deals with a feminist approach to holiday teaching. Gorsetman and Sztokman's (2013) book provides a broad and comprehensive treatment that analyzes gender practice in ECJE in US Jewish day schools and makes practical recommendations. While their research examined all age levels, the EC component is woven into the findings throughout the book. Teachers' attitudes and beliefs about gender are explored in a variety of contexts in five works. Two articles deal with the national religious schools in Israel (Achituv 2019; Manzura 2007), while others focus on the Orthodox community in the United States (Dvorin Friedman 2018) and in Israel (Yafeh 2007; Manzura 2010). A more personal treatment of gender in ECJE is found in Gorsetman and Ament's (2008) reflective document.

Special Needs

Three articles were found relating to special needs—one based on empirical research of Israeli and US teacher attitudes toward inclusion in ECJE (Alexander et al. 2016), another reporting on treatment of special education in Israeli schools (Al-Yagon, Aram, and Margalit 2016), and a third a newspaper article describing a school for special needs students in London's ultra-Orthodox community (Koppel 2011). While the three perspectives differ widely, they all express concern for Jewish schools and educational systems to provide quality education for children with special needs.

Media

Another pedagogical perspective is the use of media in the EC setting. *Shalom Sesame* has drawn the attention of researchers interested in its effect on US children's Jewish identity. Fisch et al. (2013) investigated the program's value for Jewish families and its impact beyond direct learning from the screen. In a master's thesis, Spezia (2012) studied how parents use the program to enrich their children's cultural identity.

Conclusion

Our search for research and writing about ECJE was a venture into the unknown. As active members of a community of researchers in this field, we have experienced difficulties in the past in identifying background material for our own research. Our systematic bibliographic search for this chapter led us to a wealth of materials of which we were previously unaware. On the other hand, the search results also revealed large gaps in published knowledge about several crucial topics. For example, only eight publications dealt with program evaluations, and many of those provided tools but not outcomes. If ECJE is to base practice on evidence, then we need serious evaluation of programs and curriculums.

Regarding pedagogy, two of the subthemes relate to the child per se—children's attitudes and their behavior, cognition, and development. But even viewed cumulatively, the writings in these two categories represent only 8 percent of the ECJE literature we found and draw a very partial picture of the child as a learner in ECJE. As a field, ECE is known for its outstanding emphasis on the child. The writings and research in this area as reported in this chapter provide a different message for ECJE. We suggest a reorientation and renewed emphasis on this essential category of the child as learner.

A most surprising and worrisome finding relates to writing and research about the teaching of Hebrew in ECJE. While many EC Jewish programs in the diaspora place an emphasis on Hebrew teaching, we found only two studies on the topic and no reflective writings about existing programs. Finally, we bring attention to the dearth of material addressing special needs students. The EC professional community in both Israel and the United States has recognized the need for an inclusive approach; however, the publications on this topic are glaringly sparse. We suggest that researchers address all areas of ECJE and turn their attention to these four areas in particular, both as an opportunity to contribute to the scholarly corpus of ECJE and to further the knowledge base on which sound policy can be formulated.

References

Achituv, S. 2012. "Early Childhood Educators Tell Their Stories: On the Identity of Religious Kindergarten Teachers in Israel." PhD diss., University of Haifa.

Achituv, S. 2013. "What Did the Teacher Say Today? State Religious Kindergarten Teachers Deal with Complex Torah Stories." *Journal of Jewish Education* 79 (3): 256–96.

Achituv, S. 2019. "'It Bothers Me, but I Will Not Bring It into the Kindergarten': Gender Perception Conflicts of Religious Kindergarten Teachers as Reflected in Their Work." *Religious Education* 114 (4): 1–13. https://doi.org/10.1080/00344087.2019.1600108.

Achituv, S., and S. Manzura. 2016. "How to Bridge the Gap? Teacher Educators' Approaches to the Teaching of the Biblical 'Other' in Kindergarten." *Journal of Jewish Education* 82 (3): 231–57. https://doi.org/10.1080/15244113.2016.1199255.

Alexander, S. T. 2013. "Children of the Book: Parents, Bedtime, and Jewish Identity." *Journal of Jewish Education* 79 (3): 174–98.

Alexander, S. T., D. L. Brody, M. Muller, H. Gor Ziv, S. Achituv, C. R. Gorsetman, J. Harris, et al. 2016. "Voices of American and Israeli Early Childhood Educators on Inclusion." *International Journal of Early Childhood Special Education* 8 (1): 16–38. https://doi.org/10.20489/intjecse.239574.

Al-Yagon, M., D. Aram, and M. Margalit. 2016. "Early Childhood Inclusion in Israel." *Infants & Young Children* 29 (3): 205–13.

Applebaum, L., and S. Zakai. 2020. "'I'm Going to Israel and All I Need to Pack Is My Imagination': Pretend Trips to Israel in Jewish Early Childhood Education." *Journal of Jewish Education* 86 (1): 94–119. https://doi.org/10.1080/15244113.2019.1696659.

Aram, D., and M. Ziv. 2018. "Early Childhood Education in Israel: History, Policy, and Practice." In *Handbook of International Perspectives on Early Childhood Education*, edited by J. L. Roopnarine, J. E. Johnson, S. F. Quinn, and M. M. Patte, 101–14. London: Routledge. https://doi.org/10.4324/9781315562193.

Avraham Hai, E. 2010. "Perceptions and Attitudes of Kindergarten Teachers Regarding Kabbalat Shabbat Rituals in Israeli Kindergartens." [In Hebrew.] MA diss., Hebrew University, Jerusalem. https://huji-primo.hosted.exlibrisgroup.com/permalink/f/att40d/972HUJI_ALMA21169275620003701.

Beck, P. 2002. "Jewish Preschools as Gateways to Jewish Life: A Survey of Jewish Preschool Parents in Three Cities." *Contact: The Journal of the Steinhardt Foundation for Jewish Life* 5 (1): 6–7. https://www.bjpa.org/search-results/publication/5288.

Bekerman, Z., and M. Tatar. 2009. "Parental Choice of Schools and Parents' Perceptions of Multicultural and Co-existence Education: The Case of the Israeli Palestinian-Jewish Bilingual Primary Schools." *European Early Childhood Education Research Journal* 17 (2): 171–85. https://doi.org/10.1080/13502930902951304.

Ben Avie, M., I. Vogelstein, R. L. Goodman, E. Schaap, and P. Bidol-Padva. 2011. "Early Childhood Education." In *International Handbook of Jewish Education*, edited by H. Miller, L. D. Grant, and A. Pomson, 749–65. New York: Springer.

Ben-Nun, N. 2008. "Perceptions and Attitudes of Kindergarten Teachers Regarding the Commemoration of Independence Day in Kindergartens." [In Hebrew.] MA thesis, Hebrew University, Jerusalem.

Bers, M. U., J. Matas, and N. Libman. 2013. "Livnot U'Lehibanot, to Build and to Be Built: Making Robots in Kindergarten to Explore Jewish Identity." *Diaspora, Indigenous, and Minority Education* 7 (3): 164–79. https://doi.org/10.1080/15595692.2013.787062.

Bidol-Padva, P., and R. L. Goodman. 2011. "Pursuing Excellence in Jewish Early Childhood Education: A Case Study of JECEI's Transformative Change Model." New York: JECEI.

Bidol-Pavda, P., M. Rapchik-Levin, and E. Schaap. 2006. "Project Kavod: Improving the Employment Culture for Jewish Early Childhood Education." *Jewish Education News*, Winter.

Bilu, Y. 2003. "From Milah (Circumcision) to Milah (Word): Male Identity and Rituals of Childhood in the Jewish Ultraorthodox Community." *Ethos* 31 (2): 172–203. https://doi.org/https://www.jstor.org/stable/3651935.

Bogetich, K. 2018. "L'dor Vador: Storytelling for the Holiday Cycle in a Jewish Early Childhood Setting." MSED diss., Bank Street College of Education, New York.

Brody, D. 2007. "The Experience of the Synagogue in the Development of Spirituality among Orthodox Israeli Preschoolers." *Jewish Educational Leadership* 5 (2): 7.

Brody, D. 2009. "Sailing through Stormy Seas: An Israeli Kindergarten Teacher Confronts Holocaust Remembrance Day." *Early Childhood Research and Practice* 11 (2): 13. https://eric.ed.gov/?id=EJ868535.

Brody, D. 2018. "Constructing Early Childhood Curriculum and Assessing Young Children in Israel's Mosaic of Culture." In *International Handbook of Early Childhood Education*, edited by M. Fleer and B. van Oers, 1191–1210. Dordrecht: Springer Netherlands. https://doi.org/10.1007/978-94-024-0927-7_61.

Brody, D., and N. L. Baum. 2007. "Israeli Kindergarten Teachers Cope with Terror and War: Two Implicit Models of Resilience." *Curriculum Inquiry* 37 (1): 9–31. https://doi.org/10.1111/j.1467-873X.2007.00379.x.

Brody, D., and A. Friedman. 2012. "The Effectiveness of Community of Practice in Supporting Israeli Kindergarten Teachers Dealing with an Emotionally Laden Topic." In *Early Education in a Global Context*, edited by J. A. Sutterby, 183–210. Bingley, UK: Emerald. https://doi.org/10.1108/S0270-4021(2012)0000016011.

Brody, D., and C. R. Gorsetman. 2013. "'It's Part of the Fabric': Creating Context for the Successful Involvement of an Outside Expert of Jewish Early Childhood Education in School Change." *Journal of Jewish Education* 79 (3): 199–234. https://doi.org/10.1080/15244113.2013.814985.

Comer, J. P., and M. Ben-Avie. 2010. "Promoting Community in Early Childhood Programs: A Comparison of Two Programs." *Early Childhood Education Journal* 38 (2): 87–94. https://doi.org/10.1007/s10643-010-0391-3.

Deitcher, H. 2013. "Once Upon a Time: How Jewish Children's Stories Impact Moral Development." *Journal of Jewish Education* 79 (3): 235–55. https://doi.org/10.1080/15244113.2013.814988.

Deitcher, H. 2014. "Where Is God? Critical Questions in Young Children's Lives." *EJewish Philanthropy*. July 3, 2014. https://ejewishphilanthropy.com/where-is-god-critical-questions-in-young-childrens-lives/.

Dekel, N., and R. Kark. 2019. "Universal Values in Childhood Concepts and Education in the 'New Yishuv', 1882–1914." *Israel Affairs* 25 (1): 85–101. https://doi.org/10.1080/13537121.2019.1561178.

Diesendruck, G., D. Birnbaum, I. Deeb, and G. Segall. 2013. "Learning What Is Essential: Relative and Absolute Changes in Children's Beliefs about the Heritability of Ethnicity." *Journal of Cognition and Development* 14 (4): 546–60. https://doi.org/10.1080/15248372.2012.691142.

Diesendruck, G., and L. Haber. 2009. "God's Categories: The Effect of Religiosity on Children's Teleological and Essentialist Beliefs about Categories." *Cognition* 110 (1): 100–14. https://doi.org/10.1016/j.cognition.2008.11.001.

Drori, N. 2018. "Values Education in Religious Kindergartens." [In Hebrew.] *Da'at* 15:1–19.

Dvorin Friedman, I. C. 2018. "Gender Beliefs of Teachers in Orthodox Jewish Early Childhood Programs." PhD diss., Loyola University, Chicago.

Efron, S. E. 2008. "Moral Education between Hope and Hopelessness: The Legacy of Janusz Korczak." *Curriculum Inquiry* 38 (1): 39–62. https://www.jstor.org/stable/30054722.

Feeney, S., and N. K. Freeman. 2012. "Differing Faiths in a Faith Based Program." *Young Children*, 67 (4): 82–5.

Feeney, S., N. K. Freeman, and M. Muller. 2012. "Differing Faiths in a Faith Based Program." *Young Children* 67 (3): 70–1.

Fisch, S. M., D. Lemish, E. Spezia, D. Siegel, S. R. D. Fisch, F. Aladé, and D. Kasdan. 2013. "Shalom Sesame: Using Media to Promote Jewish Education and Identity." *Journal of Jewish Education* 79 (3): 297–314. https://doi.org/10.1080/15244113.2013.815145.

Geiger, O. 2016. "Values and Ideology of a Culture as Reflected in Its Kindergarten Singing." *International Educational Scientific Research Journal* 2 (12): 88–91.

Gluschankof, C. 2008. "Musical Expressions in Kindergarten: An Inter-cultural Study?" *Contemporary Issues in Early Childhood* 9 (4): 317–27. https://doi.org/10.2304/ciec.2008.9.4.217.

Golden, D. 2006. "Structured Looseness: Everyday Social Order at an Israeli Kindergarten." *Ethos* 34 (3): 367–90. https://doi.org/10.1525/eth.2006.34.3.367.

Golden, D. 2009. "Fear, Politics and Children: Israeli-Jewish and Israeli-Palestinian Preschool Teachers Talk about Political Violence." *Etnofoor* 21 (2): 77–95. https://about.jstor.org/terms.

Golden, D., and O. Mayseless. 2008. "On the Alert in an Unpredictable Environment." *Culture and Psychology* 14 (2): 155–79. https://doi.org/10.1177/1354067X08088553.

Goodman, R. L., P. Bidol-Padva, and E. Schaap. 2006. *Community Report on Early Childhood Jewish Educators: Culture of Employment 2004–2005, Miami-Dade and Broward Counties, Florida*. New York: CAJE (Coalition for the Advancement of Jewish Education).

Goodman, R. L., and E. Schaap. 2008. "Jewish Educational Personnel." In *What We Now Know about Jewish Education: Perspectives on Research for Practice*, edited by R. L. Goodman, P. A. Flexner, and L. D. Bloombert, 199–211. Los Angeles: Torah Aura Productions.

Gor Ziv, H. 2016. "Teaching Jewish Holidays in Early Childhood Education in Israel: Critical Feminist Pedagogy Perspective." *Taboo: The Journal for Culture and Education* 15 (1): 119–34. http://search.proquest.com/docview/1789750140?accountid=12249.

Gorsetman, C. R., and A. Ament. 2008. "Anecdotes and Reflections on Gender in Early Childhood Education." *Jewish Educational Leadership* 6 (3): 40–2.

Gorsetman, C. R., and E. M. Sztokman. 2013. *Educating in the Divine Image: Gender Issues in Orthodox Jewish Day Schools*. Waltham, MA: Brandeis University Press.

Grant, L., and F. Robins. 2001. "Judaic Enrichment as a Change Agent in Early Childhood Education: Limitations and Possibilities." *Conservative Judaism* 53 (4): 52–68.

Grinspoon, J. 2002. "Building a School from Scratch." *Contact* 5 (1): 14.

Haller, R., D. Golden, and L. Tavecchio. 2018. "Negotiating Tradition and Contemporary Education: An Enrichment Center for Jewish Ultra-Orthodox Children in Israel." *Anthropology & Education Quarterly* 49 (3): 230–45. https://doi.org/10.1111/aeq.12250.

Handelman, M. S. 2000. *Jewish Everyday: The Complete Handbook for Early Childhood Teachers*. Denver: A.R.E. isbn-13: 978-0867050486.

Handelman, M. S. 2009. *Vision for Conservative Early Childhood Programs: A Journey Guide*. United Synagogue of Conservative Judaism. Accessed August 17, 2020. http://www.uscj.net/images/ECE_vision.pdf.

Harel, N. 2010. "Is Pluralism a Central Component in the Consideration of Parents Whose Children Were Educated in Kol Haneshamah Kindergartens When Choosing a Kindergarten for Second or Additional Children?" MA diss., Melton Center for Jewish Education, Hebrew University, Jerusalem.

Hass, M., S. Manzura, and S. Gavish. 2007. "A Cardboard Shofar: Jewish Identity Is Formed in Early Childhood—A Proposal for a New Deliberation." [In Hebrew.] *Hed Hagan* (2): 88–91.

Hendler, L. M. 2002. "Of Playpens and Torah." *Contact* 5 (1): 8–9.

Hod-Shemer, O., and C. Wertheim. 2011. "Promoting 'Shared Citizenship' in Kindergartens." [In Hebrew.] *Social Security* 85:71–87. https://www.jstor.org/stable/23279025.

Israelashvili, M. 2017. "Cross-Informant Evaluations of Preschoolers' Adjustment in Different Cultures." *Early Childhood Education Journal* 45 (5): 641–50. https://doi.org/10.1007/s10643-016-0808-8.

JECEI. 2011. "Making the Case for Change." http://www.jecei.org/PDF/4%20Making%20the%20Case%20for%20Jewish%20ECE.pdf.

Kelner, S. 2007. "Who Is Being Taught? Early Childhood's Adult-Centered Approach." In *Family Matters: Jewish Education in an Age of Choice*, edited by J. Wertheimer, 59–79. Waltham, MA: Brandeis University Press. http://hdl.handle.net/10192/26633.

Kennedy, D. 2006. "Configuring the Jewish Child: Intersections of Pedagogy and Cultural Identity." In *The Child in the World/The World in the Child*, edited by M. N. Bloch, D. Kennedy, T. Lightfoot, and D. Weyenbert, 43–62. New York: Palgrave Macmillan US. https://doi.org/10.1057/9780230601666_3.

Koppel, G. 2011. "How to Be Radical in the Most Traditional Locality." *Times Educational Supplement*, July 29, 2011.

Krug, C., and L. Schade. 2004. *Defining Excellence in Early Childhood Jewish Education* . Medford, MA: Center for Applied Child Development, Eliot-Pearson Department of Child Development, Tufts University.

Lachmann, L. M. 2007. *The Legacy of Max Weber*. Auburn, AL: Ludwig von Mises Institute.

Lasday, J., E. G. Spack, and E. Schaap. 2007. *The Project Kavod Covenant Foundation Grant Final Report*. Miami: CAJE (Coalition for the Advancement of Jewish Education). file:///C:/Users/19165/Downloads/17619.pdf.

Lewis, B. S. 2017. "Why Homeschool, Why Us, Why Now?: Parental Motivations for Jewish Homeschooling." PhD diss., New York University.

Libman, N. 2011. "Mi Ani? (Who Am I?): Robotics as a Medium to Express Jewish Identity." MAT diss., Tufts University, Medford, MA. https://search.proquest.com/docview/879429315?pq-origsite=gscholar.

Lindsey, C., S. Frosh, K. Loewenthal, and E. Spitzer. 2003. "Prevalence of Emotional and Behavioural Disorders among Strictly Orthodox Jewish Pre-school Children in London." *Clinical Child Psychology and Psychiatry* 8:459–72.

Manning, C. J. 2013. "Unaffiliated Parents and the Religious Training of Their Children." *Sociology of Religion* 74 (2): 149–75. https://doi.org/doi:10.1093/socrel/srs072.

Manzura, S. 2005. "The Storyteller as Interpreter: The Weekly Torah Portion in Ultra-Orthodox Early Childhood Education." [In Hebrew.] *Derech Agada* 7–8:219–33.

Manzura, S. 2007. "Kindergarten as a Mirror of Society: 'The Glass Ceiling' in the Religious Gan." In *To Be a Jewish Woman*, edited by T. Cohen, 207–17. [In Hebrew.] Jerusalem: Kolech.

Manzura, S. 2010. "Ritual and Text in the Context of Holiness: Ways of Establishing Gender Identity of Boys and Girls Ages Two to Five in Ultra-Orthodox Preschools." [In Hebrew.] PhD diss., Hebrew University, Jerusalem.

Meskin, C. W. 2001. "Keeping Up with the Crisis." *Journal of Jewish Education* 67 (3): 71–3.

Muller, M. 2010. "Kindergarten Children's Conception of Knowledge in Jewish Education." PhD diss., University of South Carolina.

Muller, M. 2013. "Constructivism and Jewish Early Childhood Education." *Journal of Jewish Education* 79 (3): 315–34. https://doi.org/10.1080/15244113.2013.816116.

Muller, M., C. Gorsetman, and S. T. Alexander. 2018. "Struggles and Successes in Constructivist Jewish Early Childhood Classrooms." *Journal of Jewish Education* 84 (3): 284–311. https://doi.org/10.1080/15244113.2018.1478533.

Nasie, M., A. H. Diamond, and D. Bar-Tal. 2016. "Young Children in Intractable Conflicts: The Israeli Case." *Personality and Social Psychology Review* 20 (4): 365–92. https://doi.org/10.1177/1088868315607800.

Pickenson-Feldman, R., and M. B. Goldsmith. 2002. "Adventures with Peer K Explorer: Preschools and the JCC." *Contact* 5 (1): 10–11.

PJ Library®. 2017. "PJ Library Impact Evaluation." Accessed November 25, 2021. https://pjlibrary.org/getmedia/f4e6712b-1b44-4676-9dea-0cdf6d9ca277/PJL_Survey_interior_web.pdf.

Pomson, A., and R. F. Schnoor. 2018. "'Growing into Our Skin as a Jewish Family': Proposing a New Approach to the Study of Jewish Self-Formation." In *Jewish Family*, 1–22. Bloomington: Indiana University Press.

RAMA (Ministry of Education the Research and Evaluation Division). n.d. "Sifriyat Pijama—2013–2014 School Year: Summary of Evaluation Report." Accessed on November 25, 2021.http://www.pjisrael.org/wp-content/uploads/2016/12/RAMA-SP-English-2013-2014-Sifriyat-Pijama-highlights-2-pages.pdf.

Robins, F. D. 2005. "Ma'alah, the Early Childhood Hebrew Immersion Project." *First School Years*, Spring 2005.

Robins, F. D. 2006. "Update and Achievements: Ma'alah, the Early Childhood Hebrew Immersion Project." *First School Years*, Spring 2005.

Rosen, M. I. 2006. *Jewish Engagement from Birth: A Blueprint for Outreach to First-Time Parents*. Waltham, MA: Brandeis University Press.

Rosen, M. I., and H. Schwartz. 2015. *How Jews Choose: A Study of Early Childhood Decisions among Jewish Parents in Greater Boston. A Research Study Report of Combined Jewish Philanthropies*. Boston: Combined Jewish Philanthropies.

Scheerens, J., C. A. Glas, S. M. Thomas, and S. Thomas. 2003. *Educational Evaluation, Assessment, and Monitoring: A Systemic Approach*, vol. 13. London: Taylor & Francis.

Schein, D. L. 2013. "Research and Reflections on the Spiritual Development of Young Jewish Children." *Journal of Jewish Education* 79 (3): 360–85. https://doi.org/10.1080/15244113.2013.817238.

Segall, G., D. Birnbaum, I. Deeb, and G. Diesendruck. 2015. "The Intergenerational Transmission of Ethnic Essentialism: How Parents Talk Counts the Most." *Developmental Science* 18 (4): 543–55. https://doi.org/10.1111/desc.12235.

Snapir, M., S. Sitton, and G. Russo-Zimet. 2012. *The Israeli Kindergarten in the 20th Century*. [In Hebrew.] Beer Sheva, Israel: Ben Gurion Research Institute for the Study of Israel and Zionism and Ben Gurion University.

Spezia, E. M. 2012. "How Parents Use Television to Enrich Their Children's Cultural Identity: The Case Study of Shalom Sesame and Jewish Life." MA diss., Southern Illinois University.

Tal, C. 2013. "What Do We Mean by Jewish Education in Professional Development for Early Childhood Education?" *Journal of Jewish Education* 79 (3): 335–59. https://doi.org/10.1080/15244113.2013.816119.

Teichman, Y. 2001. "The Development of Israeli Children's Images of Jews and Arabs and Their Expression in Human Figure Drawings." *Developmental Psychology* 37 (6): 749–61. https://doi.org/10.1037/0012-1649.37.6.749.

Tropper, A. 2006. "The Demographics of the Jewish Family in Late Antiquity." *Journal for the Study of Judaism in the Persian, Hellenistic, and Roman Period* 37 (3): 299–343. https://www.jstor.org/stable/24669762.

Valley, E., ed. 2002. "Jewish Early Childhood Education," special issue, *Contact* 5 (1).

Vogelstein, I. 2008. "Early Childhood Jewish Education: 'If Not Now, When?'" In *What We Now Know about Jewish Education: Perspectives on Research for Practice*, edited by

R. L. Goodman, P. A. Flexner, and L. D. Bloomberg, 373–85. Lewisville, NC: Torah Aura Productions.

Vogelstein, I., and D. Kaplan. 2002. *Untapped Potential: The Status of Jewish Early Childhood Education in America*. Baltimore, MD: JECE Partnership.

Wachs, S. P. 2002. "Jewish Nursery Schools: Day Schools for Little Children." *Contact* 5 (1): 12–13.

Wassom, J. 2018. "Standards of Excellence." *Exchange* May/June: 46–50.

Wertlieb, D., and M. I. Rosen. 2008. "Inspiring Jewish Connections: Outreach to Parents with Infants and Toddlers." *Zero to Three* 28 (3): 11–17.

Yafeh, O. 2007. "The Time in the Body: Cultural Construction of Femininity in Ultraorthodox Kindergartens for Girls." *Ethos* 35 (4): 516–53.

Yaffe, O., and T. Rapoport. 2013. "On Education and Secularity—Kabbalat Shabbat in the Non-religious Kindergarten in Israel." In *A Close Up Look at the Class and the School: Ethnographic Studies on Education*, edited by B. Alpert and S. Shlasky, 231–71. [In Hebrew.] Tel Aviv: MOFET Institute.

Young, M. S. 2017. "The Promise of Jewish Early Childhood Education." *Gleanings* 4 (2): 1–2.

Zakai, S. 2015. "'Israel Is Meant for Me': Kindergarteners' Conceptions of Israel." *Journal of Jewish Education* 81 (1): 4–34. https://doi.org/10.1080/15244113.2015.1007019.

Zakai, S. 2019. "'Bad Things Happened': How Children of the Digital Age Make Sense of Violent Current Events." *Social Studies* 110 (2): 67–85. https://doi.org/10.1080/00377996.2018.1517113.

Zakai, S., and H. T. Cohen. 2016. "American Jewish Children's Thoughts and Feelings about the Jewish State: Laying the Groundwork for a Developmental Approach to Israel Education." *Contemporary Jewry* 36 (1): 31–54. https://doi.org/10.1007/s12397-016-9160-y.

Zer-Zion, S. 2019. "Theater for Kindergarten Children in the Yishuv: Toward the Formation of an Eretz-Israeli Childhood." *Images* 12 (1): 70–84. https://doi.org/10.1163/18718000-12340110.

Part Two

Three Contemporary Critical Lenses

4

From the Melting Pot, to the Salad Bowl, to the Seder Plate: Moving beyond Multiculturalism in Early Childhood Jewish Education

Ilana Dvorin Friedman and Meir Muller

> *There she lies, the great Melting Pot—listen! Can't you hear the roaring and the bubbling? There gapes her mouth—the harbour where a thousand mammoth feeders come from the ends of the world to pour in their human freight. Ah, what a stirring and a seething! Celt and Latin, Slav and Teuton, Greek and Syrian,—black and yellow—Jew and Gentile—how the great Alchemist melts and fuses them with his purging flame!*
>
> —Israel Zangwill, *The Melting Pot*

Jewish author Israel Zangwill's play *The Melting Pot* opened in the Unites States in the early twentieth century. While the storyline of the play has been mostly forgotten over time, its title's message, that citizens should conform to the majority culture ("melt" together), historically and currently holds tremendous power. This is true in many areas of society, including the field of education.

This chapter describes how early childhood Jewish education (ECJE) in the United States has predominantly moved from the model of a *melting pot* to a *salad bowl* and hopefully can progress further to a *Seder plate* pedagogy. The salad bowl analogy is that of having various ingredients join to make the whole and none need to lose their uniqueness by "melting." This paradigm improves on the melting pot as it represents valuing each student's culture in the school curriculum and practices. However, in this model, as in an actual American tossed green salad, some ingredients dominate others. In one sense, the salad bowl model represents inclusivity but not equity. Berray (2019, 422) poignantly expresses that the melting pot and salad bowl are harmful and unjust "homogenous assimilation and integration metaphors" that require critique. In the context of religious education, Alexander (2019, 422) advocates for a "recovery of humanism that is grounded in the fundamental diversity, not uniformity, of human experience." As such, schools should prepare morally agentic students to become "insiders" in their own traditions while also respecting and celebrating difference within society (Alexander 2009, 2019).

Therefore, the authors of this chapter contend that a better analogy is that of a Seder plate (a special plate containing symbolic foods eaten or displayed at the Passover dinner known as a Seder). Each item on the Seder plate is essential and celebrated for its distinctive attributes. If any item is missing, the Seder plate does not meet the traditional religious guidelines. During the Passover Seder (ritual dinner), the Seder plate is utilized to elicit questions and engage the seder participants in dialogue about the story of the exodus from Egypt, which highlights issues of oppression, marginalization, and dehumanization. As such, the Seder plate *can* represent how a community honors cultural elements, thoughtfully asks questions to increase understanding that include critical questions about justice, and curates an experience that is meaningful for all the participants.

In educational terms, the melting pot represents assimilationist education, the salad bowl represents multicultural education, and the Seder plate represents culturally relevant pedagogy, which seeks to disrupt, dismantle, and replace deficit views embedded in the educational system. ECJE is grounded in several values that guide professional practice. *B'tzelem Elokim* (in the image of God), kehillah (community), and *tikkun olam* (repairing the world) all play a role in curriculum development, interactions and relationships, and expectations for children's behavior and social-emotional capacities. A Seder plate pedagogy necessitates the reimagination of these values to prepare educators and children to confront inequities and honor difference.

Early childhood (EC) centers and sites are a reflection of their sociocultural contexts that can perpetuate inequality and deficit lenses. EC educators are perfectly positioned to take the steps needed to disrupt and dismantle injustices (Long, Souto-Manning, and Vasquez 2016, 1), and some national organizations are advocating for such changes (NAEYC 2019).

This chapter, in addition to providing a description of these three pedagogical models—the melting pot, the salad bowl, and the Seder plate—offers each model's implications for Jewish programs, a set of critical questions to assist educators and school leaders in interrogating their school settings for bias, and specific strategies and examples of how to implement a Seder plate approach in ECJE.

The Three Pedagogical Models

Assimilationist Education—a Melting Pot Approach

The melting pot approach, in its most basic form, is a classic assimilation model (Brown and Bean 2006). This model encourages the stripping of cultural and linguistic differences to support the dominant culture through nationalist knowledge and pride (Gordon 1964; Jackson 2010).

In the common-school era of the nineteenth century, US schools were designed to assimilate immigrants (Carpenter 2013; Nash 2009) and Native Americans. The most insidious examples of an assimilationist view led to racist policies and practices, as evident in the Native American boarding schools in the late nineteenth century. These schools' approach was described by Captain Richard H. Pratt, who famously declared, "Kill the Indian in him and save the man" (Banks 2012). This framework also led to the exclusionary practices evidenced by the Chinese Exclusion Act of 1882, Jim Crow laws, and the development of separate "Mexican schools" in the Southwest (Grant 2010). There are overt and covert assimilationist and exclusionary practices and policies that still undergird current school systems (Calderon-Berumen 2019; Watts 2019). Backlash against the devaluing of people's culture, history, language, and ways of being in the world spurred progressive educators to develop multicultural education.

Multicultural Education—a Salad Bowl Approach

The ethnic studies and Black history movements of the end of the nineteenth century and early twentieth century, featuring the influential voices of Carter Woodson and W. E. B. Du Bois, led to the intellectual foundation for multicultural education anchored in critical literature that countered the white-focused version of history in education (Ramsey, Williams, and Vold 2003). Woodson (1933) criticized the education system's role in the perpetuation of the racial inferiority ideology. Multicultural education as a pedagogical model took shape during the Civil Rights Movement (mid-1950s and 1960s). In the 1960s, multicultural education expanded to include gender, sexual orientation, socioeconomic class, language, religion, and ability as critical components of culture, power, and schooling (Sleeter 1991). Multicultural education encompasses various educational reforms, practices, and approaches with a commitment to educational equity to prepare all students for a "pluralistic democratic society" (Banks and Banks 1995).

Though conceptualized with a critical stance to empower schools and children, multicultural education was often superficially implemented because issues of power and oppression were overlooked (Banks 1989; Gay 2013; Ramsey, Williams, and Vold 2003). Some teachers fearing backlash from families and administrators added a small measure of multicultural content to the curriculum but did not focus on the inequities in education or society.

Culturally Relevant Pedagogy—a Seder Plate Approach

Critical educational theorists strongly condemn assimilationist practices and build upon multicultural education to form Culturally Relevant Pedagogy (Ladson-Billings 2014; Paris and Alim 2017). They challenge the Eurocentric model that dominates school curricula, policies, and practices to normalize the strengths, accomplishments, values, and resources of cultural and racial communities that continue to be marginalized, misrepresented, or erased in schools (Boutte 2017; King and Swartz 2016; Ladson-Billings 2017; Wynter-Hoyte et al. 2019). Gay and Ladson-Billings propelled the field forward focusing on social justice, teachers as activists, and critical thinking (Gay 1993, 2000, 2013; Ladson-Billings 1994, 1995, 2014).

Ladson-Billings's model rests on three tenets: the development of students' (1) competence in their own and others' cultures, (2) critical consciousness, and

(3) academic expertise (1995, 160–2). She has noted that developing children's critical consciousness is the least utilized tenet in her framework (Ladson-Billings 2017). This critical consciousness asks teachers to facilitate children's ability to detect, study, and confront issues of inequity. Other scholars have surmised that educators often neglect, ignore, or avoid this component because teachers "might not fully understand it or they are unsure of their ability to engage students in a conversation about justice" (Baines, Tisdale, and Long 2018, 102).

Meir Muller (2021) has done extensive work with children ages five to ten in detecting anti-Black content in books, advertisements, and social phenomena, using critical questions (which can be used to consider any group that is minoritized or underrepresented) such as:

1. Are Black people included in this text? Why or why not?
2. Do you see anything unfair to Black people? Tell me more about this.
3. Who or what is shown as important? How was the message of importance conveyed?
4. Are Black people left out or shown as unimportant? How was this message conveyed?
5. Can this message be hurtful or unfair to Black people? Why?
6. How does the text make you feel? Why?
7. What can you do to improve this issue?

An educator who uses such questions rejects an assimilationist stance (the melting pot), builds upon multicultural education (the salad bowl), and brings to fruition the idea that every group of people is worthy, essential, and should be celebrated for their distinctive attributes (the Seder plate).

Relationship of Each Model to ECJE

Many scholars have written about young children's ability to understand issues of inequity and confront racism (Boutte and Muller 2018; Derman-Sparks and Edwards 2010). However, this critical issue is under-researched and rarely written about in the context of ECJE in the United States, except for a few calls to action (Dvorin Friedman 2020; Goodman 2020).

EC Jewish programs that consider the benefits of a Seder plate model may face several tensions. A goal of a faith-based program is to teach about one's own culture, customs, and religious practices. However, programs must be cautious lest their practices undervalue other cultures and the cultural diversity within the program. Jewish values, holidays, stories, and other aspects of the Jewish curriculum help prepare children to become inculcated in their own tradition; but the Jewish context also allows for the valuing of others and critical questioning to address injustices. With this understanding, we will hypothesize how Jewish students might fare under each model in schools where they are the majority population and in schools where they are a small percentage of the students.

The Melting Pot

The melting pot model can be harmful for Jewish students both in US public school EC programs (where they make up a small percentage of students) and in ECJE (where they are often the majority of students). Under an assimilationist model in public schools, Jewish children might be encouraged to shed Jewish attitudes and actions. The majority religion, most often Christianity, may be prominent in holiday displays, schoolwide activities, and curricula materials. Jewish students may lose opportunities when missing school days that fall on Jewish holidays and may be asked to represent a collective view of all Jewish people (Garland 2009). This can lead Jewish children to a disinterest in or even embarrassment over being Jewish. In Jewish schools (where Judaism could be the dominant culture), other cultures might be devalued and children might be taught that they are more important than other people. A similar problem could arise if the only Jewish people discussed are white Ashkenazi Jews (from Central and Eastern European Jewry), making all other groups of Jews feel omitted or marginalized. Jewish schools and public schools alike can provide for both a strong identity for Jewish children and respect for others if the melting pot method of education is rejected.

The Salad Bowl

Multicultural education is well aligned for public EC programs as this method values the cultural identities of all children. Using this model, Jewish children in public schools will have their culture reflected in the curriculum, books, websites, wall displays, and other school facets, as will other groups, even if they make up only a small percentage of students. Jewish schools that emphasize Jewish identity can incorporate practices that value other cultures and groups. Cultural knowledge and ways of being join so that children are not asked to "melt" or lose their individuality. As such, this model is beneficial for Jewish children in either public schools or Jewish schools. However, based on anecdotal reports and the authors' years of experience in the field of Jewish education, it seems that many Jewish EC centers strive to incorporate multicultural education, but the efforts often result in a "tourist approach" (Derman-Sparks and ABC Task Force 1989) that can lead to the tokenizing or stereotyping of others. This issue is also found in public schools (Hanau 2020) as they often use a superficial approach to cultural teaching that focuses solely on topics such as food, fashion, or folklore.

Jewish schools need to pay attention not only to minoritized cultures outside of Judaism but also to those within. For instance, a class studying Sephardic Jews (Jewish people who trace their roots back to the Iberian Peninsula, North Africa, or the Middle East) that only memorizes a song in Ladino (Judeo-Spanish language) and discusses how Sephardic Jews have the custom to eat rice on Passover does a disservice to this group. This salad bowl approach does not ask children of Sephardic heritage in Jewish schools to shed their identities, but schools using this approach may not offer a robust exploration of these children's culture. This deficiency can be corrected by using a Seder plate model.

The Seder Plate

The authors of this chapter call for settings of ECJE to dive deeply into all ethnicities, nationalities, and groups found within Judaism and to reflect on other community groups who are marginalized or traditionally underserved. This can be done by using the tenets of culturally relevant pedagogy (Ladson-Billings 1995), including a version of the critical questions supplied earlier in this chapter. This type of approach is represented here by a Seder plate, which is used to encourage questions to enhance understanding around issues of equity and on which each item is considered essential, celebrated for its unique features. Culturally relevant pedagogy cherishes every culture in the community and, like a traditional Seder plate, is invalidated by omitting any item (or group). Therefore, a Seder plate approach upholds Jewish values that everyone is created in the image of God, each person is required to better issues of inequity in the world, and each community must be just.

A Seder plate approach demands that educators interrogate their practices and biases to detect, study, and confront any issue of injustice. For instance, Jewish preschool children frequently hear biblical stories that bring up very complex topics that include oppression and prejudice (Achituv 2013). Yet, teachers often do not ask the children to consider these issues of inequity (for children, the term fairness might be more easily understood) or to connect these stories to modern-day incidents of injustice (Gor Ziv 2016). Table 4.1 provides specific Seder plate model strategies for ECJE, illustrated by examples collected from the field, including the work of Jewish EC organizations, schools, and educators who took a course at Gratz College on anti-bias education in 2020.

Table 4.1 Strategies and Examples of the Seder Plate Model

Seder Plate Model Strategies	Examples Collected from the Field of ECJE
Examine walls, books, websites, curriculum, and so on to ensure that all community cultures' history and language are honored	"Demonstrating diversity in the classroom as soon as one walks in" (educator in a Jewish early childhood program)
	"We are working on building our anti-bias class library" (early childhood educator in a Jewish day school)
Reflect if children are being provided the tools to look at the world and ask, "Whose voices are heard? Silenced? Omitted?" Add voices of diverse expert guests (Jewish and non-Jewish)	"Constantly asking the question: 'Whose voice is being heard and whose is silenced?' … Having guest readers … other talents of various races … Encourage asking questions and listening" (educator in a Jewish early childhood program)
	"How are people of color depicted in the classroom? How did we celebrate differences this week? Who did we introduce to the students from outside of our community? What language was used when having a conversation about race?" (early childhood educator in a Jewish day school)

(continued)

Table 4.1 Strategies and Examples of the Seder Plate Model (Continued)

Seder Plate Model Strategies	Examples Collected from the Field of ECJE
Focus on "hidden figures" (people who are often not included in the classroom conversations—Sephardic, Mizrachi, Jewish people of color, members of the Jewish Latinx community, and others)	"Ashkenazic, Sephardic, Mizrachi, Indian, and Ethiopian Jews represent some of the distinct subcultures of Judaism, but not all. We are all Jews"
	"I hope to bring guest speakers" (early childhood educator in a Modern Orthodox Jewish day school)
Consider "hidden histories"—those left out of the curriculum or picture books	"My goal is to celebrate those who have been silenced by specifically including books, videos in my room that uplift marginalized voices, and activities that focus on learning about these people's work" (educator in a Jewish early childhood program)
Inform families about the Seder plate model and how it is supported in the school	"Each week, every classroom will add a section in their class newsletter on the ways that class acted as anti-racists" (school letter to families)
Encourage children to ask questions that detect, study, and confront inequity	"A section in the newsletter with suggested questions that parents could ask their children in order to spark conversations" (early childhood educator in a Jewish day school)
	"We have to take action now ... We are committed to talk about diversity and not to be bystanders ... Together we can find ways to engage our children in this dialogue" (school letter to families)
Engage in ongoing reflection and provide professional development for professionals	"Recognize my personal biases ... stop and reflect when my biases show up ... reflect together [with colleagues] on what is going on in the classroom ... re-evaluate decisions, activities, and opportunities" (early childhood educator in a Jewish day school)
	"Through a shared commitment to creating spaces where adults and young children can speak and act against injustice and racism, this Community of Practice will support participants as they engage in anti-racism work, listening, and learning to transform their early childhood practice, classrooms, schools, and communities" (Racial Justice Community of Practice)
Share with administrators how the organization can continue long-term thinking on how we demonstrate solidarity in learning to counter a deficit perspective toward any community in every aspect of the institution	"Invite parents and educators to share their ideas, thoughts, and concerns of an anti-bias education program through a survey" (early childhood educator in a Jewish day school)

Examples of the Seder Plate Approach

In this section we offer more detailed illustrations from educators, Jewish day schools, and EC Jewish organizations of their work toward the implementation of a Seder plate model. Each of these examples unapologetically shines a light on cultures and ways of being that are omitted, marginalized, or distorted in curriculum and classrooms. These examples can be used to advocate for any marginalized group, with implications for work both within Jewish programs and non-Jewish programs.

Examples from Educators

The Seder plate model relies on the ongoing commitment, learning, and reflection of educators who apply a critical stance to their daily interactions and practices. The following examples emerged from a group of EC educators working in Jewish programs who engaged in a semester-long college course at Gratz College in the summer of 2020 for professional development around an anti-bias framework.

Course participants created plans for implementing anti-bias approaches by considering their schools' mission and culture. One educator wrote: "Diversity is represented and respected through our classroom materials, books, documentation, and the language being used throughout the classroom." She described how she planned to initiate conversations, as opposed to being reactive. This was echoed by another educator, who shared that it is "beneficial to talk about race/racism because it helps humans learn from a young age the reality of the injustices in the world and the need to always ask, 'Whose voice is being heard and whose is silenced?'" Another educator detailed the importance of "being a reflective anti-bias, anti-racist educator every day of my work and life" and added: "I recognize … that as a white individual I am in a position of power that I can use to fight for the equality of education."

These examples demonstrate the need for intentionality to avoid a surface-level approach. Instead, the educators' comments uphold a need for a Seder plate model that is best supported through the ongoing development of a critical stance. Educators described challenges and potential barriers related to methods of synthesizing multiple goals and educational philosophies in ECJE. Most concerns illuminated educators' worries about resistance from colleagues, school administrators, and families. While some educators share ways in which their schools or programs had expressed support, some feared pushback. One educator questioned, "Will parents be accepting of additions to the curriculum? Will colleagues jump on board?" It is, therefore, imperative not only for educators to share with families how the Seder plate model informs classroom practice and learning but also for schools to take an explicit position in support of the model.

Examples from a Jewish Day School and Early Childhood Center

Actions by school leaders and administrators drive systemic changes within schools and communities to best support educators as they transform their classrooms and practices. Top-down initiatives ground this important work within the school's vision with the potential for it to spread to each teacher, child, and family. In the summer of 2020, many Jewish day schools and EC centers responded to the murder of George Floyd with letters of support for the Black community with varying words of commitment toward anti-racist teaching. The Cutler Jewish Day School (CJDS) in South Carolina and Moriah Early Childhood Center in Illinois used a Seder plate approach in their letters to families. They not only offered solidarity but, more importantly, included a call to action and the naming of specific measures to advocate for a pro-Black stance that values African American history, culture, and language. The following are excerpts from the CJDS letter:

> CJDS joins other Jewish and non-Jewish organizations around the country who are outraged at the recent racial injustices including the murder of George Floyd. We stand in solidarity with the Black community that have for far too long suffered rampant racism and unfair applications of the law …
>
> We know that our words of love are not enough, and action is required. Elie Wiesel stated, "Silence encourages the tormentor, never the tormented." The following are some actions we will introduce or refocus on as we start school next year:
>
> 1. Examine our classroom and hallway walls to make sure that our representation of the African American community is well depicted.
> 2. Examine our class libraries, choice of websites, curriculum, and other materials to make sure we are honoring Black students' culture, history and language.
> 3. Reflect if we are providing our children the tools to look at the world and ask, "Whose voices are heard? Silenced? Omitted?," as doing so can lead to children confronting racial injustice.
> 4. Each week, every classroom will add a section in their class newsletter on the ways that class acted as anti-racists.
>
> These are just a few examples of the type of work we commit to do. We do this because we are responsible to educate the adults of the future so they will strive for a more racially just world.

The following is an excerpt from the Moriah Early Childhood Center letter:

> How do we educate against racism in the face of so much fear and violence? We strongly believe that we have a responsibility to take part in repairing the world (*Tikkun Olam*) and preparing our youngest citizens for a better and kinder future. We must take action now! In February, our entire staff attended a day of diversity and inclusion training, referring to racism, gender, ageism, special rights etc. We learned a lot. We are committed to talk about diversity and not to be bystanders … Together we can find ways to engage our children in this dialogue and continue to work toward a greater future for everyone affected.

In these examples each school moved beyond a salad bowl approach (superficially including cultures) to a Seder plate model, where every group of people is viewed as worthy, essential, and deserving of being celebrated for their distinctive attributes. Further, each school took a stance of advocating for activism from the school educators, families, and children. Each school was able to maintain its focus on Jewish education while incorporating this Seder plate approach.

Examples from Jewish Early Childhood Organizations

Schools were not the only EC organizations to heed the call of a Seder plate model. Three organizations—the Jewish United Fund of Metropolitan Chicago (JUF), the Paradigm Project (a network of Jewish EC practitioners), and the Jewish Education Project (an organization focused on supporting educators who work with infants through eighteen-year-olds)—also looked to move to a Seder plate model in their professional development initiatives to support educators, school leaders, consultants, and other EC professionals and stakeholders. These steps toward change signal to all community members that EC Jewish education is a necessary site for this important work.

JUF—Diversity and Equity Day of Learning

In February 2020, the JUF hosted a Diversity, Equity, and Inclusion Day of Learning (the one referenced in the letter from Moriah Early Childhood Center), organized by a planning committee of ten EC educators and leaders across six organizations and schools. Four hundred EC professionals from nineteen Jewish schools/EC programs participated in one of eleven tracks of learning focused on inclusive Jewish education. The tracks addressed a variety of areas related to multiculturalism and diversity, such as gender-expansive behaviors and gender identities; religious diversity and positionality; social justice issues and advancing diversity, equity, and inclusion; identity and oppression and institutional, differentiated instruction; intergenerational inclusion; an anti-bias lens in the examination of children's literature; and the use of arts and photography in inclusion work. Sessions encouraged deep conversation on how individual identities impact the ways in which educators interact with and support students and colleagues across race, ethnicity, gender, and (dis)ability and the study of anti-bias frameworks as a tool for promoting diversity, equity, and inclusion.

The Paradigm Project and the Jewish Education Project

Two leading Jewish EC organizations, the Paradigm Project and the Jewish Education Project, partnered during the 2020–1 academic school year to create a Racial Justice Community of Practice. They described the group's goal:

> Through a shared commitment to creating spaces where adults and young children can speak and act against injustice and racism, this Community of Practice (CoP) will support participants as they engage in anti-racism work, listening, and learning to transform their early childhood practice, classrooms, schools, and communities. As this CoP aspires to model anti-racist actions, we forefront this description with an acknowledgement that the organizers are all Euro-Americans. However, the majority of sessions will feature Black scholars and practitioners

providing access into insights and life experiences that will prepare all participants to move forward with this important work.

The Community of Practice consisted of thirty-five EC educators and leaders from Jewish EC programs across the country. Participants challenged their thinking, biases, and practices in order to enhance their critical consciousness toward change. For example, guest speakers and the Community of Practice facilitators invited participants to challenge the role of white supremacy and whiteness as a norm in children's Jewish and non-Jewish literature, utilize an anti-racist lens by asking critical questions, and reflect on anti-Blackness that is embedded in EC practices.

These EC Jewish organizations set an example for EC Jewish programs and other groups in their position that it is no longer good enough to only recognize that our schools exist in a multicultural world, but that action needs to be taken in schools to recognize and advocate for groups who are suffering injustice. The Seder plate model was shown to be an effective tool as Jewish schools were encouraged to interrogate their practices to detect, study, and confront any issue of inequity.

Conclusion

Israel Zangwill, in addition to his play *The Melting Pot*, also wrote the poem "Seder Night in London." In this sonnet he contrasts the tawdriness of a harried metropolitan city with the reverence of the Jewish home on Passover. He seems to celebrate Judaism as a counterpoint to the rest of the world. One can make the case that Zangwill vacillates between the play's message of the melting pot's assimilation and the poem's exceptionalism (which can be found in the salad bowl model). Yet, assimilation and exceptionalism are both misguided educational approaches. The analogy of a Seder plate can provide EC educators and their students with the strategies to better themselves and the world.

References

Achituv, S. 2013. "What Did the Teacher Say Today? State Religious Kindergarten Teachers Deal with Complex Torah Stories." *Journal of Jewish Education* 79 (3): 256–96.

Alexander, H. A. 2009. "Educating Identity: Toward a Pedagogy of Difference." In *Religious Education as Encounter: A Tribute to John M. Hull*, edited by S. Miedema, 45–52. Munster: Waxman.

Alexander, H. A. 2019. "Taking Back the Public Square: Peaceful Coexistence through Pedagogies of the Sacred, Difference, and of Hope." *Religious Education* 114 (4): 417–23.

Baines, J., C. Tisdale, and S. Long. 2018. *"We've Been Doing It Your Way Long Enough": Choosing the Culturally Relevant Classroom*. New York: Teachers College Press.

Banks, C., and J. Banks. 1995. "Equity Pedagogy: An Essential Component of Multicultural Education." *Theory into Practice* 34 (3): 152–8.

Banks, J. 1989. "Approaches to Multicultural Curriculum Reform." *Trotter Review* 3 (3): 17–19.

Banks, J. 2012. "Ethnic Studies, Citizenship Education, and the Public Good." *Intercultural Education* 23 (6): 467–73.

Berray, M. 2019. "A Critical Literary Review of the Melting Pot and Salad Bowl Assimilation and Integration Theories." *Journal of Ethnic and Cultural Studies* 6 (1): 142–51.

Boutte, G. 2017. "Teaching about Racial Equity Issues in Teacher Education." In *African American Children in Early Childhood Education: Making the Case for Policy Investments in Families, Schools, and Communities*, edited by T. Durden, S. Curenton, and I. Iruka, 247–66. Bingley, UK: Emerald. https://doi.org/10.1108/S2051-231720170000005011.

Boutte, G., and M. Muller. 2018. "Engaging Children in Conversations about Oppression Using Children's Literature." *Talking Points* 30 (1): 2–9.

Brown, S., and F. Bean. 2006. "Assimilation Models, Old and New: Explaining a Long-Term Process." Migration Policy Institute. October 1, 2006. https://www.migrationpolicy.org/article/assimilation-models-old-and-new-explaining-long-term-process.

Calderon-Berumen, F. 2019. "Resisting Assimilation to the Melting Pot: Validating the Cultural Curriculum of the Home." *Journal of Culture and Values in Education* 2 (1): 81–95.

Carpenter, J. 2013. "Thomas Jefferson and the Ideology of Democratic Schooling." *Democracy and Education* 21 (2): 5.

Derman-Sparks, L., and ABC Task Force. 1989. *Anti-bias Curriculum: Tools for Empowering Young Children*. Washington, DC: NAEYC.

Derman-Sparks, L., and J. Edwards. 2010. *Anti-bias Education for Young Children and Ourselves*. Washington, DC: National Association for the Education of Young Children.

Dvorin Friedman, I. 2020. "Antiracism and Jewish Early Childhood Education." e Jewish Philanthropy. July 10, 2020. https://ejewishphilanthropy.com/seeing-color-a-vision-for-anti-bias-jewish-early-childhood-classrooms/.

Garland, M. 2009. "Christian Privilege: Do Jewish Students Feel Marginalized in U.S. Public Schools?" PhD diss., Iowa State University.

Gay, G. 1993. "Building Cultural Bridges: A Bold Proposal for Teacher Education." *Education and Urban Society* 25 (3): 285–9. https://doi.org/10.1177/0013124593025003006.

Gay, G. 2000. *Culturally Responsive Teaching: Theory, Research and Practice*. New York: Teachers College Press.

Gay, G. 2013. "Teaching to and through Cultural Diversity." *Curriculum Inquiry* 43:48–70. https://doi.org/10.1111/curi.2013.43.

Goodman, R. 2020. "A Call for Action: Jewish Day Schools Address Racism by Being Multi-Cultural." e Jewish Philanthropy. July 28, 2020. https://ejewishphilanthropy.com/a-call-for-action-jewish-day-schools-address-racism-by-being-multi-cultural/.

Gor Ziv, H. 2016. "Teaching Jewish Holidays in Early Childhood Education in Israel: Critical Feminist Pedagogy Perspective." *Taboo: The Journal of Culture and Education* 15 (1): 119–34.

Gordon, M. M. 1964. *Assimilation in American Life: The Role of Race, Religion and National Origins*. Oxford: Oxford University Press.

Grant, C. A. 2010. *The Evolution of Multicultural Education in the United States: A Journey for Human Rights and Social Justice*. New York: Routledge.

Hanau, S. 2020. "Alumni Call on Jewish Day Schools to Do More to Fight Racism." *Jewish Telegraphic Agency.* June 11, 2020. https://www.jta.org/2020/06/11/united-states/alumni-call-on-jewish-day-schools-to-do-more-to-fight-racism.

Jackson, L. 2010. "The New Assimilationism: The Push for Patriotic Education in the United States Since September 11." *Journal for Critical Education Policy Studies* 8 (1): 108–36.

King, J. E., and E. E. Swartz. 2016. *The Afrocentric Praxis of Teaching for Freedom: Connecting Culture to Learning.* New York: Routledge.

Ladson-Billings, G. 1994. *The Dreamkeepers: Successful Teachers of African American Children.* San Francisco: Jossey-Bass.

Ladson-Billings, G. 1995. "That's Just Good Teaching! The Case for Culturally Relevant Pedagogy." *Theory into Practice* 43: 159–65.

Ladson-Billings, G. 2014. "Culturally Relevant Pedagogy 2.0: A.K.A. the Remix." *Harvard Educational Review* 84 (1): 74–84.

Ladson-Billings, G. 2017. "The (R)evolution Will Not Be Standardized: Teacher Education, Hip Hop Pedagogy, and Culturally Relevant Pedagogy 2.0." In *Culturally Sustaining Pedagogies. Teaching and Learning for Justice in a Changing World*, edited by D. Paris and S. Alim, 141–56. New York: Teachers College Press.

Long, S., M. Souto-Manning, and V. M. Vasquez, eds. 2016. *Courageous Leadership in Early Childhood Education: Taking a Stand for Social Justice.* New York: Teachers College Press.

Muller, M. 2021. "Preparing Black Children to Identify and Confront Racism in Books, Media, and Other Texts: Critical Questions." In *We Be Lovin Black Children*, edited by G. Boutte, J. King, G. Johnson, and L. King, 37–46. Gorham, ME: Myers Education.

Nash, M. 2009. "Contested Identities: Nationalism, Regionalism, and Patriotism in Early American Textbooks." *History of Education Quarterly* 49 (4): 417–41.

NAEYC. 2019. "Advancing Equity in Early Childhood Education Position Statement." National Association of the Education of Young Children. Accessed February 8, 2021. https://www.naeyc.org/resources/position-statements/equity.

Paris, D., and S. H. Alim, eds. 2017. *Culturally Sustaining Pedagogies: Teaching and Learning for Justice in a Changing World.* New York: Teachers College Press.

Ramsey, P., L. R. Williams, and E. Vold. 2003. *Multicultural Education: A Source Book.* Abingdon, VA: Routledge.

Sleeter, C. E. 1991. *Empowerment through Multicultural Education.* New York: State University of New York Press.

Watts, J. 2019. "Teaching English Language Learners: A Reconsideration of Assimilation Pedagogy in U.S. Schools." *Diaspora, Indigenous, and Minority Education* 15 (1): 1–9. https://doi.org/10.1080/15595692.2019.1684890.

Woodson, C. G. 1933. *The Mis-Education of the Negro.* San Diego, CA: Booktree.

Wynter-Hoyte, K., M. Muller, N. Bryan, G. Boutte, and S. Long. 2019. "Dismantling Eurocratic Practices in Teacher Education: A Preservice Program Focused on Culturally Relevant, Humanizing, and Decolonizing Pedagogies." In *Handbook of Research on Field-Based Teacher Education*, edited by T. Hodgesand and A. Baum, 300–21. Hershey, PN: IGI Global.

Zangwill, I. 1909. *The Melting Pot: Drama in Four Acts.* New York: Macmillan.

5

Educating toward Gender Awareness, Feminism, and Cultural Sensitivity in Early Childhood Jewish Education Teacher Preparation

Sharon Kaplan-Berkley and Haggith Gor Ziv

This chapter presents a reflective description of practice as experienced by two Israeli teacher educators specializing in the preparation of early childhood Jewish education (ECJE) educators. The different contexts within which the authors educate form a distinctive element of this joint study: a state-religious college of education and a state secular college of education.

Early childhood education (ECE) theory acknowledges the individual development of young children in stages positioning the developing child at the focus of educational approaches, the learning environment, and daily conduct (NAEYC 2020). It fundamentally caters to the needs of the young child while enveloping the child with support, warmth, and encouragement to grow and advance. Since Piaget (1936) first coined the notion of developmental stages, the theory of developmentally appropriate practice has evolved and changed, adapting and accommodating the theory to the education of the young child in the context of the twenty-first century. Currently, the National Association for the Education of Young Children (NAEYC) in the United States defines "developmentally appropriate practice" as methods that promote each child's optimal development and learning through a strengths-based, play-based approach to joyful, engaged learning (NAEYC 2020).

This assumption that early childhood (EC) educators should adapt to and accommodate a child's natural development and needs is accepted in teacher preparation colleges. Indeed, the content of courses and methods in the training programs with which the authors are associated are implemented according to these concepts. A similar attitude is practiced with student teachers, using self-reflection, promoting awareness, and cherishing personal growth in connection to childcare.

Furthermore, in the training of Jewish educators, traditional Jewish practice and beliefs present us with a possible conflict between conventionally observed Jewish holiday celebrations and rituals and theories of cognitive and emotional development of young children. For example, the historical story behind the celebration of a Jewish holiday is often unsuitable to the young child's cognitive perception.

In this chapter we explore different approaches to preservice teacher education in Israel by addressing traditional gender issues, the development of social critical consciousness, and gender awareness in our students. As teacher educators of EC preservice teachers, we discuss the main principles of our educational approach and the process of developing gender identity and of inspiring social change toward a gender-equal Jewish society. We wrestle with the tension between the need for belonging to a social group and the need for a safe, individual, supportive environment in which to grow. We, each in our own unique way, perceive Judaism as a moral guide to human rights, social justice, and diversity. Our shared teaching approach navigates between these tensions, resulting in our proposing a combined pedagogy illustrating our findings that secular and religious teachers in training programs deal with similar issues but through different lenses.

Background of Authors

Haggith: I am an upper-middle class Ashkenazi (from Central and Eastern European Jewry) woman, born on a kibbutz (a type of communal settlement) in Israel, holding a PhD and tenure at an academic institute; as such I have privileges that my students do not have. At the age of six, I moved with my family to Beersheba. I attended an immigrant school, where I witnessed the discriminatory practices of teachers toward children of Mizrachi (from North Africa and Middle Eastern Jewry) background. I believe that my sensitivity to social justice in education and to gender inequality stems from my experiences as a child in a poor immigrant neighborhood. When I turned twenty, I studied at the University of Judaism (now part of American Jewish University) in Los Angeles and was a member of a Conservative synagogue there. These encounters with liberal Judaism and the American feminist movement of the 1970s in California influenced me greatly.

Sharon: I am a religiously observant, liberal Orthodox Jewish woman, I hold a PhD in educational leadership, and I am a tenured ECE pedagogic mentor and lecturer at an academic institute. Upon graduating high school in South Africa, I chose to pursue my Zionist (belief in the development and protection of Israel) dream and immigrate to the State of Israel. My earliest memories of belonging to the Jewish religion take me back to the culture and climate of the family home my parents created. Ours was the home in which diverse family and friends gathered to celebrate the Jewish Sabbath and holidays. As a result, I appreciate Jewish religious observance as having values that support the growing and maintaining of family relationships within a framework that connects one to community. Moreover, I am aware that my sensitivity to identity development, multiculturalism, and social justice in education stems from my experiences as a Jewish child growing up in Apartheid South Africa.

Our Work Context

As previously mentioned, we are affiliated with and educate in different colleges of education in Israel.

Haggith: I work in a liberal, progressive college in Tel Aviv; almost all of my students are women. Many of them are the first generation in their families to graduate higher education. Ethnically, half of my students come from a Mizrachi Jewish background and half are of Ashkenazi descent. A few are Ethiopian Jews. I have very few Arab students.

Sharon: I teach at a religious-affiliated college of education, established more than ninety years ago with the sole purpose of educating young religious women to teach within the state-religious school system. The student population is mostly young, single or newly married, observant Jewish women from a culturally diverse background of Ashkenazi, Mizrahi, and Ethiopian Israelis.

Literature Review

Our work leans on two theoretical fields: critical feminist pedagogy and culturally responsive teaching.

Critical Feminist Pedagogy

Critical pedagogy seeks to understand the various ways in which knowledge is induced and constructs human consciousness through education. It also focuses on pedagogical means to promote political awareness and change in educated students to enhance equality and justice for all (Shore 1992).

Feminist pedagogy views gender issues as dominating factors that create inequality between people (Gore 1993). Traditional mainstream education tracks girls to traditional roles in society that position them in a lower place than men. Feminist pedagogy tries to change the social order that positions women in the role of the "other" (Beauvoir 2010).

In line with this, feminist critical pedagogy focuses on the way society segregates children in educational institutions into social classes, generally reflecting the social class of birth (Gor Ziv 2015). It documents practices that preserve inequality through education and tries to offer ways to change the power relationships between gender groups, class, race, ability, and other divides. By way of what it leaves outside the discourse and what it emphasizes in discussion with students, the prevailing view of knowledge advocated in schools tends to portray unequal power relationships (Zalmanson-Levy 2019).

Both critical pedagogy and feminist pedagogy aim to expose the different mechanisms that channel children to the margins of society. Both pedagogies strive to give a voice to disempowered groups. Both pedagogies raise awareness to cause social change and promote equality among all segments of society through education. Critical feminist pedagogy provides a lens through which to view society and education and interpret and act to humanize them (Gor Ziv 2013). Moreover, it views educational philosophy and praxis as one and inseparable (Freire 1970). Additionally, critical feminist pedagogy emphasizes the construction of gender inequality in a patriarchal society through education. In line with this idea, celebrations and teaching of Jewish holidays in Jewish EC centers tend to unintentionally strengthen messages of gender inequality and practices (Gor Ziv 2016). Indeed, hidden curriculum as well as overt messages of school materials and practices construct inequality that seems natural to the students and teachers (Middleton 1993).

Culturally Responsive Teaching

Culturally responsive teaching grounded in a multicultural approach to education places the students, their life histories and experiences, at the center of the teaching and learning process. It advocates employing pedagogy occurring in a context familiar to the student, while cultivating multiple ways of thinking (Gay 2018). A successful culturally responsive learning environment requires educational leaders and their staffs to create an environment of inclusion, embracing families and communities in a manner that supports diverse perspectives, values, experiences, and acceptance. A culturally responsive educational approach pervades all aspects of the educational community and organization (Derman-Sparks and Edwards 2010, 2019; Gay 2015; Ramsey 2015).

In the world of ECE, a culturally responsive perspective of education aims to help children develop positive individual identities, including the positive development of gender, racial, class, and cultural identities. It aims to help young children recognize and accept their membership within many different groups, as well as within society as a whole. In this way, a multicultural approach develops social cognition that enables the child to identify, empathize with, relate to, and respect individuals from other groups (Derman-Sparks and Edwards 2010, 2019; Ramsey 2015).

An apt example is the celebration of Jewish holidays. They are replete with sensory ceremonies, rituals, and customs. These rituals enrich the holiday celebration and encourage behaviors that create meaning and identity for participants. Actually, celebrating holidays can also offer an avenue for cultural appreciation without necessarily including religious practice (Freeman and Swim 2009; Maloney 2000).

In the secular Jewish world, these ceremonies enable growth of an identity of the Jewish people as a nation, reinforcing the development of Jewish peoplehood—a feeling of belonging and commitment to the Jewish people. Moreover, ritual is a means of exposing the young child to the rich multicultural heritage that exists among the Jewish people. Encountering diverse, ethnic ritual practices, observed in the immediate environment of the individual child, and exploring together as a community of young learners the varied ways in which other children celebrate holidays may plant the seeds for cross-cultural thinking and an ability to respect diversity among young children (Howell and Reinhard 2015).

Nevertheless, Jewish holidays and rituals might also strengthen and preserve gender inequality messages and messages of nationalism and military power (Gor Ziv 2016). The narrative of the holiday tends to place men as heroes in the center of the celebration, ignoring the existence of women. When women play a role in the narrative, they are often ignored in ECJE; for example, the courageous story of the midwives who refused to obey Pharaoh's order to kill the newborn male babies is rarely told in secular kindergartens (Gor Ziv 2016). Likewise, leading and performing rituals are generally male-focused, excluding the public participation of women.

Methodology

In researching and writing this chapter, we chose to use an autoethnographic methodology. This research method entails revealing personal insights into the culture to which one belongs and, thus, which one is examining. Autoethnography contains the personal story of the author as well as the larger cultural meaning for the individual's story (Creswell 2013). Furthermore, it allows the researcher to examine one's own individual cultural identity and analyze personal experience within the context of being a "participant observer" (Adams, Holman-Jones, and Ellis 2015).

Given that autoethnography involves engaging in a scientific study of oneself and one's culture, we employed the self as the primary research instrument for documenting and interpreting the perspectives and experiences of the Jewish preservice teachers and the classroom cultures being studied (Lawrence-Lightfoot and Davis 1997). Originally, we met one another with the intention of writing about educating for gender awareness in Israel. We dedicated our first encounter to learning about each other's beliefs and methods. We "clicked" right away and got excited, revealing the similarities and differences in our backgrounds and working situations. We decided to meet regularly to document these diverse and similar efforts to educate feminist teachers.

During this time, digital technology facilitated our collaboration. We continued our dialogue through a shared Google document in which we wrote in different colors and held weekly phone discussions. During these discussions we examined syllabi, shared students' papers, and brought forth case studies from our classroom experiences. We analyzed them together with the goal of finding the main axis that characterizes our attitudes toward gender education in a Jewish context. Thereafter, we explored and described to one another the relational practices, common values, beliefs, and experiences of our approaches to teacher preparation. Also, we applied an autoethnographic procedure to shed light on the personal and professional lives of the preservice ECJE educators and related this to our observed need to cultivate gender awareness and social justice among this particular community. We found five common themes in our educational practice (learning to view different perspectives, having a common expectation, challenging the obvious and the hegemony, expanding horizons and gaining new knowledge, and identities and power relationships) and one mutually exclusive theme (egalitarian education versus inequality in education) that characterized our approach to gender education in a Jewish context.

Collaborative, Shared Insights

Learning to View Different Perspectives

We believe that the ability to look at phenomena from different angles and accept diverse points of view is an important thinking strategy and skill to develop in the training of EC preservice teachers. We urge our students to question what they see and strive to enable their ability to think from different perspectives, thus, comprehending education as a more complex adventure. We do this in a variety of different ways.

Haggith: I try to prepare prospective teachers to be able to "get into the other's shoes." As teachers, they need this skill in order to understand children, parents, staff members, and other community members. Living in a pluralistic environment, it is essential that the teacher create an inclusive curriculum and environment. The ability to understand different perspectives and introduce them into the curriculum may be initiated in a variety of ways, including examining Jewish holidays from the perspective of girls' and boys' roles and using different points of view to look at popular children's stories.

Holidays dominate the ECJE curriculum in Israel, both in secular and religious EC centers. Two weeks, sometimes more, before each holiday, teachers introduce holiday symbols, songs, and creative activities. They hang decorations and tell stories connected to the upcoming holiday. In my course, we study each holiday in depth, with a practical perspective of how it meets the understanding of a child aged three to six.

We try to examine the holiday from a gender perspective and question the holiday's themes and hidden messages. For example, in anticipation of Hanukkah, we talk about the struggle for religious and national freedom and how to emphasize messages of peace rather than glorify wars. In advance of the holiday of Purim, we discuss the tyranny of the king and the place of women in a nondemocratic regime. We criticize the social order that permits persecution of people and ignores human rights. Before Passover, we discuss the heroism of the midwives Shifra and Pua, Pharaoh's daughter Yocheved, and Miriam, who conspired against the cruel Pharaoh together to save the life of Moses and raised him in the palace under the king's nose. Furthermore, we discuss the result of giving a slave child (Moses) the education of a prince, an education that has the potential of turning him into a leader characterized by the integrity of social justice and political consciousness.

Most Jewish holidays entail complicated narratives for young children that are not age appropriate. The heroes are mostly men, and some of the messages are nationalistic and particularistic rather than universalistic. By contrast, we try to offer ways to celebrate each holiday in a way that is understandable for young children, avoiding sexist messages and emphasizing values of equality, compassion, and solidarity.

Sharon: Focusing on the individuality and the myriad of characteristics that the ECJE educator brings to the learning environment, my students and I examine the influence of the educator's personal identity upon who they become professionally. This process demands that the preservice teacher be open to transforming who they are in relation to the world in which they educate. Moreover, it requires constant identity work, focusing on who the educator is becoming as they engage within that world, and it implies a sense of agency (Wenger-Trayner and Wenger-Trayner 2020). Thus, we implement the feminist rallying cry that "the personal is political."

We embark on a journey of identity work with assignments that obligate contemplating the various layers of culture embedded in our family roots. This delicate exercise supports the student's ability to reveal the depth and meaning of ethnic, cultural aspects subconsciously integrated in identity and life experiences. We share our personal and Jewish ethnic community identity via a childhood song, a family heirloom, or a story that has been passed down from generation to generation. Childhood memories, music, traditional clothing, ritual objects, sacred books, and food flavors fill our classroom as we educate one another concerning the diverse ethnicity that represents the personal history of the group of students.

This intimate sharing of the personal within a group of learners generates a community of practice as the students listen and react, support, and confide in one another (Wenger 1998). Moreover, this personal and social exploration of cultural rituals and traditions creates the framework within which we explore ethnic and gender awareness. They see the connection between the personal and the social, between the dominant knowledge and the marginalized ones. Indeed, the imparting of a sometimes-concealed culture can influence the context of the teaching and learning experiences of the young Jewish child. Furthermore, it can reinforce the dominant role the educator plays in communicating and portraying gender awareness within the ECJE environment.

Taught in the context of a culturally sensitive educational approach, this process entails gaining social cognitive skills regarding the differences in roles and relations between women and men in our day-to-day life in general and in the integrating of Jewish ritual practices into our lives in particular. Moreover, classroom discourse acknowledges gaining new perspectives and understandings as an essential aspect of generating an ability to respect a different point of view, cultivating social cognition. Furthermore, it addresses the educator's choice of implementing an approach integrating diversity and equality into the classroom. As opposed to one right narrative and hegemonic knowledge, such an approach strengthens the feminist concept of multiple ways of knowing (Minnich 2010).

A Common Expectation

Haggith: Unexpectedly, we discovered the existence of a tendency in both of our groups of students to approach their teaching and learning experiences believing that an ideal way of educating exists. They come to the learning experience expecting to study a one perfect way of educating young children. They presume that the practicum will provide them with a mentoring teacher who is the embodiment of this ideal practice. Instead, they encounter courses and pedagogic mentors who urge them to question what they observe, hear, and discover in their EC practicum classroom. Likewise, they are participating in courses that encourage them to challenge the mainstream way of thinking and employ personal experiences as a tool to illustrate and reflect upon personal and social cognitive strategies.

Challenging the Obvious, Challenging the Hegemony

Challenging the obvious creates resistance. It confuses our students and tends to shake their worldview. In guiding them through this process, we legitimize the need to create an educational environment that gives space to the other while making space for oneself. Ultimately, we encourage the creation of an inclusive learning environment reflecting the individual child as well as the classroom community.

Sharon: I teach within the framework of an Israeli college of education preparing preservice teachers to integrate into the state-religious educational system. To a large degree, it is expected and accepted that the learning and teaching experience I offer my students will reflect an Orthodox Jewish education. This model of education exposes the preservice teacher, herself a product of the state-religious education system, to activities that clearly should be incorporated into the daily program of the EC classroom. However, the model often creates a sense of incongruity and uncovers an ambivalence that may transcend the educator's confidence in bridging the gap between personal values and the needs of the community in which the student is training (Achituv 2019).

Since young Jewish children learn about their own and others' social identities through both overt and covert messages within the learning environment (Achituv 2019; Derman-Sparks and Edwards 2010), we frequently address this issue. I strive to make my students aware that experiences of activities may convey and support ethnic or gendered roles. Moreover, as a pedagogic mentor I aim to make students cognizant of the abstract messages the environment teaches the child.

For instance, the morning *tefila* (prayer) circle time generally begins with a girl choosing a few *shirei kodesh* (religious songs), bringing the children together with communal singing. Then the *chazzan* (cantor), a boy, dons a talit (prayer shawl) and begins the prayers, with the community of children participating. This division of girls leading an introductory sing-along of holy songs while the boys lead the prayers reinforces the need for gender parity in the classroom.

By contrast, among the communities within which my students train, we find families who support women-led prayer services. Hence, my students gain an awareness of accommodating the needs of the community within which they educate. As a student once shared,

> The mother asked if her daughter could don the tallit and lead the prayer service. I personally do not identify with this behavior but it's her daughter and if that's what she wanted, once or twice during the year, I had no problem making her happy and reinforcing her family values. But they are not the values I bring to my classroom.

In line with reinforcing an inclusive, diverse, and equal learning environment where children feel culturally supported and identified, we explore the topic of Shabbat (Sabbath). In most cases, my students choose to describe the weekly *Kabbalat Shabbat* (the ceremony or prayers welcoming the Jewish Sabbath) held on Fridays as the highlight of the school week. Typically, they describe a ceremony initiated by a young girl, designated as the *Ema shel Shabbat* (Sabbath mother), blessing two white candles and inviting Shabbat into the classroom. This is followed by a young boy, designated as the *Abba shel Shabbat* (Sabbath father), blessing the wine and challah (traditional Shabbat braided bread). Shabbat songs may be interspersed among these blessings.

In order to sensitize them to the above scenario and educate for gender awareness, my students are led through a process analyzing this ceremony. Encouraging them to dissect the accepted teaching approach and question the conventional Kabbalat Shabbat tends to create a disparity for my students. Addressing this dissonance, we try out an alternative ceremony that strives to reinforce the EC classroom as community. Here, the children sit around a Shabbat table and together, as one, led by their teacher, bless the candles, wine, and challah. They all share in drinking the wine from prepared little glasses and eat a bit of challah. Together they sing Shabbat songs and engage in communal dancing.

An additional unconventional ceremony that we initiate supports the weekly Shabbat ceremony being led by one child, either a boy or a girl. This child leads the class in all the *brachot* (blessings) without any gender differentiation. This ceremony aims to communicate gender equality and inclusiveness in the classroom community.

Along the same lines, we share interviews with the ECJE educator mentoring the practicum. Hearing the voices and stories of the mentoring teacher supports my students uncovering the conscious and unconscious penetration of personal values communicated by the culture and climate of the learning environment. It encourages them to seek out different educational approaches and grow a personal education credo generating personal harmony.

Haggith: In a secular ECE framework, the practice of designating a Shabbat father and a Shabbat mother is commonplace, and I confront my students to think about this as well. We try to challenge daily practices of gender inequality that are so common and, therefore, so obvious. My students bring from their practicum anecdotes that have identifiers regarding inequalities. We try to analyze the deep meaning of daily practices such as the use of colors (blue and pink); the space boys occupy versus the space girls occupy; general masculine language; teachers' different expectations of girls and boys; and children's literature, games, and play in class and at home. For example, in many classes, secular as well as religious, the music teacher often invites the girls to participate in dancing and then the boys. Or at the end of circle time, the teacher dismisses the girls separately from the boys. Their perceived intention is to avoid having all the children get up from their chairs at once and get crowded at the door. However, we analyze the hidden message being transferred through this practice conveying the importance of the gender divide and how natural and central it is. By contrast, we suggest other ways to deal with the need of dividing into groups. We connect small, gendered practices with theories and research, linking and integrating their observations and practices in other classes.

Expanding Horizons, Gaining New Knowledge

Haggith: In the course of the year, we explore in depth sociological divides and their manifestations in the ECE context. I start with gender inequalities in ECE, as it is the easiest for my students, who are predominantly women, to connect with. We discuss the students' experiences as girls—what messages they got at home, in school, and from their peers. We also study feminist theory and history, realizing that characteristically none of the students studied it during their high-school years. In fact, typically, their high-school history curriculum excluded the struggle of women for the right to vote, the right for education, and for entrance into the world of work. I give them tasks to observe elements of gender bias in their EC classes, such as the ratio of books in the library with male protagonists versus female protagonists. They bring to class many examples, including cloth colors, bags, games, books, and prevailing teachers' attitudes toward boys and girls. I also ask them to create activities in their practicum that promote gender equality. Later I bring up the Ashkenazi/Mizrachi divide of Israeli society and then the Jewish/Arab divide. Moreover, since my students' major is EC special education, the issue of whether or not to differentiate between children with disabilities and those without is constantly raised, with emphasis on disability studies' perspectives.

All of these themes touch the students deeply. We discuss them from a personal perspective and a social/political perspective. We realize that the personal is political in all aspects. Social inequality in our society has common characteristics: the oppression and marginalization of minority groups has aspects in common as well as differences. Contemplating these issues and looking at their manifestations in classes of young children connect with the idealism of the Jewish values that we discuss.

Sharon: Understanding the rationale behind the practice my students witness in the ECE field is an important part of my teaching approach. However, I have come to understand that for many of my students, the learning occurring within my classroom serves as their initial exposure to an educational perspective acknowledging the need to cultivate cultural sensitivity and gender awareness in contemporary Israeli Jewish Orthodox society. Moreover, it allows the preservice teacher to explore their personal attitudes, understandings, and knowledge that they bring to teaching and learning. Ultimately, my course creates a learning environment that seeks to support the growth of self-awareness, endorsing honest analyses of the personal bias preservice educators bring into the teaching and learning environment. It exposes the Jewish educator to divergent Jewish lifestyles led by their colleagues or young students, encouraging one to view the world through a lens of diversity and divergence, at the same time as advocating for the creation of a learning environment in which both young Jewish girls and young Jewish boys are given equal opportunities to express their developing Jewish identity.

Identities and Power Relationships

Haggith: Feminist theories can be perceived as a tool to examine practices in EC. We discuss the meaning of each theory in ECE frameworks and how the theory helps us to promote equality. We observe through the lens of liberal feminism how boys and girls are represented in books, on wall decorations, and in holiday stories. We inquire through social feminism how the professional world of careers is presented to young children through their parents' jobs, housework division, and work aspirations. We examine through radical feminism the hidden messages girls and boys receive and absorb about their bodies, clothing, and sexuality.

The students talk about the power relationships in the classroom, between college professors, teachers, and students; between the ECE teacher and the children; and between mainstream hegemonic knowledge and the knowledge of marginalized groups. They realize that it is not enough just to acknowledge diversity—that we have to identify power relationships and try to change them, at least in the ECE classroom. For example, many of my female students have been given customarily masculine names (e.g., Yuval, Sharon) that are very popular now, but boys never receive girls' names. It is the gender that is less powerful that strives to get the power of the more dominant and not vice versa.

Sharon: Sharing the story of one's name serves to introduce the self, while at the same time revealing the culture and folklore of one's family. Being attentive to the story behind how a person was given their name can reveal family history, together with the larger social context of the times within which their parents and grandparents lived. Hence, I choose to begin the teaching year with an introductory exercise grounded in names.

Echoing verse 25:25 in the first Book of Samuel, "*Kishmo ken hu*" (Like his name, so is he), discussing a person's name can facilitate a means to illustrate their character, individuality, and personal disposition. Most of my students are young, married, religiously observant women who tend to introduce themselves with a story about their first names or their maiden names. Although, upon marrying, they customarily take their husbands' family name, they generally choose to present themselves through their birth family, sharing the story around their parents' choice of a name and the evolution of their birth family name. At times their story begins with the words, "My parents recalled to me that they thought about a name for their unborn baby: if a boy, the name would be … However if a girl, the name would be … So I am a girl, and my name is …" This innocent admission creates a space for an initial discussion on gender roles and the influence the family environment and community to which they belong has upon the evolving gender identity and social roles of the young Jewish child.

The discussion progresses into an exploration of personal identity and social identity and of personal identity and professional identity and leads to probing whether personal identity and professional identity meet in the ECJE environment. We investigate how they influence one another. Do they mesh? Is the student aware of this meeting of the roles these types of identities play or are they one and the same? Is the professional educator's teaching approach an expression of personal identity and family values? Or is there awareness of the needs of the population they educate? In line with this, we search for identifying factors of the student population in the learning environment. Do the various learning centers reflect and, thus, validate the child's home environment or are they an expression of the EC educator's personal values and lifestyle?

For instance, we examine the sociodramatic play centers in the classroom, considering the integration of gender-specific toys or gender stereotypes communicated in the physical learning environment. We contemplate the implicit gendered message in the conventional male-oriented *Merkaz Rofeh* (doctor's playing area). Aware that all young children enjoy playing doctor, we enrich the center with multiple medical props and rename it "The Clinic" or "The Hospital." So, too, at times we relocate the block corner, placing it next to the *Merkaz Habayit* (housekeeping playing area). This physical change in the learning environment encourages children to transfer materials from the housekeeping play area to the block corner, seamlessly supporting and enriching their play. Furthermore, it encourages both boys and girls to interact, share, and create together in traditionally gendered areas of the classroom. Consequently, we actively support gender equality in the classroom's sociodramatic play area.

Gradually our students relate these explorations and discoveries to their personal experiences, realizing how identity growth and power relationships touch their own lives. They also gain knowledge of the importance of a pluralistic, gender-aware ECE environment in the identity development of the Jewish child.

Egalitarian Education versus Inequality in Education

Haggith: I start the year with the "Chocolate Game," which simulates inequality. Each player begins at a different starting point assigned to her arbitrarily on a sequenced numbered line. They roll the dice in turns in order to reach the chocolate bar at the end of the line. Thus, the ones that started at a closer number to the chocolate would win the chocolate while the others would have a lesser chance of doing so. We compare the unequal starting points of the players in the game to the unequal starting points of children in the educational system. We list the different groups that have disadvantages upon entering the system: poor children, Arab kids, girls, children of Mizrachi or Ethiopian descent, refugees and children of migrant workers, and children with disabilities. We discuss the various ways in which the educational system shortchanges these children (Svirsky 1990) and make a list of mechanisms that create inequalities, such as curriculum, grades, cultural background, unequal budgets, prejudice and stereotypes, racism, sexism, ableism, and ethnicities (Svirsky and Dagan-Buzaglo 2009).

The next step is to rebuild the "tracking" model developed by Cohen (1994, 1998) in the following way. Each group gets a big piece of paper, and they reinvent the model based on their experiences in the school system. They have to describe in a table the track of a girl called "Successa" and a boy called "Faily" as to what happens to each of them during different stages of schooling from EC until university and working life. Later on, we dive into each sociological divide for analysis. We discuss where an intervention could still be effective and when it might be too late. The Chocolate Game later on serves as a metaphor for tracking children in education (Gamoran 2011). In this way, from the beginning of my course, I start sensitizing my students to issues of social justice in education.

Sharon: As much as sharing stories and family customs is a means of encouraging my students to feel and cognize the value of diversity, it is also a tool to encourage equality in the classroom. For instance, throughout my course I alert my students to issues of social justice in education. I strive to make them aware of inequalities concealed in the curriculum. Specifically, we explore the customary teaching of a Jewish holiday or festival based on a dominant story. We examine if this practice of communicating the importance of the story simultaneously diminishes the story, heritage, customs, and knowledge of the marginalized populations of the ECJE classroom and, alternatively, what can be done so that it creates an inclusive, equal educational environment promoting the sharing and celebrating of all Jewish ethnic backgrounds.

As an illustration of this praxis, during the days preceding the Passover holiday celebration, we consider and deliberate the Passover Seder (ritual dinner) celebrated in the EC classroom. As a matter of course, the young children are exposed to the Ashkenazi Passover customs. We focus our deliberations on the Seder plate and the distinctive symbolic foods it includes. For instance, the charoset (a Passover food symbolizing the mortar enslaved Jewish people used) the children make and taste in their classroom will generally be a sweet paste made from apples and wine or grape juice. However, Mizrachi charoset is a paste made of raisins, figs, and dates. Greek and Turkish Jews use apples, dates, chopped almonds, and wine, while Italian Jews add chestnuts to their charoset. We examine and explore the idea of introducing to their classroom a charoset-making day, during which the children make and taste the various types of charoset. Similarly, we share different tunes and renditions of traditional Passover Seder-night songs and prayers.

Encouraging my students to represent the ethnic family cultures found in their classroom and to place Ashkenazi, Mizrahi, and Ethiopian traditional foods and rituals side by side during their classroom celebration, I hope to transfer to my students the significance of helping children, boys and girls alike, who celebrate in a variety of ways to be felt, seen, and represented in their classroom. Accordingly, seeking to draw attention to the women of the Exodus story in general, and to the important role played by Miriam in particular, I introduce my students to the innovative custom of Miriam's Cup (Cohen n.d.). This novel practice of placing a cup of water next to the traditional Cup of Elijah serves as a symbol of Miriam's well, whose waters are reputed to have been healing and sustaining. We discover a vehicle for representing both men and women as Jewish leaders and ensuring a means for gender equality at the Passover Seder. In this way, their Seder table becomes an inclusive celebration of the child, their family, and their ethnic culture, instead of a festivity grounded in Ashkenazi religious ritual or teacher-led traditions.

Indeed, we experience equality in education when we value one another's stories enough to integrate personal, multifaceted stories into the learning environment. When we ensure that each and every young Jewish child finds ethnic cultural aspects of their Jewish home expressed in their ECJE learning environment, we give an equal space in the curriculum to each and every child.

Conclusion

In conclusion, although the contexts of our professional environments differ from each other, we acknowledge commonalities in our feminist Jewish work. We relate to Judaism from a unique perspective in relation to ways of educating toward gender awareness and culturally sensitive teaching in ECJE in Israel.

While it is true that we use different methods and techniques, we both bewilder and surprise our students with our approach to education. We do not meet their initial expectations of getting a practical guide of dos and don'ts in working with young children. Rather, we stretch our students' human capacity to their limits. Our work is grounded in and guided by provoking in-depth critical thinking regarding gender, equality, and diversity in common practices and aspects of their personal and professional lives.

We emphasize the connection of personal experiences, themes, premises, goals, and professional practices with wider social knowledge and multiculturalism. Moreover, we integrate Jewish values that support humanism and pluralism in the teaching and learning experience. Even though we contend with initial resistance from our students, this evolves into a broadening of horizons and an eye-opener for critical feminist thinking influencing their professional identity as ECJE educators.

Takacs (2003) puts forward the idea that rather than tolerating difference, when we move to respect difference, difference helps us understand our own worldview, and the world itself, better. He questions, "How does who you are shape what you know about the world?" (27). Reaffirming Takacs's idea, we have shared examples from the processes we espouse in order to move our students to be gender aware, to respect difference, to value diversity, and to embrace the rich, colorful culture contained in multidimensional ethnic conventional Israeli society.

References

Achituv, S. 2019. "'It Bothers Me, but I Will Not Bring It into the Kindergarten': Gender Perception Conflicts of Religious Kindergarten Teachers as Reflected in Their Work." *Religious Education* 114 (4): 1–13. https://doi.org/10.1080/00344087.2019.1600108.

Adams, T., S. Holman-Jones, and C. Ellis. 2015. *Autoethnography: Understanding Qualitative Research*. New York: Oxford University Press.

Beauvoir, S. de. 2010. *The Second Sex*. New York: Random House.

Cohen, N. 1994. "Bagrut Project—Bet Dagan, Practical Model for Reducing School's Dropping Out and Increasing High School Diploma Graduates." [In Hebrew.] *Nituk le Shiluv* 6:49–66.

Cohen, N. 1998. *Study Project Method: Accelerating Gaps' Decreasing*. [In Hebrew.] Ministry of Education. Accessed November 24, 2021.https://kotar-cet-ac-il.rproxy.tau.ac.il/KotarApp/Viewer.aspx?nBookID=104439749#6.6399.6.default.

Cohen, T. n.d. "Miriam's Cup." My Jewish Learning. Accessed January 2, 2021. https://www.myjewishlearning.com/article/miriams-cup.

Creswell, J. W. 2013. *Qualitative Inquiry and Research Design: Choosing among the Five Approaches*, 3rd ed. Thousand Oaks, CA: Sage.

Derman-Sparks, L., and J. O. Edwards. 2010. *Anti-bias Education for Young Children and Ourselves*, vol. 254. Washington, DC: National Association for the Education of Young Children.

Derman-Sparks, L., and J. O. Edwards. 2019. "Understanding Anti-bias Education." *Young Children* 74 (5): 6–13.

Freeman, R., and T. J. Swim. 2009. "Intellectual Integrity: Examining Common Rituals in Early Childhood Curriculum." *Contemporary Issues in Early Childhood* 10 (4): 366–77.

Freire, P. 1970. *Pedagogy of the Oppressed*. New York: Continuum.

Gamoran, A. 2011. "Tracking and Inequality: New Directions for Research and Practice." In *The Routledge International Handbook of the Sociology of Education*, edited by M. W. Apple, S. J. Ball, and L. A. Gandin, 213–27. Oxfordshire, UK: Routledge.

Gay, G. 2015. "The What, Why, and How of Culturally Responsive Teaching: International Mandates, Challenges, and Opportunities." *Multicultural Education Review* 7 (3): 123–39.

Gay, G. 2018. *Culturally Responsive Teaching: Theory, Research, and Practice*. New York: Teachers College Press.

Gor Ziv, H. 2013. *Critical Feminist Pedagogy and Education for Culture of Peace*. [In Hebrew.] Tel Aviv: Mofet.

Gor Ziv, H. 2015. "Feminist Pedagogy in Early Childhood Teachers' Education." *Journal of Education and Training Studies* 3 (6): 197–211.

Gor Ziv, H. 2016. "Teaching Jewish Holidays in Early Childhood Education in Israel: Critical Feminist Pedagogy Perspective." *Taboo: The Journal of Culture and Education* 15 (1): 11.

Gore, J. 1993. *The Struggle for Pedagogies: Critical and Feminist Discourses as Regimes of Truth*. Oxfordshire, UK: Routledge.

Howell, J., and K. Reinhard. 2015. *Rituals and Traditions: Fostering a Sense of Community in Preschool*. Washington, DC: National Association for the Education of Young Children.

Lawrence-Lightfoot, S., and J. H. Davis. 1997. *The Art and Science of Portraiture*. San Francisco: Jossey-Bass.

Maloney, C. 2000. "The Role of Ritual in Preschool Settings." *Early Childhood Education Journal* 27 (3): 143–50.

Middleton, S. 1993. *Educating Feminists: Life Histories and Pedagogy*. New York: Teachers College Press.

Minnich, E. K. 2010. *Transforming Knowledge*, 2nd ed. Philadelphia, PA: Temple University Press.

NAEYC. 2020. Developmentally Appropriate Practice (DAP) Position Statement. April 2020. https://www.naeyc.org/resources/position-statements/dap/contents.

Piaget, J. 1936. *Origins of Intelligence in the Child*. London: Routledge & Kegan Paul.

Ramsey, P. G. 2015. *Teaching and Learning in a Diverse World: Multicultural Education for Young Children*, 4th ed. New York: Teachers College Press.

Shore, I. 1992. *Empowering Education, Critical Teaching for Social Change*. New York: Routledge.

Svirsky. S. 1990. *Education in Israel: The Region of Separate Tracks*. [In Hebrew.] Tel Aviv: Brerot.

Svirsky, S., and N. Dagan-Buzaglo. 2009. "Separation, Inequality and Faltering Leadership." Adva Center, December 15, 2009. https://adva.org/en/post-slug-1567/.

Takacs, D. 2003. "How Does Your Positionality Bias Your Epistemology?" *Thought and Action* 27. https://repository.uchastings.edu/faculty_scholarship/1264.

Wenger, E. 1998. "Communities of Practice: Learning as a Social System." *Systems Thinker* 9 (5): 2–3.

Wenger-Trayner, E., and B. Wenger-Trayner. 2020. *Learning to Make a Difference: Value Creation in Social Learning Spaces*. Cambridge: Cambridge University Press.

Zalmanson-Levy. G. 2019. "Consciousness Changing: Critical Feminist Pedagogy." In *Brilliance from Tears: Mizrahi Identifications in Educational and Cultural Contexts*, edited by N. Avisar and M. Haskin, 149–77. [In Hebrew.] Tel Aviv: Reseling.

6

Constructivism in Early Childhood Jewish Education

Meir Muller, Sigal Achituv, and Chaya Gorsetman

Rabbi Lord Jonathan Sacks, former chief rabbi of the Hebrew Congregations of the English Commonwealth, in his commentary on the Passover Haggadah (Passover text read at Passover dinner), writes: "Education means teaching a child to be curious, to wonder, to reflect, to enquire. The child who asks becomes a partner in the learning process, an active recipient. To ask is to grow" (2004, 106). Many educators in early childhood Jewish education (ECJE) would agree with this definition of education. However, the specific method that teachers can use to facilitate a child in becoming "a partner in the learning process" has long been a source of debate in both general and religious education.

This chapter proposes constructivism as a framework in both theory and application for the religious education of young children. It begins with an explanation of the theoretical underpinnings of constructivism and its pedagogical adaptation. To help situate the reader in the past decade of scholarship, a brief review of literature is then offered discussing the intersection of constructivism with religious education. This is followed by an application of constructivism to early childhood (EC) Jewish classrooms through classroom vignettes. Finally, the chapter concludes with the drawing together of theory and application in a section discussing some of the bridges and barriers of applying constructivism to religious education and specifically to ECJE.

Constructivist Theory

Constructivism concerns a specific way of understanding knowledge and a particular way of acquiring knowledge. The constructivist view comes in many variants but can be broadly represented through cognitive constructivism as developed by Piaget (1952, 1965, 1969, 1977) and social cultural constructivism as derived by Vygotsky (1978). The two theories diverge on whether the construction of knowledge is primarily internal to the individual's thought process (Piaget) or primarily constructed through a social and collaborative process within a community of learners (Vygotsky). However, at the core of both are two main foundational beliefs:

1. Knowledge is not passively received but actively constructed by the learner.
2. Knowledge is not a copy of reality but an understanding that remains true in the face of an individual's current experiences.

In other words, both constructivist models posit that knowledge is understood differently by every learner and that there is no ultimate truth that all learners will reach (Gross and Gross 2016; Krahenbuhl 2016; Muller, Buchheister, and Boutte 2017; Van Bergen and Parsell 2019). According to von Glasersfeld, a student of Piaget and founder of radical constructivism, "Knowledge is the result of an individual subject's constructive activity, not a commodity that somehow resides outside the knower" (1990, 37). Later in this chapter we will see the difficulty these ideas might present in religious education.

To further understand constructivist theory according to the Piagetian model and compatible with Vygotskian teachings it is noteworthy to understand where they diverge from two historical theories of epistemology—empiricism and rationalism. This divergence helps frame an understanding of the relationship between sensory information as championed by empiricists and reason focused on by rationalists (Kamii 2000).

Empiricists such as Locke ([1690] 1947) stress that an individual is born as a blank slate. He theorized that knowledge is located outside of the individual and is internalized through the senses. Constructivists can agree that young children experience the world through their senses and these experiences form mental structures. However, the idea that knowledge is completely external to the mind is incongruent with the tenets of constructivism (Piaget 1970).

Constructivists also found problems in the theory of rationalists such as Kant and Spinoza. Rationalists posit that children are born with innate reasoning abilities that are the foundations of all knowledge. The rationalist perspective is that the senses cannot be trusted and that reason must be used in explaining the formation of ideas (Eswine 2018). Constructivists' ideas are closer to those of rationalists than to those of empiricists. However, constructivism places more value than rationalists do on the learner's interactions with the physical world, the building of knowledge through these interactions, and the schema that is created in the learner's mind.

Types of knowledge

The authors of this chapter fully recognize that there are noted shortcomings in Piaget's work. For example, scholars point out the lack of diversity among the children he studied, that stage theory fails to capture the complexities of intraindividual and interindividual development, and an overemphasis on developmental norms applied cross-culturally (Lourenco and Machado 1996; O'Loughlin 1992). Yet, Piaget's contributions changed the field of early childhood education (ECE), and some have stood the test of time. One in particular is his ability to respect both empiricists and rationalists in explaining that sensory information and reason can be clarified through an understanding of three basic types of knowledge: physical knowledge, social knowledge, and logico-mathematical knowledge.

Physical Knowledge

Physical knowledge is gained when children use one of their five senses in interacting with an object. Examples of physical knowledge are the child feeling the lightness or roughness of an object, the sweet or bitter taste of a food, or the wetness of water. The child experiencing that a ball will bounce but a brick will not is an example of physical knowledge. Kamii (2015) explains that the ultimate source of physical knowledge is in the object.

Social Knowledge

Social knowledge is constructed through exchanges of oral or written information between people. The names of objects (e.g., a chair is called a "chair"), language in general, and the ways we should act in particular situations (e.g., in the United States, birthday candles are blown out and a wish is made) are all examples of social knowledge. Unfortunately, in some educational settings, social knowledge can take the form of children memorizing information that they do not fully understand. An example of this is the way in which many children prior to third grade learn to perform mathematical equations by memorizing the steps of an algorithm without understanding the logic behind this procedure (e.g., the rules of "carrying" and "borrowing") (Muller 2013; Muller, Gorsetman, and Alexander 2018).

Logico-mathematical Knowledge

Logico-mathematical knowledge is often thought of as higher-order thinking skills. As described, the source of physical knowledge is primarily in objects and the source of social knowledge is primarily in other people; logico-mathematical knowledge is internal to the child's thinking. Imagine a child presented with a green ball and a pink ball and asked if they are different. Many people might think that the difference between the balls is knowable through observation (physical knowledge), but this is not true. The color of each ball is knowable through observation (physical knowledge), but the difference between them is not knowable with one's eyes. The difference exists neither in the green ball nor in the pink ball or anywhere in the observable world. The difference exists due to the child's intellectual reasoning in comparing the two balls (the child has knowledge of "ball," of "green," and of "pink"). Using this understanding, the child can now deduce the difference between the balls (Muller, Gorsetman, and Alexander 2018).

Based upon these three types of knowledge, it is evident that children are active learners who reorganize their mental structures and understandings based on experience. Recognizing that children are active meaning-makers and that they learn through these three primary methods allows teachers to create classrooms based on this theory. The pedagogy of constructivism moves the classroom paradigm of memorizing information delivered by a teacher to one of knowledge that is constructed by students.

Constructivist Pedagogy

Using this theoretical understanding, constructivist pedagogy capitalizes on opportunities for children to construct their own understandings using the three types of knowledge. Krahenbuhl writes that this is indeed occurring in schools: "Constructivism is the dominant pedagogical theory in contemporary educational circles … such policies promote constructivist pedagogical practice such that evaluators must explicitly witness the students physically engaged in doing something and not receiving information" (2016, 98–9). In other words, children are expected to be using physical knowledge (which can be done through active learning, often termed "discovery," "inquiry," and/or "collaboration"), with a decrease in memorizing social knowledge through frontal teaching, to facilitate higher-order thinking skills in forming ideas.

Equally important is that in classrooms teachers understand that "knowledge is a human construct" (McPhail 2016, 298). While according to radical constructivists there is no absolute truth, most constructivist educators believe that when we construct knowledge, we are advancing our understandings of an external truth. Therefore, most constructivist pedagogy agrees with the religious education belief that there is an external reality that people continuously strive to understand (Pradhan 2016).

Baviskar, Hartle, and Whitney (2009) provide four critical elements in constructivist learning. First, the learner's previous knowledge should be the basis for new learning. Second, new knowledge is presented in a manner that causes students to reorganize their current thinking. Third, opportunities are made available to apply new knowledge with peer or teacher feedback (to ensure that the knowledge is not simply memorized or rejected). Finally, time to reflect on new understandings is provided. Fosnot summed up constructivism as an "approach to teaching that gives learners the opportunity for concrete, contextually meaningful experiences through which they can search for patterns; raise questions; and model, interpret, and defend their strategies and ideas" (2005, ix). Hence, the goal of constructivist learning is to interact with materials, ideas, and people that challenge existing understandings to construct new insights that are gained not through memorization but by using higher-order thinking skills in making logical connections and deductions.

Religious Education and Constructivist Theory

Religious education can be seen as being at odds with constructivist theory and pedagogy (Demirel Ucan and Wright 2019; Liagkis 2015; Muller 2010). Sigal Achituv (2013) describes the role of religious education as transferring bodies of knowledge that are accepted as religious truth to students, whereas constructivism does not accept an ultimate truth or the ability to pass a replica of knowledge from the mind of the teacher to the student. She writes that *gananot* (teachers in Israeli preschools for children aged three to six) are constantly torn between implementing the traditional approach and the constructivist approach (256):

> According to the "traditional approach" (Dewey 1938) the role of school is to transfer to the student the bodies of knowledge that were created in the past. The student is considered passive and his aim is to absorb a copy of the knowledge existing within the teacher or within the written subject matter. The source of the knowledge conveyed by the teacher to the student is the tradition, and the teacher is considered a source of authority for its transmission. The progressive approach, or as it was later called—the constructivist approach—recognizes the central role of the student himself in organizing the subjects to be learned and in constructing them. In this approach, the child himself chooses, arranges and interprets the knowledge perceived from interactions with his surroundings.

As mentioned earlier, this idea is further illuminated by von Glasersfeld (1995), who uses the term "radical" for constructivism, as he believes that the function of cognition serves to organize a person's experiences of the world but that it cannot discover any ultimate truth. In other words, there is a strong undercurrent in constructivism that goes against the idea that there are principles, texts, or dogmas that should be believed as inarguable truth.

Literature Review of Religious Education and Constructivist Pedagogy

In the late 1990s and early 2000s, articles discussing faith-based schools and constructivism often described religious education as embracing a teacher-centered, didactic approach over a child-centered, constructivist pedagogy (Berliner 1997; Lederhouse 1998; Knowlton 2002; Knowlton and Shaffer 2004). Few articles discussed constructivism directly with regard to religious education, which remains an under-researched topic with only a dozen articles published in the past decade or so. These recent articles do address a range of views, though.

First is a trend in accepting that constructivist education can lead to children creating personal engagements with religious topics and increasing their understandings of religious goals (Court 2013; Deulen 2013; O'Grady 2018). This includes instances where constructivism is accepted but narrowed in scope. For instance, Kaymakcan (2007, 203) suggests that "constructivist learning theory be used in the teaching of living dimension of religion (experience and practice by individual and society) rather than the doctrinal dimension in religious education" (2007, 203).

By contrast, there are also articles warning that constructivism can be vague, causing confusion in religious education (Liagkis 2015). Other research goes so far as to say that constructivism is used to hide the true intent of the aims of religious teaching.

> A controversial issue such as the theory of evolution has been situated in the context of constructivism that allows other perspectives to be presented under the guise of providing equal time and space to alternative perspectives on aspects of

science and religion such as theory of evolution. I believe that some participants are willing to use constructivism as a tool to disguise attempts to teach creationism and/or intelligent design in science courses. (Taşkın 2014, 870)

This debate and the fact that these articles represent religious education in at least six different countries demonstrate that constructivism and religious education are of interest and importance to educators.

In the field of ECJE, most of the work on applying constructivist education to the classroom has been published by the editors of this book and the authors of this chapter (Achituv 2002, 2013; Muller 2010, 2013; Muller, Gorsetman, and Alexander 2018). Achituv has researched how educators use a constructivist approach when teaching difficult biblical stories (see Chapter 7 of this book for her most recent treatment of this topic). Muller has looked at how children use Piaget's three types of knowledge in understanding the holiday of Passover. And Muller, Gorsetman, and Alexander have researched the challenges teachers in a Jewish EC center faced in implementing constructivist pedagogy.

In Jewish education outside of the EC years, Hassenfeld (2018) reports how two Orthodox Talmud (the body of Jewish civil and ceremonial law and legend) teachers respond to constructivist pedagogy and the underlying factors in accepting or rejecting the model. Researchers such as Katzin (2015) provide data from a longitudinal study on new teachers and the methods they use to teach Jewish subjects. While there are other articles looking at the emphasis of asking questions in Jewish education (Sigel, Kress, and Elias 2007) and struggling with texts, those reported here are the only ones found that include direct connections to constructivist pedagogy.

Constructivism in Early Childhood Jewish Classrooms

This section explores constructivist pedagogy through observations of young children's experiences in the classroom, in particular their reactions to Jewish holidays. Chaya Gorsetman uses here the following three anecdotes to shine light on how children can misinterpret stories delivered through teacher-centered direct instruction. They support the constructivist approach of not using stories (social knowledge) as the sole method of instruction but implementing them together with hands-on experiences (physical knowledge) to lead to higher-order thinking skills.

Story One: After hearing the story of *Purim* [a Jewish holiday recorded in the book of Esther], a four-year-old girl suddenly refused to go home with her non-Jewish babysitter who had cared for her since she was an infant. When her parents finally arrived at school to pick her up and asked why she wouldn't go home, she said, "*Haman* [the Purim story's villain who plotted to destroy the Jewish people] wasn't Jewish, and he didn't want the Jewish people to celebrate Jewish holidays. I don't want to go with her because she is not Jewish and will not let me be Jewish. I don't like people who are not Jewish!"

Story Two: Before Passover, a mother of a five-year-old boy enrolled in a day school lamented that her son no longer wanted to be Jewish. With great certitude, the child said to his mother, "All they ever want to do is kill the Jews!" When asked what he meant, he said, "On Hanukkah they wanted to kill us! On Purim they wanted to kill us and now on Passover they want to kill us again! That's why I don't want to be Jewish!"

Story Three: A four-year-old child overheard her father and grandfather talking about the Garden of Eden. She said that she learned about that in her preschool. Her father asked, "What did you learn about the Garden of Eden?" The child responded that she learned that there was an apple in the garden. Her father asked, "What else did you learn?" The child said, "The teacher just kept talking, blah blah blah."

Each of these cases occurred as a result of children being "taught" religious content or stories through direct instruction without being provided time to wonder, question, or reflect on the information; the results were not positive. These three anecdotes illustrate how young children are sometimes confused or even frightened or simply tune out when told stories as historical incidents. Furthermore, events that occurred years, even centuries, ago might be confused as being events that are occurring now.

Additionally, young children are egocentric and literal, and they connect to what they hear in a deeply personal and intense way. For example, Gorsetman reports how one young girl, after hearing about the days of the Messiah and how the Messiah will awaken the dead, suddenly was unable to sleep. It seems that she was terrified that the stuffed alligator on her dresser would come to life while she was sleeping and eat her up during the night.

These characteristics of young children (namely, an embryonic sense of time compounded by developmentally egocentric and literal stages) require they be provided with age-appropriate experiences. Since young children are attentive to the here and now, once they are engaged and interested in what is going on around them in a classroom (or at home or elsewhere), they can learn in a deep and intense manner. Applying the principles of constructivist theory to the learning environment can not only enable children to gain the meta messages of these biblical and holiday stories but also help connect them to their own lives.

Gorsetman, to illustrate the importance of this concept, also uses the example here of a teacher who, as a prelude to teaching the holiday of Hanukkah, asked her students what they already knew about the holiday. The children responded enthusiastically about lighting candles, the colors of the candles, dreidels (spinning top-like toys), presents, eating latkes (potato pancakes), and other aspects of holiday experiences. The teacher then asked what the class wanted to learn about Hanukkah. Interestingly, the class continued with the tangible and experiential quests for knowledge, such as different ways to light the *hanukkiah* (ritual candelabrum for Hanukkah), the difference between lighting on the first day and each day thereafter, how to make a dreidel, how to make it spin better, and how to fry traditional holiday foods. Surprisingly, at least to the teacher, not one of her twenty-two children mentioned wanting to hear the story of Hanukkah.

Stories, like other pieces of social knowledge (information gained by children through someone else), are important tools in teaching young children. Constructivist teachers use stories to facilitate children in making connections between texts (one story to another), text to self (personal connections), and text to world (helping to make sense of how the world works). This holds true for stories of historical events (e.g., biblical accounts, holidays, etc.) where the story is told to both share information and provide opportunities for students to ask probing questions and reflect. When storytelling, teachers can enhance this learning experience by asking probing open-ended questions such as the following:

1. What questions do you have about the story of the holiday?
2. What else would you like to know?
3. What part of the story interests you?
4. What other questions do you have?
5. If you were telling the next part of the story, what would it say?

In this way, students have the opportunity to construct the knowledge that is being presented to them.

Furthermore, a constructivist approach would recommend that holiday stories be accompanied with opportunities for children to learn through customs and rituals that they could experience. These would include foods they could eat, objects they could explore, and songs they could sing. For instance, young children would benefit from the concrete experiential activities of baking and cooking, to smell the aroma of the holiday; exploring authentic artifacts, to inspire wondering about the "what ifs" of the holiday; and singing songs, to gain a connection with generations past and those today singing similar holiday songs.

These recommendations, along with the story of the children expressing how they want to experience Hanukkah, are well aligned with constructivist pedagogy in the ECJE context and the children becoming a partner in their own learning process. When children are given objects to construct physical knowledge and provided social knowledge that they cannot otherwise deduce (the name of the top is a dreidel, the holiday custom is to eat food fried in oil, the story of the holiday, etc.), they will use higher-order thinking skills to raise questions, connect learning with prior ideas, make connections across Jewish experiences, consider various problem-solving strategies, and gain new insights.

Educators and Implementation of Constructivist Pedagogy

Bridges and barriers of using a constructivist pedagogy extend beyond the issue of storytelling. Achituv has observed that in Israeli *ganim* (pre-elementary schools for children aged three to six), successes in constructivist activities in EC classrooms are equated with facilitating conversations about Jewish values and putting these values into practice within the local community. EC teachers' innovations in this area include visiting nursing homes, adopting elderly people who become the *gan*'s (pre-elementary school for children aged three to six) "grandpa" or "grandma," establishing relationships with IDF (Israel Defense Forces) soldiers by sending letters and packages especially around *Yom Ha'atzmaut* (Israel independence day), and implementing joint activities with classes for children with special needs. During periods characterized by security tensions, many ganim create connections with three- to six-year-olds that are in the tension zones through delivery of drawings and encouraging messages.

In the field of constructivist community activities, the ganim that are located in kibbutzim (a type of communal settlement) are particularly noteworthy. One of the main principles of the EC kibbutz educational philosophy is the connection between the EC programs and the community (Haas and Gavish 2008) through hands-on constructivist-type learning experiences. Achituv provides here the example of Rivka, a 62-year-old retired *ganenet* (preschool teacher) who worked in a kibbutz and described the way these unique relationships are expressed:

> What characterizes the gan in the kibbutz is the very strong community. The gan is an integral part of the kibbutz. The children share the fabric of life in the community (very exciting to see them come to visit the nursing home located in the heart of the kibbutz. My mother is there now, and often when I was with her, the preschoolers came to visit, and her two great-grandchildren happily came to her room). Before *Rosh Hashanah* [Jewish New Year], they come to see how Assaf is practicing in the *shul* [synagogue] on the *shofar* [a ram's horn blown on the Jewish New Year], and the *gabai* [prayer service proctor] opens the Holy Ark and shows them the white coats of the *Torah* [a holy scroll containing the Five Books of Moses], which are special for the High Holidays. Before *Sukkot* [one of the three biblical holidays celebrated by building huts] the children come to see how Aryel'e the carpenter builds the large *sukkah* [a hut built for usage during the holiday of Sukkot] next to the dining room. On *Simchat Torah* [a holiday celebrating the annual completion of reading the Torah scroll] evening, they come to see how the Torah scroll coats are changed again, to the colorful coats with which they will happily dance; before *Shavuot* [Jewish festival occurring seven weeks after Passover] they come to see how the shul is being decorated with green branches.

In contrast to these positive ways of implementing constructivist pedagogy through community-based projects focused on values, there are challenges in implementing constructivist Jewish activities in EC classrooms. The overarching challenge in facilitating a constructivist classroom reported in previous research (Muller, Gorsetman, and Alexander 2018) is that while teachers are successful in using physical knowledge (objects) and provide opportunities for children to create logico-mathematical knowledge (higher-order thinking), they are not confident that children can construct knowledge without providing an abundance of facts (social knowledge) to the children. The conflict of wanting to tell the children information that they might otherwise deduce on their own is a struggle in both general and religious education. The following are examples of where this might be observed in the classroom.

One area this plays out in is art activities. Some teachers find it difficult to let children use art materials freely (without direction), in particular with regard to Jewish content and holiday curriculum (Achituv 2013). They often provide templates and ready-made educational kits in an attempt to impress the children's parents. For example, one study (Achituv 2013) cites a teacher named Noa who admitted: "I guide them and sometimes cut certain templates such as Jerusalem city buildings or New Year's circles for the apple [one of the Jewish New Year's symbols]." Unfortunately, this pedagogic approach limits the child's personal expression and construction of knowledge.

A second challenge to constructivist pedagogy seen in ECJE programs deals with performances given for family members that are organized for the holidays, especially around Hanukkah. The encounter with the families puts pressure on the teachers to "train" the children in a way that prevents constructivist learning. Achituv (2013) interviewed Israeli teacher Avigail, who described the situation like this: "The closer we get to the performance, the more the rehearsals grow in frequency. I try to start rehearsals a month before. The week before the performance the rehearsals are more often … every two days until the performance arrives." In the same study, another teacher expressed her need to impress the parents by explaining, "You invite parents to the performance. You need the gan to look right. You can't do something that looks like half a job."

Three other challenges deal with subjects that are described in detail in other chapters of this book, so we will address them only briefly here. The first is Jewish ceremonies that take place in schools, such as *Kabbalat Shabbat* (the ceremony or prayers welcoming the Jewish Sabbath), the Passover Seder (ritual dinner) and *Tu Bishvat* (Jewish Arbor Day), which take place in classrooms prior to the actual time celebrated with the family or the community. This causes the school celebration to be somewhat decontextualized in that it is disconnected from a truly authentic experience. Furthermore, the purpose of these celebrations is to convey the ritual practices of the holiday, but it does so without providing time for children to construct meaning (see Chapter 9 of this book for an in-depth discussion of Jewish holidays and ceremonies).

The second challenge deals with children's Jewish literature, which often tends to be didactic in approach and focused on instilling Jewish values and content at the expense of literary quality. Stories that do not engage children in employing higher-order thinking skills are often not remembered or lack high value in constructing knowledge. Fortunately, in the past decade, the Jewish communities in the United States and Israel have seen a number of significant initiatives that have led to high-quality Jewish EC literature becoming available (see Chapter 8 of this book for an in-depth discussion of these literature initiatives).

The third challenge to implementing a constructivist pedagogy for ECJE deals with telling Bible stories to young children. In Chapter 7 of this book, which explores teaching the Bible in ECJE, Achituv discusses the propensity of educators' orientation to instill absolute values while telling Bible stories and avoiding open discussions, along with educators' tendencies to glamorize biblical characters' behavior when dealing with cases of moral conflicts.

Common to all these challenges is the aforementioned focus of teachers on imparting factual knowledge because they do not fully trust that children can construct their own knowledge. Educators seemingly prefer to create learning experiences in the classroom where they have more control over the exposure to predetermined social knowledge in both abstract and concrete areas. Use of art and literature as learning tools, in addition to open discussions around values and morals, are often perceived as challenges for the educator to accomplish curricular goals.

A Possible Way Forward

We have seen in this exploration of constructivism in contemporary ECJE some of its many assets and challenges. We suggest, in conclusion, that religious educators focus on Baviskar, Hartle, and Whitney's (2009) critical elements in constructivist learning:

1. Content is connected to a learner's prior knowledge.
2. New knowledge is presented in a manner that causes a student to reorganize their current thinking.
3. Opportunities are made available to apply the new knowledge with peer or teacher feedback and time to reflect.

We further recommend a step beyond Kaymakcan's (2007) suggestion that constructivist learning be used only in teaching the living dimension of religion rather than the doctrinal dimension. It is our view that religious customs, stories, doctrine, law, philosophy, and ways of being in the world can all be included in a constructivist classroom. Pekarsky (2006) explains that some religious educators challenge the notion that children should be allowed to construct their own knowledge, because this might lead the children to construct ideas outside of Jewish tradition or undercut the idea that Jews should perform the mitzvot (directives found in the written and oral Torah). But he claims the opposite to be true: Using a constructivist pedagogy is more likely to result in children growing up to be adults who have a deep appreciation and engagement with Judaism.

Sacks expands his perception of educating the child as a partner in the learning process by writing that "in Judaism, to be without questions is not a sign of faith, but a lack of depth" (2004, 105). We challenge all educators who teach about religion to trust in the remarkable abilities of young children to construct knowledge that can lead to lifelong religious engagements.

References

Achituv, S. 2002. "Kindergarten Teachers Exposed to a Pedagogy of Listening." MA diss., University of Haifa.
Achituv, S. 2013. "What Did the Teacher Say Today? State Religious Kindergarten Teachers Deal with Complex Torah Stories." *Journal of Jewish Education* 79 (3): 256–96.
Baviskar, S., T. Hartle, and T. Whitney. 2009. "Essential Criteria to Characterize Constructivist Teaching: Derived from a Review of the Literature and Applied to Five

Constructivist-Teaching Method Articles." *International Journal of Science Education* 31 (4): 541–50.

Berliner, D. 1997. "Educational Psychology Meets the Christian Right: Differing Views of Children, Schooling, Teaching, and Learning." *Teachers College Record* 98:381–416.

Court, D. 2013. "Religious Experience as an Aim of Religious Education." *British Journal of Religious Education* 35 (3): 251–63.

Demirel Ucan, A., and A. Wright. 2019. "Improving the Pedagogy of Islamic Religious Education through an Application of Critical Religious Education, Variation Theory and the Learning Study Mode." *British Journal of Religious Education* 41 (2): 202–17. https://doi.org/10.1080/01416200.2018.1484695.

Deulen, A. 2013. "Social Constructivism and Online Learning Environments: Toward a Theological Model for Christian Educators." *Christian Education Journal: Research on Educational Ministry* 10 (1): 90–8. https://doi.org/10.1177/073989131301000107.

Dewey, J. 1938. *Experience and Education*. New York: Collier.

Eswine, S. 2018. "The Exertion of a Choice: An Ecofeminist Vision ~ Aesthetic, Embodied, and Connected Learning." PhD diss., Georgia Southern University.

Fosnot, C. 2005. *Constructivism: Theory, Perspectives and Practice*. New York: Teachers College Press.

Gross, K., and S. Gross. 2016. "Transformation: Constructivism, Design Thinking, and Elementary STEAM." *Art Education* 69 (6): 36–43. https://doi.org/10.1080/00043125.2016.1224869.

Haas, M., and T. Gavish. 2008. *Mother Look, It's Real*. [In Hebrew.] Tel Aviv: Hakibbutz Hameuchad.

Hassenfeld, Z. 2018. "Resources of Jewish Culture: A Case Study of Two Talmud Teachers." *Religions* 9 (22): 221–35.

Kamii, C. 2000. *Young Children Reinvent Arithmetic: Implications of Piaget's Theory*. New York: Teachers College Press.

Kamii, C. 2015. "Selected Standards from the Common Core State Standards for Mathematics, Grades K-3: My Reasons for Not Supporting Them." *Defending the Early Years*.

Katzin, O. 2015. "Teaching Approaches of Beginning Teachers for Jewish Studies in Israeli Mamlachti Schools: A Case Study of a Jewish Education Teachers' Training Program for Outstanding Students." *Journal of Jewish Education* 81 (3): 285–311. https://doi.org/10.1080/15244113.2015.1065633.

Kaymakcan, R. 2007. "Pluralism and Constructivism in Turkish Religious Education: Evaluation of Recent Curriculum of Religious Culture and Ethical Knowledge Lesson." *Educational Science: Theory and Practice* 7 (1): 202–10.

Knowlton, D. 2002. "A Constructivist Pedagogue's Personal Narrative of Integrating Faith with Learning: Epistemological and Pedagogical Challenges." *Journal of Research on Christian Education* 11 (1): 33–57.

Knowlton, D., and S. Shaffer. 2004. "Shifting toward a Constructivist Philosophy for Teaching Biblical Principles in K-12 Christian Schools." *Christian Education Journal* 1 (3): 116–29.

Krahenbuhl, K. 2016. "Student-Centered Education and Constructivism: Challenges, Concerns, and Clarity for Teachers." *Clearing House: A Journal of Educational Strategies, Issues and Ideas* 89 (3): 97–105. https://doi.org/10.1080/00098655.2016.1191311.

Lederhouse, J. N. 1998. "Caught in the Middle: Evangelical Christian Public Elementary Educators." *Anthropology and Education Quarterly* 28 (2): 182–203.

Liagkis, M. 2015. "Religious Education in Greece: A New Curriculum, an Old Issue." *British Journal of Religious Education* 37 (2): 153–69. https://doi.org/10.1080/01416 200.2014.944093.

Locke, J. (1690) 1947. *Essay Concerning Human Understanding*. England: Oxford University Press.

Lourenco, O., and A. Machado. 1996. "In Defense of Piaget's Theory: A Reply to 10 Common Criticisms." *Psychological Review* 103 (1): 143–64.

McPhail, G. 2016. "The Fault Lines of Recontextualisation: The Limits of Constructivism in Education." *British Educational Research Journal* 42 (2): 294–313.

Muller, M. 2010. "Kindergarten Children's Conception of Knowledge in Jewish Education." PhD diss., University of South Carolina.

Muller, M. 2013. "Constructivism and Jewish Early Childhood Education." *Journal of Jewish Education* 79 (3): 315–34.

Muller, M., K. Buchheister, and G. S. Boutte. 2017. "Multiple Perspectives on Cognitive Development: Radical Constructivism, Cognitive Constructivism, Sociocultural Theory, and Critical Theory." *Constructivist* 26 (1): 2–34.

Muller, M., C. Gorsetman, and S. T. Alexander. 2018. "Struggles and Successes in Constructivist Jewish Early Childhood Classrooms." *Journal of Jewish Education* 84 (3): 284–311.

O'Grady, K. 2018. *Religious Education as a Dialogue with Difference: Fostering Democratic Citizenship through the Study of Religions in Schools*. New York: Routledge.

O'Loughlin, M. 1992. "Rethinking Science Education: Beyond Piagetian Constructivism toward a Sociocultural Model of Teaching and Learning." *Journal of Research in Science Teaching* 29 (8): 791–820.

Pekarsky, D. 2006. *Vision at Work: The Theory and Practice of Beit Rabban*. New York: Jewish Theological Seminary of America.

Piaget, J. 1952. *The Origins of Intelligence in the Child*. New York: International University Press.

Piaget, J. 1965. *The Child's Conception of the World*. New Jersey: Littlefield, Adams, and Company.

Piaget, J. 1969. *The Child's Conception of Time*. London: Routledge & Kegan.

Piaget, J. 1970. *Science of Education and the Psychology of the Child*. New York: Viking.

Piaget, J. 1977. *The Development of Thought: Equilibration of Cognitive Structures*. New York: Viking.

Pradhan, N. 2016. "Constructivist Pedagogy: A Need of the Hour." *Scholar* 1 (2): 32–9.

Sacks, J. 2004. *The Chief Rabbi's Haggadah: Hebrew and English Text with New Essays and Commentary*. London: HarperCollins.

Sigel, I. E., J. S. Kress, and M. J. Elias. 2007. "Beyond Questioning: Inquiry Strategies and Cognitive and Affective Elements of Jewish Education." *Journal of Jewish Education* 73 (1): 51–66. https://doi.org/10.1080/15244110601175178.

Taşkın, Ö. 2014. "An Exploratory Examination of Islamic Values in Science Education: Islamization of Science Teaching and Learning Via Constructivism." *Cultural Studies of Science Education* 9 (4): 855–75.

Van Bergen, P., and M. Parsell. 2019. "Comparing Radical, Social and Psychological Constructivism in Australian Higher Education: A Psycho-philosophical Perspective." *Australian Educational Researcher* 46 (41): 41–58. https://doi.org/10.1007/s13 384-018-0285-8.

Von Glasersfeld, E. 1990. "Environment and Communication." In *Transforming Children's Mathematics Education: International Perspective*, edited by L. P. Steffe and T. Wood, 30–8. Hillsdale, NJ: Lawrence Erlbaum.
Von Glasersfeld, E. 1995. *Radical Constructivism: A Way of Knowing and Learning.* London: Falmers.
Vygotsky, L. 1978. *Mind and Society*. Cambridge, MA: Harvard University Press.

Part Three

Core Jewish Subjects through the Three Contemporary Critical Lenses

7

Teaching the Bible in Early Childhood Jewish Education

Sigal Achituv

Teaching Bible stories to young children can be seen as at the crossroads of a number of developmental and theoretical spheres, generating particular dilemmas for the teacher. The telling of these types of stories relates to aspects central to sociological and social realms as an opportunity for a mutual encounter between child and teacher. It also has deep roots in the educational domain as an act of socialization and the inculcation of cultural values. Its religious and Jewish observance aspects provide an occasion to understand the values of faith and tradition. Furthermore, it is imbedded in the field of hermeneutics as the teacher mediates Bible stories for children, especially when the child is hearing them for the first time (Achituv 2012).

In light of all of this, the early childhood education (ECE) teacher, while telling a Bible story, must deal simultaneously with various educational, hermeneutical, religious, and cultural issues (S. Achituv 2013). According to Levisohn (2008), there is limited research concerning teachers' perspectives and dilemmas relating to Bible teaching. This gap is particularly significant when it comes to ECE, and the purpose of this chapter is to help fill it.

In keeping with the focus of this book, this chapter will explore the issue of teaching the Bible in the Israeli early childhood Jewish education (ECJE) system through the contemporary critical pedagogical lenses of constructivism, multiculturalism, and gender. It will begin with a description of different approaches to teaching the Bible, followed by a representative picture of the current state of teaching the Bible in Israeli ECJE frameworks. The next section will explore some of the challenges arising from teaching the Bible, particularly having to do with teachers' ideologies, concentrating on the contemporary lenses of multiculturalism and gender, as well as constructivism. The chapter will include relevant references and examples from recent studies of Bible instructors and students in ECE departments at Israeli education colleges and of Israeli ECJE teachers. It will conclude with a summary highlighting the major conclusions arising from this exploration.

Approaches to Teaching the Bible

A number of different approaches can be distinguished in the practice of teaching the Bible (Adar 1954; Holtz 2003). Shkedi and Nisan (2006) present three main methods: disciplinary, normative-conceptual, and cultural.

1. The disciplinary approach maintains that the Bible is a universal work and should, therefore, be related to as a text open to examination and historical-scientific study, rather than as a source of requisite values for the teacher or students. Thus, studying the Bible according to this method does not involve any moral dilemmas.
2. The normative-conceptual approach views the Bible as a holy text given to the Jewish people. Accordingly, the Bible contains traditional religious values that obligate both teachers and students. These values are considered sacred and, therefore, represent an absolute good and right that is the basis of Jewish moral attitudes. The student is obligated to interpret the content of these values and must refrain from projecting his or her own modern values onto the Bible.
3. The cultural approach views the Bible as a national cultural work that expresses a variety of humanistic and national values. The Bible represents a common Jewish cultural language in which various ethical questions can be addressed. The cultural approach can be divided into three sub-perceptions, which orient the formation of discussions within the Bible studies framework. The first of these views the Bible as a source for bestowing national or moral and social values; the second emphasizes the tension between the Bible's values and those of modernity and liberalism; and the third stresses the personal dimension, which enables a modern person to find in the Bible an echo of his or her own personal feelings and values.

Various challenges faced by ECE teachers stem, in part, from their belief in a particular approach to telling Bible stories. Before considering these challenges in depth, though, it will be helpful to have a brief overview of the general field of teaching the Bible in Israeli ECJE systems.

Teaching the Bible in ECE in Israel

> All curricula composed in Israel, including those in the pre-state period of the Yishuv, and since the establishment of the State 1948, included an initial acquaintance of the pupils in the formal or compulsory education systems with the stories of the Bible starting at a very early age … not just the state-religious education system but also the general state education system placed the study of the Bible at the center of its curriculum. (Ilan 2011)

These words of Moshe Ilan, the former director of the curriculum development department in the Israeli Ministry of Education, indicate the centrality of the Bible in ECE in Israel. According to Ilan, recent years' curricula also have "not renounced the centrality of the Bible as constitutive literature, and not relinquished the *gan* [pre-elementary school for children aged three to six] as a place in which we meet ... the stories of the Bible" (Ilan 2011). Koboby expresses a similar sentiment: "Many of the Bible stories are repeatedly told to the children starting in the gan" (1992: 144). The fact that the pupil encounters the same stories again and again is sufficient "for the influence of the Bible on the child's soul to be significant." Biblical stories, therefore, constitute part of the official curriculum of the gan.

The teaching of the Bible is treated very differently, though, in the two official Jewish educational streams in Israel—state and state-religious. (The third Jewish educational stream in Israel, Haredi—ultra-Orthodox—has its own Bible curriculum and is not dealt with in this chapter.) For example, there is a marked difference in the mission statement that appears at the beginning of the two official curricula.

In the state *ganim* (pre-elementary schools for children aged three to six), the Bible is depicted as the Book of Books, the cultural infrastructure of the Jewish people and its heritage. The text tells the story of the people's evolution and their connection to the Land of Israel. The child's exposure to the story and its content is seen as an essential element in the formulation of one's national-cultural makeup. Here, the gan's main emphasis is on the personal and cultural experience in encountering the Bible story and its heroes (Israel Ministry of Education 2003). This curriculum presents the cultural approach to teaching the Bible.

In the guide for teachers of Israeli state-religious ganim, study of the Torah (the holy scroll containing the Five Books of Moses) is considered a religious obligation and the basis for religious education as a whole. The Torah is the foundation and nucleus of belief and the fulfillment of divine commandments, forming the basis of Jewish culture and life that have developed over the generations. It is depicted as the incumbent source of national values and rights over the Promised Land. It is the core of the ideas, concepts, symbols, and rationale for state-religious education (Israel Ministry of Education 2002). This curriculum presents the normative and the cultural approaches to teaching the Bible.

Thus, Bible stories have a central role in the Israeli state-religious gan (Ben-Or 2005). Some of the teachers tell the stories according to the order of the *parshat hashavuah* (the weekly Torah reading) read in the synagogue but most adopt the "Bible story" approach, which focuses mainly on the stories in the Books of Genesis and Exodus (Israel Ministry of Education 2002, 2013), as well as the stories of the Books of Esther and Ruth.

Although Bible stories are also told in Israeli state ganim, they occupy a less central role. It is common for children aged five to six to hear Bible stories regularly throughout the year. Children aged three and four are most often told stories of creation, the flood, forebears, and Jewish festivals, including stories of the Patriarchs, the story of the Exodus from Egypt (Passover), the giving of the Torah and the Book of Ruth (Shavuot), and the Book of Esther (Purim) (Israel Ministry of Education 1982a,b, 1992). Dori (2019) found that when Bible stories were told by ECE teachers in Israeli state ganim, they were mostly from the Book of Genesis, but a substantial number of teachers in those ganim chose not to tell Bible stories at all. According to Dori, this was a factor both of parent expectations and the teacher's personal willingness to teach content from the Bible.

Accordingly, ECE departments at Israeli education colleges include courses in Bible proficiency, aimed at deepening the knowledge of the Bible of those training for teaching in ganim, as well as providing didactics courses intended to cultivate tools for applied teaching of the Bible in ganim. These tools relate to selecting appropriate Bible stories and to coping with the ancient language of the Bible, emotionally complex stories, and concepts remote from the world of children in ECE (Achituv and Manzura 2016).

Teachers' Ideologies and Challenges

Shkedi and Nisan (2009) classify teachers' ideologies as belonging to "a living ideology" (Billig et al. 1988) that constitutes a combination of overt and hidden beliefs that evolve from the experience of a particular cultural context. This ideology is interactive and includes perceptions regarding various fields. The sum total of these perceptions crystallizes in the teacher's consciousness as an ideal all-inclusive view, despite the fact that in the perceptions there are inconsistencies, internal contradictions, and vague formulations (Elbaz-Luwisch 2005). Researchers point to the fact that elementary school and ECE teachers' personal ideologies influence their perceptions relating to the teaching of the Bible as well as their ways of teaching it in practice (Achituv 2012; Shkedi and Nisan 2009). In other words, teachers' approach to Bible studies is guided by both their religious identity and their educational orientations.

Many challenges are faced by ECE teachers who include Bible stories in their teaching practice. They are required to deal with huge disparities that exist between the ancient way of life and tradition and the present-day world of the child. They face inaccessible language, chronological and cultural gaps, moral complexities, and stories involving violent events. Furthermore, they must cope with religious issues that are complex for both the teacher and the child, such as the existence of God. A common denominator of these challenging issues is the fact that the Bible was written for adults, not for young children. ECE teachers have the responsibility of adjusting these texts for their unique audience. They must "translate" the language of the Bible into modern-day language and explain in simple terms the differences between the ancient biblical way of life and the contemporary circumstances of the young children's lives. By doing so they serve, both consciously and unconsciously, as interpreters of the Bible.

Achituv and Manzura (2016) found that some of the challenges in telling Bible stories in ECJE settings are similar for religious and secular EC teachers in training. Both groups showed a disinterest in Bible studies and apprehension in dealing with biblical language and complex content. While secular students were concerned about the content of stories that may cause anxiety in the children, religious students were mainly concerned with the need to recognize the imperfection of the Bible's heroes.

Other challenges have emerged as sectorial. For instance, secular students were characterized as having only superficial knowledge of the Bible and as having a sense of alienation stemming from the assumption that the Bible obligates a normative-conceptual approach (Shkedi and Nisan 2006), which could be perceived as "religiousizing." One of the secular ECE students interviewed as part of a study about attitudes toward the teaching of the biblical "other" in ganim (Achituv and Manzura 2020) described the irrelevance of the Bible for her:

> I grew up my whole life in the Shomer HaTzair system [a youth movement that was considered anti-religious], with anti-Bible education; I don't believe in it, I'm not religious and I don't want anything to do with it. It wasn't something that had any significance for me or that I wanted to get close to. (273)

Religious students, on the other hand, were characterized as having difficulties in accepting alternative interpretations. This was described by one of the lecturers teaching Bible in an ECE religious faculty: "Every year I wait for someone to say that they have a difficulty or problem with the war and the command to kill everyone, and it surprises me anew every year. They don't ask … because it's not a problem" (Achituv and Manzura 2020, 277).

Constructivism and Telling Bible Stories

ECE teachers are often torn between implementing a traditional approach or a constructivist approach in their practice (Achituv 2002; Muller, Gorsetman, and Alexander 2018). Muller's findings claim that "by using constructivism as a theory and pedagogy to guide Jewish EC programs and choosing topics that are contextualized, children will employ higher order thinking" (2013, 330). The challenge presented by telling Bible stories to young children in the spirit of the constructivist approach is mainly expressed by religious ECJE teachers (Achituv and Manzura 2016), who will be the focus of this section.

A major difference between a constructivist approach and "traditional" approaches can be seen in the role of the child during the storytelling. Does the child participate passively in the story or play an active part through engaged listening, interpretation, and discussion? Because religious values are usually perceived as absolute, there is often a prevailing view that the role of the teacher is to instill these values as they are and avoid any associated discussion and debate. This perception is most prevalent among dogmatic religious approaches, whereas modern religious approaches recognize the relative nature of their values (Alexander 2001). Farjoun-Kadosh (2005), for example, expresses an approach tending toward traditionalism, which instructs ECE teachers in giving the children the "right answer" while telling Bible stories. Accordingly, some religious teachers regard themselves as responsible for molding the children's religious beliefs in a certain way, which contradicts constructivist principles (Muller, Gorsetman, and Alexander 2018).

These teachers generally are not willing to risk a child interpreting a story in a way the teacher believes to be mistaken. One example of this is a strategy these teachers choose when they deal with cases of moral conflicts related to biblical characters' behavior. S. Achituv (2013) and Ben-Or (2005) found that religious teachers' most common approach in dealing with this issue was attempting to glamorize the characters' behavior by emphasizing the positive and minimizing the negative sides of the behavior, while avoiding a discussion of the topic with the children. For instance, Gila, one of the teachers in a study of state-religious kindergarten teachers and their experience dealing with complex Bible stories, said regarding the story of Jacob pursuing his father's blessing (Genesis 27): "I tried to glamorize ... His mother ordered him and he did it, his mother asked him and he did it" (S. Achituv 2013, 275). Gila's attempt at glamorization was expressed by her justification of Jacob's cheating, stressing he was only doing his mother's bidding.

This conflict is not unique to the Jewish religious context; it has also been shown to exist in Christian religious education. Studies regarding religious perceptions in Christian religious schools have stated that they adopt a didactic, teacher-focused approach, as opposed to a constructivist-pedagogic, student-focused approach (Berliner 1997; Knowlton 2002; Lederhouse 1998). These studies claim that religious belief in an absolute truth is aligned with positivistic educational approaches and is counter to personal interpretation, which characterizes a constructivist approach. The problem, emphasized by these researchers, focuses on the critical pedagogical question of how the teacher can convey personal values and beliefs to the children while simultaneously cultivating some form of independence, as demanded by the constructivist approach.

Muller, Gorsetman, and Alexander (2018) found that teachers' feelings of uncertainty and lack of self-efficacy in implementing a constructivist pedagogy stem from, among other things, their religious obligation to teach as much Jewish content as possible. Furthermore, S. Achituv (2013) found that the conflict of religious ECE teachers, whose beliefs sometimes include dogmatic approaches, is often between their religious identity and their educational identity. Constructivist approaches that are part of their educational identity are taken from Western thought and not from the classical Jewish thought that shaped their religious identity. The teachers face tension between their familiarity and identification with modern academic approaches reflecting Western thought, on the one hand, and their affinity to connect with and believe in the Jewish tradition that they grew up with, on the other. This tension reflects an ever-present inner turmoil felt by the teachers regarding their different identities. The fact that religious ECE teachers in Israel mostly teach in the state-religious sector adds to their conflict, since they regard their job as including responsibility for instilling religious Zionist (belief in the development and protection of Israel) values in the children. These teachers often find themselves pulled in two directions as to their responsibilities: the children and their development, on the one hand, and the instilling of religious Zionist values, on the other (S. Achituv 2013).

This discussion of constructivism and the telling of Bible stories has concentrated on the question of *how* ECE teachers tell these stories to the children. In contrast, multiculturalism and gender issues in this context relate to the content of the stories and lead to the question of *what* teachers tell the children.

Multiculturalism and Telling Bible Stories

According to Grant and Ladson-Billings, multiculturalism includes "the diverse life experiences, traditions, histories, values, world views, and perspectives of the diverse cultural groups that make up a society" (1997, 185). These groups sustain a dialogue with one another without having to sacrifice their particular identities. Indeed, the Bible includes stories about different cultures. Nevertheless, it perceives the Israeli liberated male as the only ultimate cultural role model. Whoever does not fit into this definition is considered the "other." In this sense, the discourse concerning multiculturalism and the telling of Bible stories should focus on the question of the Bible's attitude toward the "other" and the way in which ECE teachers cope with telling young children Bible stories dealing with the "other."

The term "other" is most often defined as the following: dissimilar, different, other person, not the same person, stranger, or gentile. Who then is the biblical "other"? If we refer to most of the Bible's chapters, the biblical "other" is anyone other than one of the men belonging to the people of Israel. This could include a child, a woman, a slave, a gentile, and more. Initial scrutiny of the Bible reveals its attitude toward these "others." The Bible contains striking moral commands relating to the orphan, the widow, the disabled, and the convert. However, the solutions it provides to the ethical problems regarding other groups or individuals may occasionally arouse reservations and be difficult for the contemporary reader to digest (Achituv 2012; Cohen 1997). Within the category of "gentiles as others," the Bible does not treat everyone equally (Carmon 2007; Elitzur 2001; Kamm 2001; Sagi 1994). For the reader coming from a modern-day philosophical and moral world, questions regarding the gentile "other" may color not only the human heroes of the Bible in a problematic light but even God himself.

Israeli ECE teachers holding multicultural attitudes and facing multicultural classes ask themselves how to present these complex issues to young children. The main difference between the various strategies for dealing with this challenge is rooted in the teacher's approach to teaching the Bible and her personal ideology. For the one who sees the Bible as a source for imparting national, moral, or social values (Shkedi and Nisan 2006), a conversation on the biblical "other" may serve as a means for raising different views, for coping with moral dilemmas, and for attaining softened judgment.

Studies that have examined early childhood (EC) educators dealing with the "other" while telling Bible stories present a complex picture. Achituv and Manzura (2016) found that lecturers teaching the Bible in both ECE secular and religious faculties followed a cultural approach. These lecturers fostered thought development by asking questions and casting doubt, which promoted a moral, value-based education and the student's search for meaning. For the lecturers who taught in religious faculties, the cultural approach was found to be in harmony with their personal religious philosophy, based on the perception of the Bible as a sacred source as well as one on free choice of opinions and values (Alexander 2001).

Moreover, Achituv and Manzura (2016) discovered that issues related to the attitude toward the "other" did not interest most ECE students. The reasons for this varied between religious and secular students. Similar to the religious teachers described in the previous section, religious ECE students objected to a critical observation of the Bible and to the raising of doubts surrounding its model characters. Faced with the general conception of dichotomy, many of them had difficulty viewing the complexity of different situations in relating to the biblical "other." For example, one of the students claimed: "Esau is the wicked one … Ishmael is the villain" (Achituv and Manzura 2016, 245).

S. Achituv (2013) found that it was easier for religious ECE teachers to tell the children Bible stories of immoral acts performed by Bible characters when those characters were "others" rather than Israelites. For instance, Amalia, one of the teachers, explained how she would tell the story of Lavan the Aramite: "With Lavan, well Lavan the Aramite it was easy for us to tell, because *he* did it" (245, original emphasis). Yardena, another teacher, admitted that her level of criticism of Hagar was different than it would be of an Israelite: "It is a little easier for me to talk of Hagar as she is ungrateful, than to talk of Jacob or such."

A central cause found for secular students ignoring the issue of the biblical "other" was their adoption of the "mythical lens," which taints the text in a manner that does not enable the students to see its literal meaning, such as in describing Israelite success as overpowering strength in the phrase "the few versus the many." For example, one of the lecturers teaching Bible in a secular ECE faculty said:

> It never happened that someone said, "Yes, that's exactly how we are with the foreign workers." It's not a pressing issue for them to discuss but by contrast, there are those students for whom it's very important to prove how evil our enemies are. (Achituv and Manzura 2016, 246)

These studies present evidence of a gap between the moral perspectives of ECE lecturers and teachers and their ideologies. It can be seen that beyond the challenges inherent in the biblical text when referring to the biblical "other," examining the teaching of the Bible in a multicultural context must take into account the ideology of the educators themselves in this area. For teachers, this would include their cultural, religious, and educational identity and the group of children they educate, which itself is often multicultural. Whatever the identity of the teachers and the children, it would be beneficial for teachers to engage in moral discussions encouraging the children to think critically. Learning to make moral distinctions enables the fashioning of a self-identity as a prerequisite for a real encounter with the "other" and one's culture (Alexander 2001, 2005, 2009; Rosenberg 2005).

Gender and Telling Bible Stories

According to Manzura (2007), ECE teachers' attitudes toward gender perceptions are expressed through both their visible and their covert educational activities in every sphere of the classroom. Their position on gender issues is reflected in such things as the literature they choose to read to the young children, the design of the play area, and even simple verbal messages. For instance, this might be a typical question: "What did your mom prepare for you for lunch?" These gendered attitudes influence young children's perceptions regarding their gender roles and identities.

This is certainly the case with regard to the present discussion. Attitudes toward Bible stories that teachers tell children express their perspectives toward gender issues (Achituv 2019). As with multiculturalism, gender issues that emerge from Bible stories present challenges for ECE teachers. The discrepancies between the status of women in antiquity and their status today not only are rooted in historical and technological changes but also are discrepancies in values. One notable example of this is the masculine narrative that dominates Bible stories and the feminine narrative that is usually hidden (Levi 2017). Here, too, there is a need to take into account the ideology of the teachers themselves.

Achituv (2019), in examining gender perception conflicts of Israeli Orthodox ECE teachers, points to two types of coping strategies that have been employed in an attempt to bridge these discrepancies. The first is acceptance and reconciliation. Teachers who employ this strategy explain the discrepancies according to the uniqueness of the women of antiquity. For example, Amalia (who participated in a larger study on teaching Bible stories in ganim and was quoted previously from S. Achituv's [2013] study) referred to the phenomenon of polygamy in the Torah:

> Today it may not be appropriate, then they were special women, who were willing to be several wives of one husband, but, no, not me. Today I would not be willing to live like that … to be a wife together with another wife of someone. Definitely not. But it must have been suitable for those times. (Achituv 2019, 9)

Amalia demonstrated acceptance and reconciliation regarding polygamy, which in her opinion was good for that era. She added an explanation rooted in the uniqueness of the women of antiquity, who agreed to live in a polygamous family structure. She ignored the fact that polygamy did not require the consent of the women, but she admitted that she herself would not agree to it, acknowledging that times had changed.

The second coping strategy is being aware of the discrepancy and downplaying it to the children. For example, Hannah, another teacher in the study (Achituv 2019), referred to the story of Abraham's hospitality (Genesis 18) in a way that showed she was aware of the gaps between her gender perception and the situation described in the Bible stories, while choosing not to express feminist ideas to the children:

> I don't connect with it, and therefore, I will not include it in the Bible stories … I will not make an issue of it because I don't know if, as a kindergarten teacher, I am allowed to … with what Avraham said to Sarah, "Get [the food for the guests] ready quickly." Why did he have to tell her? Couldn't he prepare the food himself? These kinds of things are the feminist issue. Well then, because I'm not connected to it. I mean, if I really were into the feminist thing and if it were important to me. (9)

Hannah was aware of the difficulties that the story raises and the possibility of a feminist reading of the story, but nevertheless chose not to expose the children to such a reading. This is because she did not connect to the "feminist thing" and did not think she had permission to introduce feminist ideas into the kindergarten.

There are two plausible reasons for these teachers' choices not to deal with this discrepancy with young children. The first is the claim made by Gross (2011) that women live and operate in an "androcentric culture" characterized by a chauvinistic patriarchy, where the social order is determined by men. This claim is given support by Rapoport, Garb, and Penso, who specifically apply it to religious education: "The imperative of this education is to construct a woman's subjectivity that is subject to divine law and the male world" (1995, 58). The second reason is the concern that this will stamp them as feminists, which is still considered revolutionary and questionable in some groups within the Jewish Orthodox world (Irshai and Zion-Waldoks 2013).

Schneider (2016) found a third coping strategy used by Israeli ECE teachers working in religious kibbutzim (a type of communal settlement) to bridge the discrepancies between the status of women in antiquity and their status today. These teachers gave voice to feminine characters who are often absent from Bible stories by letting the children discuss and play these women's roles, thereby expressing their feminist agendas. Yonit, an ECE teacher in a religious kibbutz (a type of communal settlement), described this strategy:

> The voices of the foremothers who are not heard in the bible. There must have been mothers' voices. The fact that the bible was written by a male doesn't mean that we weren't heard. It's a trend that has been outrageous ever since, and we can add to it. (Schneider 2016, 163)

Yonit's remarks challenge the exclusion of the female voice in the Bible. Her views lead her to social-pedagogical activism. She calls for social correction, while using the biblical text from the past that she blames for excluding women. Schneider (2016) suggests that this strategy testifies to the emergence of a more liberal pattern reflecting the direction of the Israeli religious Kibbutz Movement (a term describing the various kibbutz organizations), which advocates for postmodern values and sees no contradiction between secular culture and religion (Y. Achituv 2013).

Summary

Amir (2004) argues that you cannot understand Jewish culture without recognizing its connection to the biblical text. This text requires deciphering the meanings hidden between its lines and translating it into the reader's language according to the contemporary generation's sensitivities and needs. ECJE teachers who live in a postmodern world tell Bible stories to young children who often are hearing them for the first time. These teachers try to work their way through tensions that exist between different values: constructivist educational beliefs versus dogmatic religious beliefs and liberal values (e.g., multiculturalism and feminism) versus the Bible's perspective toward "the other" and the status of women. The identity of these teachers and the communities in which they live and work influence their conduct and the professional choices they make regarding the field of Bible teaching.

These choices concern fundamental questions relating to hermeneutics. The teacher who tells Bible stories to young children acts consciously or subconsciously as a commentator. In order for the stories to be meaningful, the teacher must try to perceive them from one's own world by seeking out the story that disturbs him, the events that are exciting her, and the connections that relate to one's own life story. It is the awareness of the essential connections between each of these facets of the teacher's lens and the world of the children hearing the stories that will determine the power of this educational tool in a given learning context.

References

Achituv, S. 2002. "Kindergarten Teachers Exposed to a Pedagogy of Listening." MA diss., University of Haifa.

Achituv, S. 2012. "Early Childhood Educators Tell Their Stories: On the Identity of Religious Kindergarten Teachers in Israel." PhD diss., University of Haifa.

Achituv, S. 2013. "What Did the Teacher Say Today? State Religious Kindergarten Teachers Deal with Complex Torah Stories." *Journal of Jewish Education* 79 (3): 256–96.

Achituv, S. 2019. "'It Bothers Me, but I Will Not Bring It into the Kindergarten': Gender Perception Conflicts of Religious Kindergarten Teachers as Reflected in Their Work." *Religious Education* 114 (4): 1–13. https://doi.org/10.1080/00344087.2019.1600108.

Achituv, S., and S. Manzura. 2016. "How to Bridge the Gap? Teacher Educators' Approaches to the Teaching of the Biblical 'Other' in Kindergarten." *Journal of Jewish Education* 82 (3): 231–57. https://doi.org/10.1080/15244113.2016.1199255.

Achituv, S., and S. Manzura. 2020. "'They Are Undergoing a Makeover … I Gave Them In-Depth Glasses and Suddenly They See Three-Dimensional': Teachers' Attitudes to the Bible in Relation to the Processes of Change Expected from Students in Early Childhood Departments." [In Hebrew.] *Dapim* 73:261–88.

Achituv, Y. 2013. "Wind Gusts in the Religious Kibbutz." In *A Critique of Contemporary Religious Zionism—Selected Writings*, edited by Y. Englander and A. Sagi, 174–90. [In Hebrew.] Jerusalem: Hartman Institute.

Adar, Z. 1953. *The Educational Values of the Bible*. [In Hebrew.] Tel Aviv: Neuman.

Alexander, H. A. 2001. *Reclaiming Goodness: Education and the Spiritual Quest*. Notre Dame, IN: University of Notre Dame Press.

Alexander, H. A. 2005. "Education in Ideology." *Journal of Moral Education* 34 (1): 1–18.

Alexander, H. A. 2009. "Educating Identity: Toward a Pedagogy of Difference." In *Religious Education as Encounter: A Tribute to John M. Hull*, edited by S. Miedema, 45–52. Munster: Waxman.

Amir, M. 2004. "From Hermeneutics to Deed: The Biblical Text as a Factor That Evokes Ethical Reflection in Teacher Educators." [In Hebrew.] *Dapim* 37:120–44.

Ben-Or, S. 2005. "The Modes of Adapting the Biblical Text for the Purpose of Storytelling in the State Religious Kindergarten." [In Hebrew.] MA diss., Bar-Ilan University.

Berliner, D. 1997. "Educational Psychology Meets the Christian Right: Differing Views of Children, Schooling, Teaching, and Learning." *Teachers College Record* 98:381–416.

Billig, M., S. Condor, D. Edwards, M. Gane, D. Middleton, and A. Radley. 1988. *Ideological Dilemmas: A Social Psychology of Everyday Thinking*. London: Sage.

Carmon, A. 2007. "Agreement, Difference, Otherness." In *On the Judaism of a Democratic Country*, edited by A. Ravitzky and Y. Z. Stern, 471–94. [In Hebrew.] Jerusalem: Israel Democracy Institute.

Cohen, G. H. 1997. "Moral Judgment of Biblical Characters? An Evaluation of the Character of Sarah." In *Ways in the Bible and its Teaching*, edited by M. Ahrend and S. Feuerstein, 199–213. [In Hebrew.] Ramat Gan: Bar-Ilan University.

Dori, N. 2019. "Educating Jewish Values in State Kindergartens." [In Hebrew.] *Atar Daat* 15:1–15.

Elbaz-Luwisch, F. 2005. *Teachers' Voices, Storytelling and Possibility*. Greenwich, CT: Information Age.

Elitzur, A. 2001. "'But We Are Guilty for Our Brothers'—the Other in the Book of Genesis." In *The Other: Between Man, Himself and His Fellow*, edited by C. Deutsch and M. Ben-Sasson, 307–41. [In Hebrew.] Tel Aviv: Department for Jewish Culture, Center for Educational Technology.

Farjoun-Kadosh, D. 2005. "A Complicated Story." [In Hebrew.] *Hed Hagan* 70 (1): 30–41.

Grant, C. A., and G. Ladson-Billings. 1997. *Dictionary of Multicultural Education*. Phoenix, AZ: Oryx.

Gross, Z. 2011. "The Consolidation of Civic Identity in a Particularistic Religious Setting." In *Citizenship, Education and Social Conflict: Israeli Political Education in Global Perspective*, edited by H. A. Alexander, H. Pinson, and Y. Yona, 172–86. New York: Routledge.

Holtz, B. W. 2003. *Textual Knowledge: Teaching the Bible in Theory and in Practice*. New York: Jewish Theological Seminary Press.

Ilan, M. 2011. *Bible in Kindergarten*. [In Hebrew.]. Leah Mazor. Accessed August 27, 2014. http://mikrarevivim.blogspot.com/2017/11/blog-post_49.html#more.

Irshai, R., and T. Zion-Waldoks. 2013. "Modern Orthodox Feminism in Israel—between Nomos and Narratives." [In Hebrew.] *Mishpat Umimshal* 15:1–94.

Israel Ministry of Education. 1982a. *Book of Esther Guide for the Kindergarten Teacher*. [In Hebrew.] Jerusalem: Ministry of Education, Pedagogical Administration.

Israel Ministry of Education. 1982b. *Exodus from Egypt and the Giving of the Torah Guide for the Kindergarten Teacher*. [In Hebrew.] Jerusalem: Ministry of Education, Pedagogical Administration.

Israel Ministry of Education. 1992. *Stories of the Patriarchs and Stories of Jacob Guide for the Kindergarten Teacher*. [In Hebrew.] Jerusalem: Ministry of Education, Pedagogical Administration.

Israel Ministry of Education. 2002. *Starting from Genesis Guide for the Kindergarten Teacher*. [In Hebrew.] Jerusalem: Ministry of Education, Pedagogical Administration.

Israel Ministry of Education. 2003. *Bible Curriculum for State Kindergartens*. [In Hebrew.] Jerusalem: Ministry of Education, Pedagogical Administration.

Israel Ministry of Education. 2013. *Continuing with the Book of Exodus Guide for the Kindergarten Teacher*. [In Hebrew.] Israel: Ministry of Education, Pedagogical Administration.

Kamm, M. 2001. "The External and Internal Other—the Story of Jacob and Esau: From the Bible until the Modern Age." In *The Other: Between Man, Himself and his Fellow*, edited by H. Deutsch and M. Ben-Sasson, 342–66. [In Hebrew.] Tel Aviv: Department for Jewish Culture, Center for Educational Technology.

Knowlton, D. 2002. "A Constructivist Pedagogue's Personal Narrative of Integrating Faith with Learning: Epistemological and Pedagogical Challenges." *Journal of Research on Christian Education* 11 (1): 33–57.

Koboby, D. 1992. *Sifru-therapia*. [In Hebrew.] Jerusalem: Magnes.

Lederhouse, J. N. 1998. "Caught in the Middle: Evangelical Christian Public Elementary Educators." *Anthropology and Education Quarterly* 28 (2): 182–203.

Levi, D. 2017. "Language Creates Reality, on Gender Awareness in Educational Practice." [In Hebrew.] *Adam Olam* 47:32–7.

Levisohn, J. A. 2008. "Introducing the Contextual Orientation to Bible: A Comparative Study." *Journal of Jewish Education* 74 (1): 53–82.

Manzura, S. 2007. "Kindergarten as a Mirror of Society: 'The Glass Ceiling' in the Religious Gan." In *To Be a Jewish Woman*, edited by T. Cohen, 207–17. [In Hebrew.] Jerusalem: Reuven Mas.

Muller, M. 2013. "Constructivism and Jewish Early Childhood Education." *Journal of Jewish Education* 79 (3): 315–34.

Muller, M., C. Gorsetman, and S. T. Alexander. 2018. "Struggles and Successes in Constructivist Jewish Early Childhood Classrooms." *Journal of Jewish Education* 84 (3): 284–311.

Rapoport, T., Y. Garb, and A. Penso. 1995. "Religious Socialization and Female Subjectivity: Religious-Zionist Adolescent Girls in Israel." *Sociology of Education* 68 (1): 48–55.

Rosenberg, J. M. 2005. "From 'Bible Stories' to Teaching Torah." [In Hebrew.] *On the Bible and Its Teaching* 8:11–29.

Sagi, A. 1994. "The Punishment of Amalek in Jewish Tradition: Coping with the Moral Problem." *Harvard Theological Review* 87 (3): 323–46.

Schneider, O. 2016. "The State-Religious Kindergarten in a Whirlwind of Identities." [In Hebrew.] *Shnaton Shaanan* 21:151–78.

Shkedi, A., and M. Nisan. 2006. "Teachers' Cultural Ideology: Patterns of Curriculum and Teaching Culturally Valued Texts." *Teachers College Record* 108 (4): 687–725.

Shkedi, A., and M. Nisan. 2009. "The Influence of Teachers' Personal Ideology on Bible Teaching Methods." [In Hebrew.] *Theory and Practice in Planning Studies* 20:53–77.

8

Strengthening Jewish-Israeli Identity and Promoting a Common Cultural Canon through Children's Literature: The Experience of Sifriyat Pijama

Sylvia Kamowitz-Hareven

Over the course of history, humankind has transmitted its beliefs, values, and cultural heritage through storytelling. This tradition carries on today when adults read aloud picture books with children. Many of us remember stories read to us when we were young: books that sparked our imagination, folktales passed down from generation to generation, fables that highlight the distinctions between right and wrong and good and evil. Why do these stories leave such long-lasting impressions? Is it the plot or characters, the rhyming verse, or the endearing illustrations? Or perhaps the fond memory of cuddling up close to adults as they read aloud, or the emotions evoked by their voices?

The significance of early exposure to books for children's development has been studied extensively in recent years. Research has shown that shared reading experiences in the early years can have transformative effects on children's language development, budding literacy, knowledge of the world, and emotional development (Doyle and Bramwell 2006; Flack, Field, and Horst 2018; Saracho 2017; Wasik, Hindman, and Snell 2016).

Moreover, like the legends and stories retold throughout the ages, shared reading can do much more than promote literacy skills and scholastic readiness. A children's book can act as a springboard for conversation surrounding values and belief systems, an expression of common cultural heritage, and a unifying force in ethnically diverse societies. As such, literature plays a central role in values education and in the cultural socialization of young children (Deitcher 2013; Narvaez 2002; Trousdale 2004).

Acting upon the many benefits of shared reading, the Harold Grinspoon Foundation (HGF), a philanthropic nongovernmental organization (NGO) based in the United States and founder of PJ Library˚ (a sister program described in the following section), created a unique book-gifting program to promote shared reading and conversations around Jewish-Israeli heritage and values for children and their families in Israel: Sifriyat Pijama (Pajama Library). The program, initiated as a pilot intervention in a hundred classrooms in the 2009–10 school year, has since blossomed into an integral component of the Israeli state curriculum, cofinanced by the Ministry of Education and reaching over 85 percent of children in public preschools and first and second grades across the country.

History and Development

Sifriyat Pijama is a sister program of PJ Library®, a Jewish values-based family book program launched in North America in 2005 by HGF. PJ Library® distributes monthly read-aloud books in English, Spanish, Portuguese, German, Russian, and Ukrainian to some two hundred thousand families in North and South America, the UK, Australia, Russia, the Ukraine, and Mexico. As articulated on its website, "PJ Library® shares Jewish stories that can help your family talk together about values and traditions that are important to you."

Sifriyat Pijama, like PJ Library®, suggests that reading together can encourage family conversations around values, but it does not send books directly to families. Due to postal constraints, mailing books to individual homes throughout Israel is not feasible. However, education in Israel is compulsory and free from the age of three, and almost all children attend public school from that age. Thus, when conceiving the Israeli program, its developers identified an opportunity to create a combined school-and home-based model in partnership with the Ministry of Education, directly engaging educators and incorporating the program into Israel's mainstream early-years curricular guidelines. Sifriyat Pijama aspires to further HGF's goal of empowering parents to hold meaningful conversations with their children, while at the same time enriching values-based education in the classroom, encouraging a culture of family reading and expanding classroom and home libraries for Israeli children.

How the Program Works

Sifriyat Pijama provides eight different, age-appropriate children's books annually to more than 250,000 Israeli preschoolers and 110,000 first- and second-graders, initially introducing the books in the classroom and then distributing personal copies to each child. The program in first and second grades is limited to four read-aloud books per year, as many children acquire the ability to read independently in these grades. Over a period of five years, Sifriyat Pijama ultimately provides each child with a collection of thirty-two read-aloud picture books. Most families receive the books free of charge, while those in more affluent communities pay a highly subsidized fee. Each year a new booklist is selected, so children do not receive books that were previously delivered to their older siblings.

The books are delivered monthly to preschools in parcels containing multiple copies of that month's selection. Each book is accompanied by parent and teacher guides with suggestions for conversations and activities relating to the Jewish-Israeli values or cultural themes emerging from the story. Teachers are encouraged to read aloud the book and carry out discussions and play/crafts activities in the classroom. Then each child receives a personal copy as a gift for their home library. The books serve as a bridge between the home and the classroom, as teachers work together with parents to empower families and reinforce the values reflected in the stories.

A parallel program for Arabic-speaking Israeli children, Maktabat al-Fanoos (Lantern Library), was initiated by HGF in 2014 and operates in collaboration with Israel's Ministry of Education in all Arab public schools in Israel. The program annually provides books to about two hundred thousand Arabic-speaking children between the ages of three and eight.

Creating a Common Literary Canon in a Culturally Diverse Society

Jewish-Israeli society is an ever-changing, linguistically and culturally diverse mosaic ranging from ultra-Orthodox to secular and with many Israelis being first-generation immigrants. Alongside the cultural and linguistic differences are socioeconomic divides as well.

The Jewish-Israeli public education system is highly centralized and operates on two parallel tracks, state-religious and state, from preschool through high school. While some subject matters are common to both tracks, other disciplines (e.g., Bible; Jewish thought, history, and literature) have distinct curricula, teaching methods, and textbooks. Most Haredi (ultra-Orthodox) schools in Israel are independent and not part of the public education system. As such, they do not participate in many state-financed programs and do not take part in Sifriyat Pijama. (For further information on the Israeli school system, see Chapter 1 in this book.)

Israel's dual-track education system allows schools a measure of autonomy regarding Jewish subject matter and suggests a closer fit between schools and the beliefs and practices of the families they serve. Yet the system also reinforces cultural disparities between subgroups, creating a society in which graduates of Israeli public schools, religious and secular, have an ever-shrinking cultural foundation in common. Sifriyat Pijama is one of the only Ministry of Education programs overtly dealing with Jewish identity that provides identical curricular materials to the two parallel tracks of Israeli schools. By distributing the same books and training guides to schools in both tracks, the program is addressing the vital need to forge a broad common literary and cultural canon among Israeli children and their families.

Considerations in Book Selection

Sifriyat Pijama is constantly challenged to identify quality, age-appropriate children's books, relevant for diverse populations, that invite conversations around Jewish-Israeli values and heritage and are welcomed by families from different walks of life. As the program is cofinanced and pedagogically supervised by the Ministry of Education, the books also require the approval of the ministry's early childhood (EC) division.

One of the early tasks of the program developers was to compile a corpus of child-appropriate "Jewish-Israeli values" relevant for a wide swath of the Jewish population in Israel: Orthodox, traditional, and secular; wealthy and economically disadvantaged; immigrant and Israeli-born. Against the backdrop of Israel's evolving Jewish character and increasing divisiveness between religious and secular Israelis, the list is dynamic and is revisited from time to time.

Sifriyat Pijama has expanded the menu of what is considered Jewish content beyond holidays, beliefs, rites, and ritual. Its selection of books includes stories about Israeli historical events, biblical figures, and Jewish folktales from around the world—as well as secular children's books that address humanist Jewish values and invoke conversations on character development, moral dilemmas, interpersonal relations, and social justice.

The program has also played an important role in highlighting the Hebrew language by reviving classical Israeli children's literature, bringing back into print and at times reillustrating books that were no longer available. Close attention is paid to the illustrations of old and new books to ensure that they reflect a broad diversity of people and landscapes.

Each year a committee comprising representatives of the Ministry of Education, together with independent specialists in children's literature, illustrations, Jewish family education, and EC, peruses hundreds of existing books and unpublished manuscripts in search of eight new titles for each age group. Selecting books for a nationwide program requires focused intent surrounding issues of cultural authenticity and sensitivity, ethnic diversity, and gender roles. The process is complex as the committee members strive to collectively define criteria for quality children's literature and deliberate on a myriad of questions, such as the following:

1. Which biblical figures and legends are meaningful for twenty-first-century Israeli children?
2. Will some religious parents or educators resist modern adaptations of traditional texts?
3. How will overtly "Jewish" books be received by nonreligious families, who may have concerns over religious coercion or indoctrination?
4. How can we mediate the sometimes archaic language of classical children's literature and give it relevance today?
5. What is the role of nostalgia in a multicultural society, and is nostalgia shared by all?
6. Do social trends, political agendas, contemporary parenting attitudes, or the relative popularity of authors or illustrators impact the selection process?
7. To what degree do the committee members' personal tastes, life experiences, and biases affect the choice of books?
8. Is it necessary that all the books reflect current perceptions of family structure, gender roles, and social equity? How can we ensure fair

representation of strong female characters when the protagonists in most children's books are boys?
9. Are we equally sensitive to the needs of different subgroups in Israel? How do we respond to tensions among groups and not be swayed by the preferences or pressures of a particular community?
10. What is the appropriate balance between art and agenda in children's literature? How do we guarantee that a book selected for its "message" is not overly simplistic or didactic?
11. Finally, we must also ask ourselves about which books are *not* selected. Which topics, language usage, or illustrations are considered taboo or inappropriate for the program? How daring or cautious are we in our choice of books?

Table 8.1 displays a sampling of books that have been selected for Sifriyat Pijama. A comprehensive list of all Sifriyat Pijama titles and values can be found on the program's website: https://eng.pjisrael.org/book-search/.

Table 8.1 Sampling of Sifriyat Pijama Books

Title	Author/Date	Genre	Value
A Sick Day for Amos McGee	Philip Stead (2010)	Contemporary prose (translated)	Visiting the sick
Hannah Banana's Granny Cooked Porridge	Ora Ayal (1999)	Contemporary prose (Israeli)	Hospitality, generosity
Snow of Dandelions	Rinat Primo (2017)	Contemporary prose (Israeli)	Social activism, caring for the environment
Itamar Meets a Rabbit	David Grossman (1988)	Contemporary prose (Israeli)	Stereotypes, xenophobia
The Chickens and the Fox	Haim Nachman Bialik (1922/2005)	Classical prose (Israeli)	Unique contributions to society, special needs
Bone Button Borscht	Aubrey Davis (2016)	Folktale (translated)	Community, being charitable to strangers
King Solomon and the Bee	Uriel Ofek (2019)	*Agada* (Jewish legend)	King Solomon, wisdom
A Garden on a Donkey	Devora Busheri (2020)	Midrash (Rabbinic text)	Rachel and Rabbi Akiva, knowledge
Grandpa Sabih	Tami Shem-Tov (2018)	Contemporary prose (Israeli)	Ethnic pride, *aliyah* (immigration to Israel)
I Gave a Flower to Nurit	Miriam Yalan-Shteklis (2005)	Classical poetry (Israeli)	Varied themes, Hebrew language
Feathers in the Wind	Shlomo Abbas (2014)	Folktale	The power of words
A Hole in the Ship	Adi Zelichov-Ralevi (2018)	Rabbinic text (Midrash)	Collective responsibility

Navigating the Religious and Cultural Divide

The distribution of the same books to thousands of Israeli families is not in itself sufficient to generate a common literary culture. To enhance engagement, supplementary materials accompany the books. These materials include teacher and parent guides, a website, and presence on social media platforms, aimed at encouraging and facilitating "beyond the book" activities and conversations in homes and in classrooms. The materials are grounded in the following guiding principles and conceptual frameworks:

1. Personalizing the reading experience by applying multiple lenses to texts ("United yet Unique" and "Mirrors and Windows")
2. Highlighting family enjoyment of conversational reading
3. Empowering parents to read aloud and share their own heritage and belief systems with their children

Cultivating common bonds among Israelis should not replace individual and family identity, beliefs, or practices. When families read together, they are encouraged to relate the plots and characters to their own experiences. Conversational reading gives parents opportunities that may not arise in everyday routines to share with their children the beliefs and heritage that guide their lives. This in turn invites young children to take pride in their budding cultural identity.

Personalizing the Reading Experience by Applying Multiple Lenses to Texts

United yet Unique

From the outset the conceptual framework "United yet Unique" was proposed to guide Sifriyat Pijama in achieving a healthy balance between the personal and the communal. "United" was the goal for the books, their creators, and their content to foster a sense of belonging to a shared community and help generate a common cultural-literary canon. "Unique" meant the parent and teacher guides would intentionally encourage readers to create specific meaning from the stories through their own personal lenses and empower parents to discuss their belief systems and pass down to their children their traditions, aspirations, and worldviews.

An example of applying the lens of "United yet Unique" is *The Missing Spice*, a rabbinic (based on the Talmud [the body of Jewish civil and ceremonial law and legend]) tale dating from the period of the Roman Empire, adapted for children by the Israeli author Dvora Omer (2013). In the story, the Roman governor Antoninus shares a Sabbath meal at the home of Rabbi Judah the Patriarch, a renowned rabbi and chief editor of the Mishna (the first major written collection of Jewish oral traditions). The governor relishes the meal, although the food was served cold because of the biblical prohibition against lighting fire on the Sabbath. When he returns for another visit on a weekday, the same food is served but the meal is not nearly as tasty. The rabbi explains to Antoninus that the "missing spice" in the weekday meal is the Sabbath atmosphere—a spice that cannot be purchased in any market.

The legend, which had previously appeared in an anthology long out of print, was retold as a picture book created for Sifriyat Pijama. The book acquainted parents and children with a prize-winning Israeli author and introduced them to Rabbi Judah, to the special friendship between the Roman governor and the rabbi, and to the history and landscape of the period. The accompanying guide invited families to discuss together their own traditions and to identify and enrich the "spices" that make the Sabbath day unique for them, which may include traditional rituals, family customs, or simply spending time with family and friends.

The conceptual framework of "United yet Unique" enabled Sifriyat Pijama to distribute an ancient legend about the holiness of the Sabbath day, while simultaneously encouraging families across the religious-secular divide to take pride in their particular lifestyle. Framing the story within this construct helped facilitate respectful, thoughtful conversations surrounding a potentially volatile topic in Israeli society—how the Sabbath is celebrated in public and private spaces—in a manner appropriate to all walks of life.

Mirrors and Windows

Rudine Sims Bishop (1990), whose work has focused on multicultural children's literature, uses the imagery of mirrors and windows to describe the rich contribution of books to young and adult readers. According to her framework, literature serves as a mirror when readers view themselves as reflected in the story and acts as a window when exposing them to new worlds and experiences and encouraging empathy toward others. A good book, according to Sims Bishop, should be both a mirror and a window:

> Books are sometimes windows, offering views of worlds that may be real or imagined, familiar or strange. These windows are also sliding glass doors, and readers have only to walk through in imagination to become part of whatever world has been created and recreated by the author. When lighting conditions are just right, however, a window can also be a mirror. Literature transforms human experience and reflects it back to us, and in that reflection we can see our own lives and experiences as part of the larger human experience. Reading, then, becomes a means of self-affirmation, and readers often seek their mirrors in books. (ix)

Sims Bishop's imagery can be useful in explaining how, time and again, thousands of Israeli families with vastly different belief systems and life experiences can find relevance in the same book. Her construct also encourages us to expand our perception of "what or who is this book about," as quality literature surely has multiple meanings. A good book touches upon a variety of themes, values, and emotions.

An example of the value of looking at children's literature through the lens of "mirrors and windows" is *Mr. Minasa's Shoes*, a traditional Ethiopian folktale retold by Israeli author Ronit Hacham (2018). The story tells of a man who departs on a journey to a faraway country. Upon arrival in his new home, our hero tries to rid himself of his old shoes, in the belief that they are no longer needed and are not appropriate for the new country. He buys new shoes and tosses the old pair, only to have them returned to him time and time again, on each occasion being reminded by others that the shoes belong to him and he must surely miss them.

After reading the book, adults and children may ask themselves: When in my life have I acted like Mr. Minasa and set upon a journey to a new home? Did I ever wish to start afresh and leave something behind, only to be reminded that it is an integral part of my identity? How have I felt and behaved toward newcomers in a setting that I consider my home?

Seen through these lenses, the legend surpasses the experience of an Ethiopian Jew in Israel and may resonate with a large and varied readership: adults and children, immigrants in a new country, those comfortable and welcomed in their setting, and people who feel marginalized or separate from mainstream society. The book also encourages parents to compare their own family's immigration story with that of Mr. Minasa and to share their ethnic heritage with their children.

Highlighting Family Enjoyment

Messages urging today's parents to read with their children are articulated through an abundance of public campaigns and popular parenting columns, often citing as motivators school readiness or success in life (American Academy of Pediatrics 2014; Chamberlin 2012; Leppert n.d.; LitWorld n.d.). Most parents "know" the value of reading and surely want the best for their children (Preece and Levy 2018). So why do so many parents not take the time to read aloud to their children? For some this may be due to a lack of books, but for many others it is a scarcity—real or perceived—of time. In today's age of computerized technology and the outsourcing and organization of children's leisure hours, when overworked parents themselves rarely sit down to read a book for pleasure, reading with one's children may feel like a chore to be squeezed into the family's already busy schedule.

Sifriyat Pijama attempts to change home reading habits by emphasizing the benefits of shared reading for the whole family—the joy and the closeness of reading books together. It follows these guidelines:

1. The books encourage multiple readings and conversations. They are not intended to "teach a lesson" but rather to be enjoyed together.
2. Teachers play a central role by incorporating the books into a play-based classroom curriculum and associating reading with fun. When children bring their copies home, they anticipate continued enjoyment around them with their parents.
3. The parent guides offer a variety of optional games and experiential activities, relaying the message that shared reading can lead to family enjoyment.
4. Other supplementary materials include videotaped tips on reading with young children, conversation-starter card games, community story-time events, and more.

Empowering Parents

The name "Pajama Library" intimates a culture of bedtime stories, encapsulating the image of calm and happy parents and children, following the family dinner and a moment before heading off for bed, as they sit cuddled together on the child's bed or the living room couch. Yet this image does not apply to everyone, and shared reading need not be limited to bedtime.

In order to reach out to all families, including parents who work night shifts and may not be home at their children's bedtime, adults who do not have a tradition of reading, who cannot read in Hebrew, or who struggle to cope with an array of childrearing challenges, simply handing out books is not enough to bolster a culture of meaningful and fun conversational reading. As family reading is the focal point of the program, a variety of ways are sought to build *all* parents' confidence and capability to read and enjoy the books with their children.

As an example, many Sifriyat Pijama families are non-Hebrew-speaking, first-generation immigrants. To enhance the books' accessibility to these families, the parent guides have been translated into other languages, special training for teachers is offered, and the program has collaborated with welfare and nonprofit organizations that incorporate the books into parent training and home intervention programs. The message relayed is that parents have a unique role in passing down their own childhood memories and family traditions to their children, and they are encouraged to use the books to launch such conversations. Immigrant parents are also reminded that, like them, young children cannot read the Hebrew text, and guidance is provided on "reading" the illustrations in picture books.

These steps have been applauded by many immigrant families and those who work with them. As Israeli society continues to evolve, yet more inclusive and culturally sensitive steps should be taken at the community level to ensure that the books are truly accessible to all and that they do not reinforce structural inequalities within Israeli society. With appropriate mediation, the books may provide immigrant and marginalized families with an entry ticket into society, acquainting them with classical Jewish texts and contemporary Israeli stories and generating a common ground among all families.

Indicators of Success—National Participant Surveys

HGF sends out annual online surveys to all Sifriyat Pijama teachers, with return rates averaging 56 percent. Summaries in English of teacher surveys and evaluation reports can be found on the Sifriyat Pijama website: https://eng.pjisrael.org/.

Additionally, the Ministry of Education's evaluation division, the National Authority for Education Assessment and Evaluation (known by its Hebrew acronym as RAMA), periodically conducts studies of Sifriyat Pijama as part of its comprehensive evaluation of all ministry programs. The RAMA studies use telephone interviews to survey random samplings of both teachers and parents, and their findings are remarkably consistent with the cumulative results of the HGF online surveys. Of particular value are RAMA's parent interviews, as they provide insight into the program's impact on shared-reading practices in homes.

The data that follows is drawn from the 2015 RAMA survey findings. Responses to both HGF and RAMA studies have consistently demonstrated very high regard for the program and the books delivered, echoing strong anecdotal evidence arising from the field. With minor exceptions, no conspicuous variance among participants was found.

Overall Satisfaction

The overwhelming majority of teachers expressed a very high level of satisfaction with the program, identified with its goals, and viewed it as an integral component in their professional practice aimed at promoting children's emergent literacy, fostering socio-emotional development and values education, and encouraging parent involvement. Notably, 96 percent of the teachers stated that they believed the program should be compulsory for all preschools, and a significant proportion stated that they thought discontinuing the program would have a negative impact on children's engagement with books, both in the classroom (62 percent) and at home (78 percent). The RAMA survey showed a similar level of satisfaction among parents. Figure 8.1 shows 95 percent of the parents and 96 percent of the teachers reporting their satisfaction with the program overall as between four and five on a scale of one to five.

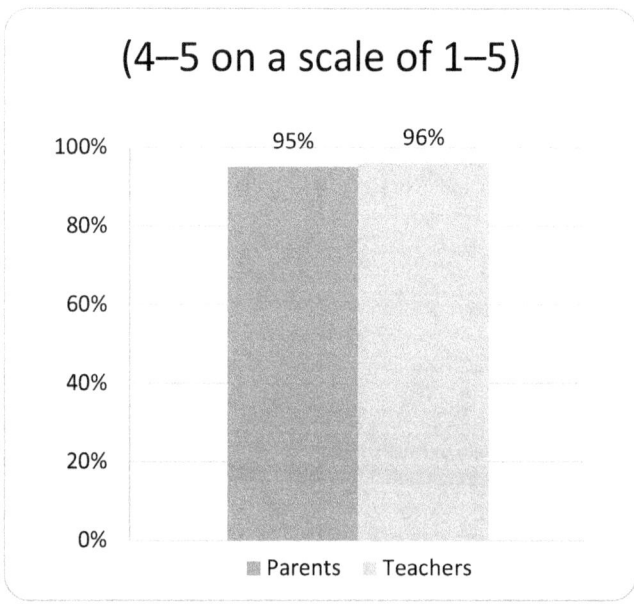

Figure 8.1 Satisfaction with the program.

Note: Results of 2015 RAMA survey.

Satisfaction with Book Selection, Reading Practices, and Classroom Activities

In its first decade of operation, Sifriyat Pijama distributed almost two hundred different titles. With minor variations among the selections, the books were very highly regarded by teachers and parents. Figure 8.2 shows 88 percent of the parents and 83 percent of the teachers reporting their satisfaction with the book selection as between four and five on a scale of one to five. Virtually all the teachers reported that they had read the books multiple times in the classroom before distributing copies to the children to take home. Ninety-four percent of teachers reported conducting conversations surrounding the books with the children. Most conversations (79 percent) touched upon values, heritage, or moral dilemmas arising in the stories.

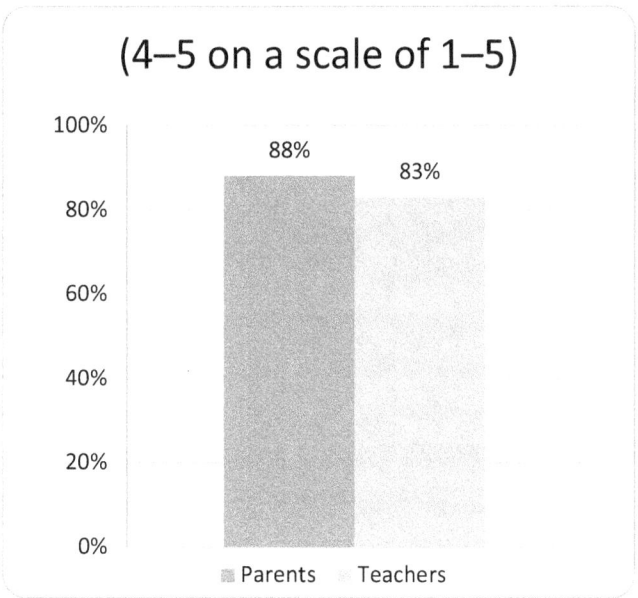

Figure 8.2 Satisfaction with the books.
Note: Results of 2015 RAMA survey.

Teachers initiated other book-related activities as well. Predominant activities were acting out the stories, arts and crafts projects, and social action based on the story. (For example, a book on visiting the sick prompted a teacher to initiate a practice of having children call sick classmates.) Figure 8.3 shows how teachers used other book-related activities in the classroom.

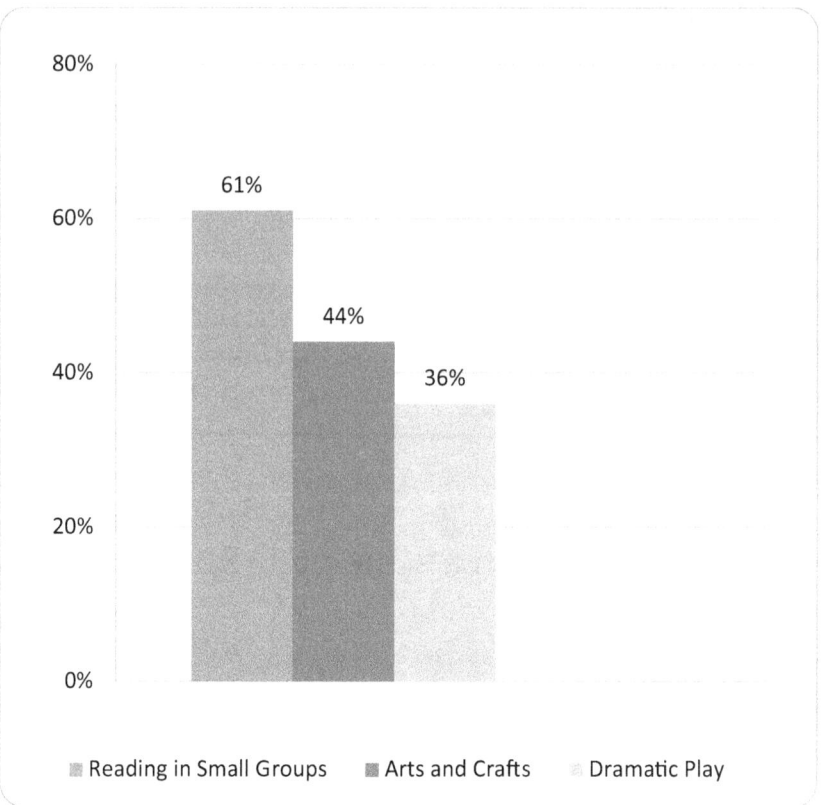

Figure 8.3 Other book-related classroom activities.

Note: Results of 2015 RAMA survey.

Perceived Impact of the Program

A significant percentage of the teachers reported that the program enhanced the centrality of books and an increase in the scope of reading in their classrooms and in the homes. Reported highlights of the program's perceived impact were:

1. Exposure to quality children's literature and formal language
2. Increase in teacher-initiated and children's independent reading
3. Increase in conversations around values and heritage
4. Children's enhanced enjoyment from listening to stories
5. Increase in language-/literacy-related activities and increased reading in the home and awareness among parents of the importance of reading aloud

Figure 8.4 shows the percentages of teachers who rated the impact of particular activities as between four and five on a scale of one to five. Figure 8.5 shows the percentages of parents who rated the impact of particular activities as between four and five on a scale of one to five.

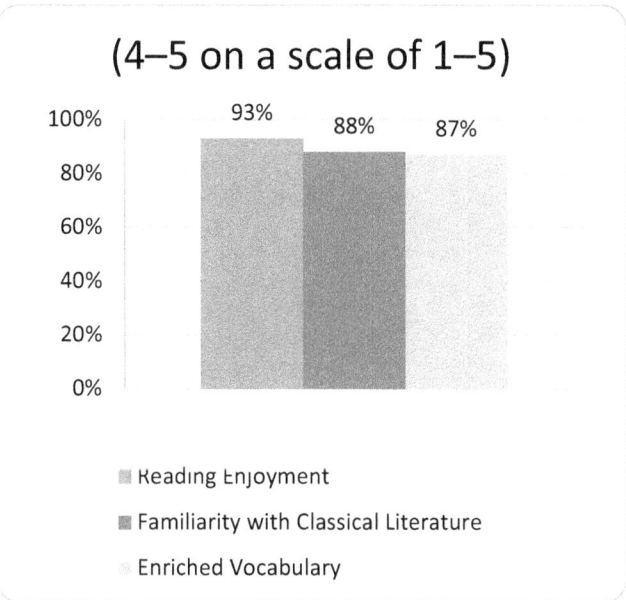

Figure 8.4 Perceived program impact—teachers.

Note: Results of 2015 RAMA survey.

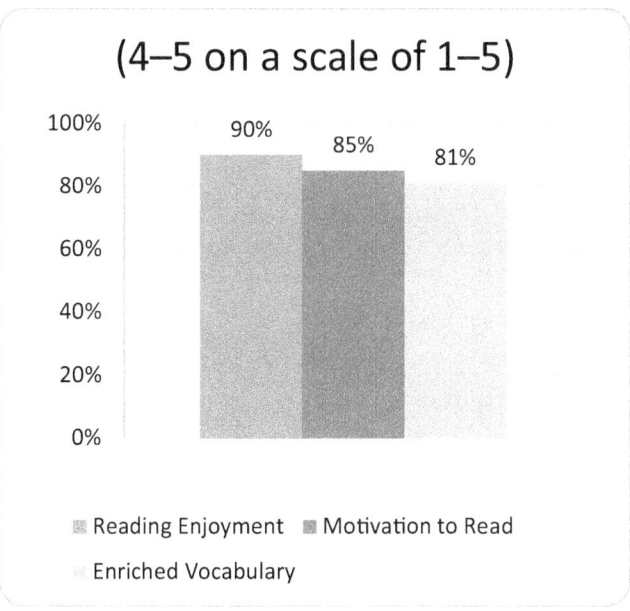

Figure 8.5 Perceived program impact—parents.

Note: Results of 2015 RAMA survey.

Insights from Parent Surveys Regarding Home Reading Practice

The RAMA parent interviews revealed that nearly 90 percent of Sifriyat Pijama parents read most or all books at least twice and 31 percent of the families who had been in the program for several years frequently read previous years' books with their children. Parents also reported an increase in the frequency of family reading and in parent-child conversations about the books. Figure 8.6 shows the changes in home reading practices.

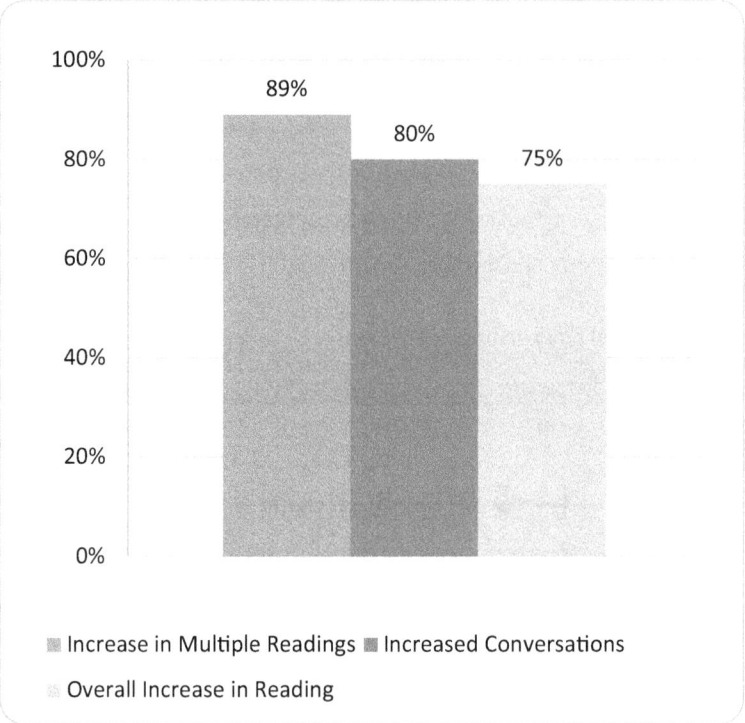

Figure 8.6 Changes in home reading practices.

Note: Results of 2015 RAMA survey.

Eighty percent of the parents reported that the program had contributed greatly or very greatly to expanding their home libraries. This is particularly significant for underserved families. When asked to quantify how many children's books they had in their homes, 20 percent of the parents indicated they had *only* Sifriyat Pijama books, and 12 percent reported Sifriyat Pijama books comprised 50–80 percent of the children's home libraries.

The high regard of Sifriyat Pijama as reflected in the nationwide surveys is encouraging. Further exploration is still needed, however, to gain a richer and more nuanced understanding of the program. This may be achieved through longitudinal studies on sustained effects, as well as qualitative research giving voice to children's perceptions and shedding light on the quality of parent-child interactions around the books, variance in experiences among different cultural groups, best practices when working with immigrant and historically underserved families, and more.

Conclusion and Future Challenges

Meta-analyses of book-gifting programs and shared reading interventions have shown that they can be effective in improving children's language skills and encouraging reading in the home, particularly among at-risk populations (de Bondt, Willenberg, and Bus 2020; Dickinson and Morse 2019; Neyer, Szumlas, and Vaughn 2018). Indeed, Sifriyat Pijama has demonstrated success in advancing the agenda of the Ministry of Education's emergent literacy curriculum for Israeli preschoolers.

Looking back on its first decade of operation, it is possible to affirm that Sifriyat Pijama is acting as an agent of social change by stimulating family conversations around Jewish-Israeli values and heritage through shared reading. Due to its scale of activity, the program is also playing an ongoing role in generating a common literary canon among Israeli children, forging positive ethnic identity and cultural knowledge. Time will tell the lasting scope and range of these effects.

These achievements are significant when considering the nature of contemporary Western culture, for we are living in an era of extreme individualism (Triandis 1995; Santos, Varnum, and Grossmann 2017), in a society that highlights the particular, embraces the unique, and provides a vast array of choices. From infancy onward, today's children are encouraged to cultivate their personal preferences and identity. Individualism is carefully nurtured by the adults who raise them and is echoed throughout society. One needs to go no further than the pasta aisle in the neighborhood supermarket, peruse popular parenting websites, or browse the myriad of Netflix channels to witness the pervasiveness of this celebration of the individual.

Emphasis on individualism is reflected in Jewish life as well, as families in Israel and in the Diaspora seek to express their faith, heritage, and practice in ways that are uniquely meaningful for them. This, of course, is not a recent phenomenon. As is written in the Midrash, there are "seventy faces of the Torah" (Bamidbar Rabbah 13:15).

Within this culture of individualism, Sifriyat Pijama has taken an audacious stance by distributing the same book to thousands of Israeli homes, connecting young children and their families to a common heritage, and accentuating values that bind Israeli Jews as a community. The fact that the same picture books are being read by religious and secular children is de facto creating common ground among families with disparate values and lifestyles. Indications that readers by and large like all or most of the books lend hope to the possibility of forging some sense of cultural unity.

Childhood and family relations cannot, however, be separated from societal or global trends. Changes on the macro level will continue to necessitate ongoing dialogue with the field, operational adaptations, and fine-tuning of the program's selection of books. And as Israeli society continues to evolve and its common Jewish-Israeli ethos changes, new tensions will certainly arise.

Alongside the ongoing development and adaptation of Sifriyat Pijama, two major societal trends pose challenges to the program and should be given consideration: demographics and technology.

According to the 2018 report of Israel's Central Bureau of Statistics, 14 percent of all Jewish-Israelis self-identify as Haredi and send their children to independent schools (Central Bureau of Statistics 2018). It is likely that this percentage will rise in coming years. Despite some attempts to adapt the program to their cultural needs, most Haredi children do not participate in Sifriyat Pijama. Questions to be considered are: Could a comparable program be designed for this population? Is it feasible to identify a corpus of books that would be welcomed in all Haredi schools and homes? What are the ramifications of separate booklists for Haredi and state schools—the clouding of Sifriyat Pijama's desire for commonality within Israeli society weighed against the ongoing risks of not providing for this sector?

Regarding technology, screen time is here to stay, and many parents and educators are concerned by the ubiquity and attraction of digital media in the lives of young children. New technologies and changing perceptions have led to a wealth of recent studies seeking insight into parent-child interactions around e-books (Korat and Falk 2017; Korat and Shamir 2012; Ozturk and Hill 2018; Troseth et al. 2020). How will this technological revolution affect the future of books? What effects will it have on the book publishing industry, on reading habits, and on parent-child shared reading?

These challenges are not unique to Sifriyat Pijama and will surely pose dilemmas for many in the field of early childhood Jewish education (ECJE) in Israel. Meanwhile, we continue to seek deeper understanding of the social ramifications of the program. As the first generation of Sifriyat Pijama readers grow into adulthood, one may anticipate the day when Israelis from all walks of life will look back fondly on the books they received as children, be secure in their Jewish-Israeli identity, feel a strong collective bond, and invite their own children into the magical world of books and stories.

References

Abbas, S. 2014. *Feathers in the Wind*. [In Hebrew.] Hod Hasharon. Israel: Agur.
American Academy of Pediatrics. 2014. "Literacy Promotion: An Essential Component of Primary Care Pediatric Practice." *Pediatrics* 134 (2): 404–9. https://doi.org/10.1542/peds.2014-1384.
Ayal, O. 1999. *Hannah Banana's Granny Cooked Porridge*. [In Hebrew.] Jerusalem: Ayalot.
Bialik, H. N. (1922) 2005. *The Chickens and the Fox*. [In Hebrew.] Tel Aviv: Hakibbutz Hameuchad.
Busheri, D. 2020. *A Garden on a Donkey*. [In Hebrew.] Tel Aviv: M. Mizrahi.

Central Bureau of Statistics. 2018. *Religion and Self-Definition of Extent of Religiosity: Selected Data from the Society in Israel Report No. 10*. [In Hebrew.] June 27, 2018. https://www.cbs.gov.il/he/mediarelease/DocLib/2018/195/32_18_195b.pdf.

Chamberlin, J. 2012. "Bringing Books to Life: Psychologists' Research Points to New Ways to Nurture Young Readers." *Monitor on Psychology* 43 (9): 40. American Psychological Association. October 2012. http://www.apa.org/monitor/2012/10/books.aspx.

Davis, A. 2016. *Bone Button Borscht*. Toronto: Kids Can.

de Bondt, M., A. Willenberg, and A. G. Bus. 2020. "Do Book Giveaway Programs Promote the Home Literacy Environment and Children's Literacy-Related Behavior and Skills?" *Review of Educational Research* 90 (3): 349–75. https://doi.org/10.3102/0034654320922140.

Deitcher, H. 2013. "Once Upon a Time: How Jewish Children's Stories Impact Moral Development." *Journal of Jewish Education* 79 (3): 235–55. https://doi.org/10.1080/15244113.2013.814988.

Dickinson, D. K., and A. B. Morse. 2019. *Connecting through Talk: Nurturing Children's Development with Language*. Baltimore: Paul H. Brookes.

Doyle, B. G., and W. Bramwell. 2006. "Promoting Emergent Literacy and Social-Emotional Learning through Dialogic Reading." *Reading Teacher* 59 (6): 554–64. https://doi.org/10.1598/rt.59.6.5.

Flack, Z. M., A. P. Field, and J. S. Horst. 2018. "The Effects of Shared Storybook Reading on Word Learning: A Meta-Analysis." *Developmental Psychology* 54 (7): 1334–46. https://doi.org/10.1037/dev0000512.

Grossman, D. 1988. *Itamar Meets a Rabbit*. [In Hebrew.] Tel Aviv: Am Oved.

Hacham, R. 2018. *Mr. Minasa's Shoes*. [In Hebrew.] Tel Aviv: Agam.

Korat, O., and Y. Falk. 2017. "Ten Years After: Revisiting the Question of e-Book Quality as Early Language and Literacy Support." *Journal of Early Childhood Literacy* 19 (2): 206–23. https://doi.org/10.1177/1468798417712105.

Korat, O., and A. Shamir. 2012. "Direct and Indirect Teaching: Using e-Books for Supporting Vocabulary, Word Reading, and Story Comprehension for Young Children." *Journal of Educational Computing Research* 46 (2): 135–52. https://doi.org/10.2190/ec.46.2.b.

Leppert, K. n.d. "Why You Should Read Aloud to Your Children." Parenting. Accessed October 5, 2020. http://www.parenting.com/article/world-read-aloud-day-march-5.

LitWorld. n.d. "World Read Aloud Day Activity Hub." Accessed October 5, 2020. http://www.litworld.org/wrad.

Ministry of Education. 2015. "Evaluation of Sifriyat Pijama." [In Hebrew.] RAMA Evaluation Division. Accessed October 5, 2020. http://cms.education.gov.il/Education CMS/Units/Rama/HaarachatProjectim/idud_kriaa.htm.

Narvaez, D. 2002. "Does Reading Moral Stories Build Character?" *Educational Psychology Review* 14 (2): 155–71. https://doi.org/10.1023/a:1014674621501.

Neyer, S. L., G. A. Szumlas, and L. M. Vaughn. 2018. "Beyond the Numbers: Social and Emotional Benefits of Participation in the Imagination Library Home-Based Literacy Programme." *Journal of Early Childhood Literacy* 21 (1): 60–81. Sage Journals. November 12, 2008. https://doi.org/10.1177/1468798418810765.

Ofek, U. 2019. *King Solomon and the Bee*. [In Hebrew.] Tel Aviv: Sifriyat Ofer.

Omer, D. 2013. *The Missing Spice*. [In Hebrew.] Tel Aviv: Modan.

Ozturk, G., and S. Hill. 2018. "Mother–Child Interactions during Shared Reading with Digital and Print Books." *Early Child Development and Care* 190,

2020 (9): 1425–40. Taylor Francis Online. November 14, 2018. https://doi.org/10.1080/03004430.2018.1538977.

PJ Library˙. n.d. "About PJ Library." Accessed February 2, 2021. https://pjlibrary.org/about-pj-library.

Preece, J., and R. Levy. 2018. "Understanding the Barriers and Motivations to Shared Reading with Young Children: The Role of Enjoyment and Feedback." *Journal of Early Childhood Literacy* 20 (4): 631–54. https://doi.org/10.1177/1468798418779216.

Primo, R. 2017. *Snow of Dandelions*. [In Hebrew.] Tel Aviv: Yediot.

Santos, H. C., M. E. W. Varnum, and I. Grossmann. 2017. "Global Increases in Individualism." *Psychological Science* 28 (9): 1228–39.

Saracho, O. N. 2017. "Parents' Shared Storybook Reading—Learning to Read." *Early Child Development and Care* 187 (3–4): 554–67. https://doi.org/10.1080/03004430.2016.1261514.

Shem-Tov, T. 2018. *Grandpa Sabih*. [In Hebrew.] Tel Aviv: Kinneret.

Sims Bishop, R. 1990. "Mirrors, Windows, and Sliding Glass Doors." *Perspectives* 1 (3): ix–xi.

Stead, P. 2010. *A Sick Day for Amos McGee*. New York: Roaring Brook.

Triandis, H. C. 1995. *New Directions in Social Psychology: Individualism & Collectivism*. Boulder, CO: Westview.

Troseth, G. L., G. A. Strouse, I. Flores, Z. D. Stuckelman, and C. R. Johnson. 2020. "An Enhanced EBook Facilitates Parent–Child Talk during Shared Reading by Families of Low Socioeconomic Status." *Early Childhood Research Quarterly* 50:45–58. https://doi.org/10.1016/j.ecresq.2019.02.009.

Trousdale, A. M. 2004. "Connections, Concepts, Critiques: Using Children's Literature for Spiritual Development." In *Spirituality and Ethics in Education: Philosophical, Theological, and Cultural Perspectives*, edited by H. A. Alexander, 130–9. East Sussex, UK: Sussex Academic.

Wasik, B. A., A. H. Hindman, and E. K. Snell. 2016. "Book Reading and Vocabulary Development: A Systematic Review." *Early Childhood Research Quarterly* 37:39–57. https://doi.org/10.1016/j.ecresq.2016.04.003.

Yalan-Shteklis, M. 2005. *I Gave a Flower to Nurit*. [In Hebrew.] Tel Aviv: Dvir.

Zelichov-Ralevi, A. 2018. *A Hole in the Ship*. [In Hebrew.] Tel Aviv: Yediot.

9

Holidays and Ceremonies in Israeli Early Childhood Jewish Education

Shulamit Hoshen Manzura

This chapter focuses on the ways in which the holidays are celebrated in Israeli *ganim* (pre-elementary schools for children aged three to six). The suggestions for analysis of the celebrations are based on the author's years of experience as a teacher, counselor, and researcher. This examination of holidays in Israeli early childhood Jewish education (ECJE) is carried out through the prism of ritual practice of ceremonies, celebrations, and processions.

The purpose of the chapter is to present as broad a picture as possible and connect what happens in Israeli early childhood education (ECE) to Israeli society's attitudes toward its holidays and ceremonies. It begins with a short historical survey about celebrating holidays in ganim throughout the past century and then deals with the example of Shavuot (a Jewish festival occurring seven weeks after Passover) as celebrated in the past few decades. It concludes with an examination of the holiday and ceremonies in Israeli ganim in general as a reflection of contemporary Israeli society.

Some of the examples that appear in this chapter are taken from observations and interviews in ganim conducted by students as part of their requirements in courses that the author taught at Oranim College of Education in 2016–18. The use of the database for research and writing was done with the approval of the teachers and the students and according to the ethical codes of the Research and Evaluation Authority at Oranim College.

Historical Background

Prior to Israel's independence and early years as a state, celebrations and rituals were the major educational tools used by the Zionist (belief in the development and protection of Israel) leadership to create an authentic culture that would differ from diaspora culture (Arye-Sapir 2006; Shavit and Sitton 2004; Shoham 2014a,b). The expression "renewed holidays" arose to refer to holidays with a long-standing tradition (e.g., Shavuot and Hanukkah) and to "young" holidays (e.g., *Tu Bishvat*—Jewish Arbor Day) that were adapted to the Zionist ideology. Documents from that time and interviews indicate that the holidays were proclaimed by the Teachers' Council for the

Jewish National Fund (JNF) to strengthen the national identity of Israeli children and, through them, of the public (Arye-Sapir 2006).

For example, during Shavuot, the towns and kibbutzim (a type of communal settlement) would reenact the ceremony of bringing in the *bikkurim* (first harvested fruits, referred to as "first fruits") to the Temple as described in Jewish sources. The first fruits were brought in by schoolchildren and their proceeds given to the JNF. The following describes some related memories of Tel Aviv senior citizens:

> Shavuot was a very big holiday with all the schools coming out with the wreaths, with the First Fruits … At the head of the procession marched the Gymnasia Herzliya student orchestra, and a cart drawn by two oxen carried "all the best" of Mikve Israel [an agricultural school]. (Arye-Sapir 2006, 83)

The national religious movement objected to the transformation of Shavuot, a holiday commemorating *Matan Torah* (the giving of the Torah [the holy scroll containing the Five Books of Moses]), into a secular, national holiday. This had an immediate but partial influence on the educational system by deemphasizing the religious aspect of the holiday. Yet, the impression of the processions of bikurim remained the most significant in the collective memory. It was still vivid in the memories of the Tel Aviv senior citizens, whereas Matan Torah was not even mentioned by them (Arye-Sapir 2006).

Although research on the role of the education system in these processes focuses on elementary and secondary schools, the testimonies we have about ganim in the first half of the twentieth century indicate that young children took part in the school celebrations. A primary source for this comes from testimonies of the first *gananot* (preschool teachers) in the Yishuv (pre-state Israel) (Shchori-Rubin 2002, 2015).

Prior to Israel's independence and during its early years, the traditional cheder (all-boys Jewish schools where only religious studies were taught) continued to operate, including boys from the age of three. At the same time, ganim in the spirit of Pestalozzi, Fröbel, and Montessori were established beginning in 1898. In the fifty years henceforth, until the enactment of the 1949 Israel Compulsory Education Law, ganim became a major cultural agent of the Zionist movement (Dayan 2016; Shchori-Rubin 2002, 2015). Hassia Feinsod-Sukennik (1966) described her goal as a *ganenet* (preschool teacher) and supervisor to unify the different cultures of Israeli-born and immigrant children by having contemporary poets and writers compose poems, stories, and plays in Hebrew about the holidays.

In certain cases, the ganim unintentionally influenced the public, as in the case of *Kabbalat Shabbat* (the ceremony or prayers welcoming the Jewish Sabbath) in the Kibbutz Movements' (a term describing the various kibbutz organizations) ganim in the 1920s and 1930s. The observance of Kabbalat Shabbat by ganim led to a new tradition of celebrating it in the kibbutz dining room, despite serious objections at the time to the introduction of any Jewish ceremonies or symbols into kibbutzim (Horowitz 2016; Marks 2018). A Kibbutz Degania leaflet from this period reads: "Within the kindergarten and school special ceremonies are held … The hurried and preoccupied parents also relish them from afar and are full of longing for Shabbat themselves" (Horowitz 2016, 13).

In ganim of the general and workers' streams, observance of holidays in that period were intended to strengthen national and pioneering values—work, closeness to the land, collectivism, and national solidarity. However, in the programs of the Mizrachi stream (the political religious Zionist movement that was established in 1902), religious traditions were preserved at the same time these *ganim* applied modern progressive educational approaches (Arye-Sapir 2006; Steinberger 2013). (For a description of these streams of Israeli education in existence prior to 1953, see Chapter 1 of this book.) For instance, in the religious Zionist Ohel Yaakov ECE network, established in 1933, Shavuot is described thus:

> While all kindergartens in the city attended the First Fruits ceremony, Ohel Yaakov in Jerusalem decided to celebrate the holiday differently, in a manner that would illustrate the meaning of the holiday signifying Matan Torah. On the eve of Shavuot, the kindergarten children visited the Chief Rabbis ... Following the visit, the kindergarten children went on to the Central Yeshurun Synagogue ... and they were shown the Torah scrolls. (Steinberger 2013, 311)

An interesting example of the tension between the different streams in Jewish society during that period is the change that took place in the celebration of holidays in the religious kibbutzim. These kibbutzim belonged both to religious society and to the secular Kibbutz Movement. During the 1940s and 1950s, for a period of about fifteen years, the main objective of religious kibbutzim was to celebrate the agricultural aspect of holidays alongside full observance of Jewish law. However, the voices opposing these agricultural celebrations, such as the reenactment ceremony of bringing first fruits on Shavuot and the Omer (wheat harvest) on Passover, prevailed, and these celebrations gradually faded due to religious opposition to their secular character (Fishman 1990).

The effect of the renewed-holiday trend was also evident during the 1970s and 1980s. Studies about celebrations in state secular ganim reveal nationalism to be the main component both in collective events, such as holidays and commemorative days, as well as in celebrations where individuals and their families were supposedly centered, such as birthdays and Mother's Day. As an agent of culture, the teacher was perceived to be at the top of the hierarchy. She or he led all the ceremony's participants, children and parents alike, in accordance with the ceremony's program, which reconfirmed and strengthened values, ideology, and social hierarchies (Furman 1994; Shamgar-Handelman and Handelman 1986, 1991).

Ceremonies and Holidays in Ganim in the Twenty-First Century

In all types of ECJE in Israel for children aged three through six, Jewish time constitutes a central axis in educational planning: the Hebrew yearly and monthly cycles, the center of which are the holidays, and the weekly cycle, the climax of which is Shabbat. All of the Jewish educational streams—state, state-religious, and

Haredi (ultra-Orthodox)—build their programs in this way (for a description of these educational streams created in 1953, see Chapter 1 of this book). This cultural infrastructure common to almost all ganim is a unique Israeli characteristic in ECE, which so far has been studied only in the context of a certain stream or a certain event (Ben-Nun 2008; Gluschankof 2011; Manzura 2010; Yaffe and Rapoport 2013).

In addition to the common characteristic of educational planning around the Jewish time axis, there is integration of ritual practice to one degree or another. The ritual naturally increases the learning experience through senses and emotions and intensifies its effect on the children, as well as having the potential for cross-generational transfer. According to Bell (1997), rituals organize the passing of time and give it social meaning. An interesting example of cultural structuring of time can be seen in ultra-Orthodox ECE, where the gender messages conveyed in the rituals are intended to preserve the values of ultra-Orthodox society, such as can be seen in the significant differences between birthday celebrations of boys and girls (Manzura 2010; Yaffe 2004).

Beyond these shared characteristics that create "familial similarity" (Ben-Rafael and Ben-Chaim 2006), there are great differences among ganim as to how they relate to holiday content and practices. The difference depends on the educational stream (e.g., the centrality of the biblical text with regard to Shabbat and holidays in ultra-Orthodox and religious education), the cultural location (e.g., the emphasis given in holiday activities to the context of physical and social environments in rural programs), and the educational approach of policy leaders and teachers and their personal connection to the topic.

While some holidays are celebrated in all early childhood (EC) programs (Rosh Hashanah, Passover, Hanukkah, and Purim), others are undergoing changes in hierarchy following shifts in attitudes toward them in Israeli society (Shoham 2014b). For instance, Yom Kippur (Day of Atonement), a major holiday in ultra-Orthodox and religious education, is changing character and gaining importance in many state ganim, while Jerusalem Day (a national Israeli holiday celebrating the unification of Jerusalem after the 1967 War) has undergone the opposite process over the past decade and is mostly celebrated in religious Zionist programs and only in some state ganim. The *Sigd* (a holiday of Ethiopian Jews) is undergoing yet another process, turning from a holiday celebrated only by Ethiopian Jewry into one celebrated in many educational programs, while remaining completely unknown in others.

The attitude toward Independence Day in ganim is an interesting example of cultural diversity in Israeli society. In most ultra-Orthodox ganim, there is no marking of national holidays, such as days of remembrance (for Holocaust martyrs, fallen soldiers, and victims of terror) and Independence Day. In state ganim, Independence Day is celebrated as a secular national holiday, unlike most other holidays, which include a religious aspect. On the other hand, most state-religious programs view this day as both a national and a religious holiday, combining singing *Hatikva* (the Israeli national anthem) with saying the Hallel (liturgy praising the Lord).

The attitude toward Shabbat is also diverse. Friday practices usually reflect and reconfirm the old order that preserves religious traditions, but sometimes a new order is established that challenges conventional hegemony. In many ganim, the Friday practice includes the baking of challah bread and cakes and a festive gathering. At one end of the continuum, one can find Kabbalat Shabbat rituals characterized by many significant traditional symbols, most of which carry social gender messages through the roles of "father" and "mother" of Shabbat. These rituals take place in ultra-Orthodox ganim (Manzura 2010; Yaffe 2004) and in state-religious programs (Manzura 2007), but also in many state ganim with mostly traditional or secular populations (Yaffe and Rapoport 2013). At the other end of the continuum, the Oranim College research revealed Kabbalat Shabbat rituals with very few traditional symbols and with no mention of any traditional blessing, in addition to no gender division of roles. Instead, the rituals emphasize the values of nature, family, rest, and so on. Some of these ceremonies have a spiritual orientation, as in some anthroposophical programs, while others have a secular orientation, as in many kibbutz ganim.

Shavuot as a Case Study

The descriptions of celebrating the holiday of Shavuot that follow are from seven ECJE programs. Two are from research literature (Furman 1994; Yaffe 2004), one from an interview the author conducted with a ganenet, and four from the Oranim College research. They illustrate a wide range of perceptions regarding celebrating the holiday, reflecting the variety of attitudes toward it during Israel's pre-independence period and early years of statehood—from observing Shavuot as Matan Torah, according to Jewish tradition, to celebrating it as a national holiday focused on the harvest and first fruits.

At One End—Celebrating the Giving of the Torah

A Shavuot Ceremony in an Ultra-Orthodox Program for Girls Aged Five to Six

The girls, in white blouses and blue skirts, are wearing identical paper crowns adorned with images of Mount Sinai, the Tablets of the Covenant, and the inscription "Matan Torah." They start the day by walking to the synagogue and listen to the voices of men studying Torah in the adjacent room. Then, differing from custom, each one of them steps forward to kiss the Torah scroll in the open Holy Ark and make a wish out loud. In the gan party after their return, they eat dairy food, which, according to their teacher, symbolizes the revelation at Mount Sinai. The girls sing some songs about the Torah and then dance, following the teacher's instruction to imagine they are holding Torah scrolls.

This ceremony (Yaffe 2004) addresses only the commemoration of Matan Torah. All parts of the practice are designed to form a memory that joins together the past (the revelation at Mount Sinai) and the present (the men studying Torah). Through this holiday ceremony and others, for example, Simchat Torah (a holiday celebrating the annual completion of reading the Torah scroll), Kabbalat Shabbat, and so on, the perceived message is: We belong to the nation that received the Torah. Yet studying the Torah and dancing with Torah scrolls is for boys only (Manzura 2010; Yaffe 2004).

A Shavuot Ceremony with Eight Secular State Ganim Taking Part

Unlike the previous ultra-Orthodox ceremony, this one includes a procession of children with first fruits. However, this is marginal and not mentioned in the main event, which was in fact devoted totally to Matan Torah. In addition, the complex gender message that characterized the ultra-Orthodox ceremony is also present in this multi-participant celebration. It was shared that after "the important man who was supposed to come never showed up," a female teacher opened the Holy Ark herself but still said, "A woman is not allowed to open and touch a Torah scroll. In fact, a woman is not allowed to be here." She took out a Torah scroll but quickly put it back when she was told that the rabbi was coming (Furman 1994, 169–71). This illustrates the discrepancy between the religious symbols and norms the female teacher wishes to teach the children and the performative actions she is taking by standing before them in the main section of the synagogue, which is the men's section.

At the Other End—Celebrating with First Fruits

A Waldorf Program for Children Aged Four through Seven in an Agricultural Settlement

The preparation throughout the month preceding the holiday is dedicated to harvesting the wheat that has grown in the gan yard, preparing the flour, and baking bread. On the day of the celebration, the children, dressed in white, are adding greenery to decorate shelves on which they will place the fruit baskets they have prepared at home. The children set the long feast table, around which all the children and staff members will sit. The ceremony is the peak of the holiday activity, beginning with a first fruits procession into the gan and the placing of baskets on the shelves. The ceremony involves a unique adaptation of the story of the first fruits being brought to the Temple, blessings, songs, and tastings of symbolic holiday food. The Temple is referred to as "a holy, illuminated place," and the teacher recites the blessings ("Thank you sun, rain, land and God!") that represent the ideology of the gan.

The teacher explained in the interview, "For me the Temple is not a religious place, rather a symbol of plenty, of light and sanctity." In this way she chooses the elements that are suitable for the place and for the gan's approach, with the purpose of creating a spiritual and emotional experience. There is no mention of anything related to the Mount Sinai revelation, Matan Torah, or the Jewish people. The holiday is stripped of all historical, religious, national, communal, and cultural contexts and becomes a story with symbolic-mythical, out-of-time meanings.

A State Secular Gan for Children Aged Four through Six in a Moshava (Privatized Farming Community Established in the Pre-Israeli State)

As part of the preparations for Shavuot, the children build a model Western Wall (remnant of the ancient Temple) out of cubes. (The teacher explained in the interview that the reason for this was that Jerusalem was the annual topic chosen by the Ministry of Education and, therefore, the celebration this year was different than usual.) The children, wearing festive clothes for the occasion and carrying wreaths of greenery prepared at home, decorate the gan with them and set the tables. Afterward they come in from the yard with their fruit baskets in a procession, singing. They place the baskets on the tables and sit in a circle near the tables to present the bringing of the first fruits. As preparation, they divide themselves into two groups: priests and first fruit bearers. The priests put on cloaks and stand by the "Western Wall," while the first fruit bearers march around the tables until they reach the Wall and hand their baskets to the priests. Finally, they all dance with tambourines and drums and sit down at the tables for a dairy meal. Unlike the Waldorf teacher, this teacher gives her students the historical and religious background of the first fruits, mostly due to the commitment to the yearly topic. There is no mention of traditional blessings during the meal and there is no reference to Matan Torah.

And in Between—Celebrating First Fruits and Also Marking Matan Torah

A State Secular Gan for Children Aged Three and Four in an Immigrant Absorption Town

In this case, the special shared food (rather than personal food boxes) marks the uniqueness of the occasion. The children bring flower wreaths, a kiddush (sanctification of wine) goblet, two candlesticks, and a central basket with fruit and stalks of wheat. They enter the room from the yard, carrying their own baskets, singing, and walking around the table. The procession around the table continues with several stops. In one of them, the teacher lights the candles and says the traditional blessing for lighting the holiday candles. After another walk around the table, she mentions the holiday names learned in the preceding weeks and their significance. Matan Torah is marked, she says, "because the children of Israel received the Torah at Mount Sinai." The children continue to walk around the table singing, and the teacher tells them about the city of Jerusalem being a holy city and the ancient custom of pilgrimage made three times a year. Finally, the children lay their baskets on the table and sit down. They all say the traditional blessing over grape juice, and the meal begins. The centrality of the first fruits celebration and pilgrimage is conveyed through the prolonged walking done by the children throughout most of the ceremony. Matan Torah and Mount Sinai are mentioned only in passing.

A State Secular Gan for Children Aged Three and Four in a Moshav (Settlement with Individually Owned Farms or Businesses That Share Some Communal Aspects)

Prior to the holiday, each of the routine walks outside is dedicated to searching for one of the "seven species" that were traditionally brought to the ancient Temple as first fruits. In addition, various activities are carried out around each of the species, such as grinding wheat grains with a pestle and mortar.

On the day of the celebration the children arrive dressed in white, with a wreath made of branches and flowers and a fruit basket. The ceremony is conducted with the children and staff sitting around a long table and, as in the previous example, is accompanied by songs and explanations about why the holiday is named what it is. They eat a meal of dairy products and fruit, and the teacher recites some traditional blessings over the food. In the interview, the teacher explained, "The children are not 'close to faith' and neither am I … but you have to give them a bit of a holy atmosphere. At Kabbalat Shabbat we also say the blessings … It's important to expose them to that."

Programs combining the first fruits holiday with Matan Torah, such as in these two examples, characterize 70 percent of the Shavuot programs described by gananot in Dori's (2019) study, which examined the attitude of state secular gananot toward Kabbalat Shabbat, holidays, and Bible stories.

And Also—Celebrating Matan Torah and Hinting at First Fruits

A State-Religious Gan for Children Aged Four through Six in a Religious Kibbutz

Sometime before Shavuot the teacher tells the children the story of the Book of Ruth, although the focus is on the revelation at Mount Sinai and the Ten Commandments. Like for other holiday preparations, their daily walk is to the synagogue, which is now (only for this holiday) decorated with green branches. One of the children's father or grandfather is already waiting for them inside the synagogue. He takes a Torah scroll out of the Holy Ark and reads the Ten Commandments, which the children have heard in stories at the gan and which they will hear again with their parents in the synagogue the following day. On their way back to the gan, the teacher looks for seven-species trees and the children pick up branches to decorate the gan "like in the synagogue." She says that "at the end of the day, sometimes all the ganim get together to sing Shavuot songs, and the kibbutz rabbi comes to teach them a bit of Torah."

The holiday celebration in this gan is focused on Matan Torah and not on first fruits. According to the teacher, to be historically precise, Shavuot is the wheat harvest holiday in which a sacrifice of wheat was brought into the Temple, while the first fruits were brought to the Temple between Shavuot and Sukkot (one of the three biblical holidays celebrated by building huts). She claims that in the gan they grind wheat grains and make flour after witnessing the wheat harvest. In the period between Shavuot and Sukkot, during daily walks, some gananot in religious kibbutzim additionally tell the children about bringing the first fruits into the Temple, mark the first fruits trees they come across with a ribbon, and talk about "a first pomegranate and a first fig," a reference to the Mishna (the first major written collection of the Jewish oral traditions) passage relevant to the holiday.

Unlike in the previous examples, the emphasis in this program, similar to those in other ganim in religious kibbutzim, is on the holiday experience in the context of the community and its customs (Hoshen Manzura and Achituv, forthcoming). Although nature and agriculture are central to the gan experience, in this example, Matan Torah is the heart of Shavuot and the first fruit from the seven species is only hinted at through decorative greenery. In contrast to the other examples presented, there is no special ritual before the holiday.

The Different Uses of Symbols and Ceremony

The different use made in the various ganim of key physical symbols (e.g., wreaths, challah breads, candles, fruit baskets) reflects their power to enfold and summarize the complex meanings of the various practices (Ortner 1973). For example, in relation to the common use of a wreath and a crown, they serve in various transition ceremonies to emphasize a change of hierarchy of the main participant, such as a crown in a coronation or a veil on a bride. However, in Shavuot gan ceremonies, the wreath and the crown serve as socialization agents to strengthen the sense of solidarity and collectivity. The individual green wreaths made by the children and their parents in some cases symbolize the first fruits holiday and highlight nature and national values, whereas the identical crowns on all the girls' heads in the case of the ultra-Orthodox gan symbolize Matan Torah, serving to highlight religious values and emphasize the collective.

Another difference between ganim is the teacher's choice of ceremony: high or low (Henry 1992; Maloney 2000). In most ganim the holiday ceremonies are essentially high-ritual. They have a certain style, are relatively fixed, are filled with meaningful symbols, and provide a climax to an emotionally stirring event. However, in the religious kibbutzim programs, the practices prior to the holidays have low-ritual characteristics. They are part of the routine of the gan and more functional than symbolic.

The Gan as a Reflection of Jewish-Israeli Society

To what extent do holidays and ceremonies in Israeli EC programs reflect Israeli Jewish society? In some cases, the holiday reflects the customs and way of life familiar to the children from their families and surroundings. In other cases, the celebration of the holiday remains solely in the framework of the gan. In many cases, it seems that the messages the children receive at home and in the gan differ and are even contradictory in aspects such as religion, gender, and so forth.

According to Fruman (2004), in the case of the secular public today, the holidays have completely lost both the religious and the national Zionist aspect. A new hierarchy has formed in which some of the more "national" holidays are perceived as "children's holidays" that do not go beyond the boundaries of the educational system. By contrast, other holidays that are celebrated among the secular public (e.g., Passover and Hanukkah) fulfill secular functions of esthetics, family, ecology, and a sense of identity with the Jewish collective but are completely empty of the meanings of the past and are moving from the public to the family sphere. In this secular public, liberal democratic values have replaced Jewish tradition as a source of national cohesion, and individual autonomy and freedom have replaced common social values (Almog 2004).

It could be concluded from this that in the secular population, in many cases the children move between the educational framework and their homes in parallel cultural lines that hardly ever meet. This conclusion seems reasonable in view of studies examining issues in Israeli society, in general, and the educational system, in particular, in terms of social rifts, power struggles, and educational work that is a direct product of state mechanisms (Azariahu 1995; Gur 2005; Nasie and Bar-Tal 2020). However, other studies, based on, among other sources, the third Guttman Report (Arian and Keisar-Sugerman 2012), indicate that a complete loss of religious and national aspects does not characterize the majority of the "secular public" in an era that Shenhav (2018) has called "post-secular." The picture that emerges from that 2009 Guttman report is that of a scale. At each end is a group of respondents who defined themselves as either "religious" (including ultra-Orthodox) or "secular" as to beliefs, practices, and group affiliation. At the center of the scale is a very large group—more than half of the respondents—with a huge variety of and all possible intersections between religious and secular beliefs and practices and a variety of forms of community affiliations, through which the respondents defined their place with regard to religious and secular sectors (Shoham 2014a, 38).

Following this approach, it can be seen that in recent decades a new Jewish culture has formed to be the majority group and mainstream of Israeli culture, independent and separate from other Jewish cultures and yet connected to them. This is neither a religious nor a secular culture, but a Jewish culture containing religious and secular elements, which conducts a cultural exchange with other Jewish cultures in Israel. A main feature of this new culture is free, personal acceptance of symbols, holidays, and ceremonies (Arian and Keisar-Sugerman 2012; Ben-Rafael and Ben-Chaim 2006; Rosner and Fuchs 2018; Wolf 2019).

The picture emerging from the examples described here of holiday celebrations in ganim reflects Israeli Jewish society with a secular majority with strong ties to tradition:

> The religious lives of Israeli Jews, in belief and in practice, are far from being governed by the religious establishment. The Israeli Jews usually pick components of the tradition according to their preference, and even the meaning of these beliefs and practices to them is not necessarily in line with Orthodox interpretation. They do not identify with the religious group … but that is not out of principled objection to religion in its entirety as a content world, but because the modern era allows them to personally choose what they want out of religion, according to their educational, cultural, political, economic, psychological needs, etc. (Shoham 2014a, 35)

Regarding parts of the secular public that are opposed to integrating Jewish aspects into public life and the educational system, it is safe to say that they are not well represented among ECJE teachers. In Dori's (2019) study, most participants reported they were teaching religious values out of their own free will and not out of an obligation imposed by the system, just as the gananot chose how to relate to the national holidays according to their free will (Ben-Nun 2008).

The views of a kibbutz ganenet interviewed in the Oranim College research are in accord with Dori's findings:

> The very fact that we put on special clothes, and the very fact that we made challah breads already made us feel that this was a very special and holy day … Of course, I would like to have Friday as a day off, but on the other hand I say that in the secular

society I live in, there is no one else to convey this message ... My role on Friday is the most important one.

In Conclusion

It is important also to observe the various holiday practices from the perspective of the pedagogical culture in Israel. How autonomous ECJE teachers consider themselves to be in planning holiday ceremonies is a factor of the degree and style of supervision within the educational stream for which they work; differences in their individual personalities; and the religious, social, and educational ideologies that motivate them.

The teachers who rely on traditional methods of education refer to holiday practice as one unbreakable unit whose components are interdependent. In this way, the ceremonies are fixed and identical throughout the years and loaded with symbols, regardless of the backgrounds of the children, parents, and educational staff. The accepted view of practice in this case is that there is an appropriate model for Shabbat and the holidays, and the children should learn about that ideal.

In contrast, at the constructivist end of the scale, we find the ECJE teachers with autonomous perceptions and awareness of their role as the designers of objectives and work methods. They seek to create a blend of old and new traditions, while trying to examine deeper meanings. This blend is unique, flexible, and attentive to the needs and initiatives of the gan community—the children, their families, the educational staff, and the surrounding community. Awareness of the pedagogical, religious, gender, and cultural aspects of the holidays and their effect on shaping identities in EC plays an important role in how these gananot think about their practices (Haas, Manzura, and Gavish 2007; Schweid 1984, 1996; Scully and Howell 2008).

In the introduction to their book *Israeli Judaism: A Portrait of a Cultural Revolution*, Rosner and Fuchs present Israel as a startup venture, which they refer to as "a future for the Jewish people in a national state" (2018, 10). They state that like any startup venture, "the idea exists—but the product is still under development." The research presented in this chapter demonstrates that Israeli ganim are active agents in this startup venture— "incubators" of a variety of approaches toward the holiday ceremonies and rituals of the next generation. As such, ECJE in Israel is of the utmost importance.

References

Almog, O. 2004. *Saying Farewell to Srulik: A Change in the Values in the Israeli Elite*. [In Hebrew.] Haifa: University of Haifa and Zmora Bitan.

Arian, A., and A. Keisar-Sugarman. 2012. *Israeli Jews—a Portrait: Beliefs, Observing Tradition and Values of Jews in Israel 2009*. [In Hebrew.] Jerusalem: Guttman Institute and Israel Democracy Institute. Accessed March 30, 2021. https://www.bac.org.il/content/sites/bac/flash/isrelity/data/Gutman-Report.pdf.

Arye-Sapir, N. 2006. "The Shaping of Urban Culture and Education: The Stories of Ceremonies and Celebrations in Tel Aviv in the Early Years." [In Hebrew.] *Dor*

Ledor: Anthologies of Research and Documentation of the History of Jewish Education in Israel and in the Diaspora 36:201–13.

Azariahu, M. 1995. *State Rituals: Celebrations of Independence and Commemoration of the Fallen 1948–1956*. [In Hebrew.] Beersheva: Ben-Gurion University.

Bell, C. 1997. *Ritual, Perspectives and Dimensions*. Oxford: Oxford University Press.

Ben-Nun, N. 2008. "Mindsets and Attitudes of Kindergarten Teachers about Independence Day in the Kindergarten." [In Hebrew.] MA diss., Hebrew University of Jerusalem.

Ben-Rafael, E., and L. Ben-Chaim Rafael. 2006. "Contemporary Jewish Identities: Still One People?" [In Hebrew.] *Iyunim Be-Tekumat Israel* 16:463–98.

Dayan, Y. 2016. "The Invention of Kindergarten from Friedrich Fröbel to the Hebrew Kindergarten." [In Hebrew.] *Bema'agali Hinuch* 6:124–34. https://www.dyellin.ac.il/sites/default/files/journals/journaleducation/edition6/yaeldayan-7.pdf.

Dori, N. 2019. "Educating Jewish Values in State Kindergartens." [In Hebrew.] *Atar Daat* 15:1–15.

Feinsod-Sukennik, H. 1966. *Chapters on Kindergarten: Memories and Actions*. [In Hebrew.] Tel Aviv: Otzar Hamore.

Fishman, A. 1990. *Between Religion and Ideology: Judaism and Modernization on the Religious Kibbutz*. [In Hebrew.] Jerusalem: Yad Ben-Zvi.

Fruman, R. 2004. "What Do They Do on Holidays? The Secular and the Jewish Holidays." In *Unbelievable: A Different Look at Religion and Secularism*, edited by A. Kleinberg, 205–63. [In Hebrew.] Tel Aviv: Keter.

Furman, M. 1994. *Childhood as a Concoction: Violence and Obedience in Early Childhood*. [In Hebrew.] Tel Aviv: Hakibbutz Hameuchad.

Gluschankof, K. 2011. "Hanukkah Online: Continuity and Change in Kindergarten Hanukkah Parties as Expressed in YouTube Videos." [In Hebrew.] *Hokrim@GilHarach* 1:28–47. https://kindergarten.levinsky.ac.il/wp-content/uploads/sites/13/2018/01/HanukkahOnNetClaudia.pdf.

Gur, H. 2005. *Militarization in Education*. [In Hebrew.] Tel Aviv: Babel.

Haas, M., S. Manzura, and Z. Gavish. 2007. "A Cardboard Shofar: Jewish Identity Is Shaped during Early Childhood." [In Hebrew.] *Hed Hagan* 2:40–5.

Henry, M. E. 1992. "School Rituals as Educational Contexts: The World, Others, and Self in Waldorf and College Prep Schools." *Qualitative Studies in Education* 5 (4): 295–309.

Horowitz, R. 2016. "The Place of Religion and Tradition in Kibbutz Settlement: Kabbalat Shabbat as a Test Case." [In Hebrew.] Seminar paper presented at Bar Ilan University, Ramat Gan, Israel.

Hoshen Manzura, S., and S. Achituv. Forthcoming. "The Kindergarten in the Religious Kibbutzim." In *Early Childhood Education: A Pedagogical Tradition at Oranim College*. [In Hebrew.]

Maloney, C. 2000. "The Role of Ritual in Preschool Settings." *Early Childhood Education Journal* 27 (3): 143–50.

Manzura, S. 2007. "The Kindergarten as a Social Mirror: The 'Glass Ceiling' in the Religious Kindergarten." In *To Be a Jewish Woman: Proceedings of the Fourth International Conference on "A Woman and Her Judaism,"* edited by T. Chen, 207–17. [In Hebrew.] Jerusalem: Kolech—Religious Women's Forum.

Manzura, S. 2010. "Ritual and Text in the Context of Holiness: Ways of Establishing Gender Identity of Boys and Girls Ages Two to Five in Ultra-Orthodox Preschools." [In Hebrew.] PhD diss., Hebrew University of Jerusalem.

Marks, D. 2018. "Kabbalat Shabbat on the Kibbutz: Secular Religiosity." [In Hebrew.] *Jerusalem Studies on Jewish Folklore* 31:93–134.
Nasie, M., and D. Bar-Tal. 2020. "Political Socialization in Kindergartens: Observations of Ceremonies of the Israeli Jewish Holidays and Memorial Days." *European Journal of Social Psychology* 50:685–700.
Ortner, S. B. 1973. "On Key Symbols." *American Anthropologist* 75 (4): 1338–46.
Rosner, S., and K. Fuchs. 2018. *Israeli Judaism: A Portrait of a Cultural Revolution*. [In Hebrew.] Jerusalem: Dvir and Institute for Jewish People's Policy.
Schweid, E. 1984. *The Goal of Appointed Times: The Meaning of Jewish Holidays*. [In Hebrew.] Tel Aviv: Am Oved.
Schweid, E. 1996. *Zionism in a Post-Modernistic Era*. [In Hebrew.] Jerusalem: Hasifria Hazionit.
Scully, P., and J. Howell. 2008. "Using Rituals and Traditions to Create Classroom Community for Children, Teachers, and Parents." *Early Childhood Education* 36:266–1.
Shamgar-Handelman, L., and D. Handelman. 1986. "Holiday Celebrations in Israeli Kindergartens: Relationships between Representations of Collectivity and Family in the Nation State." In *Political Anthropology—the Reality of Authority*, edited by V. M. Aronoff, 71–103. New Brunswick: Oxford.
Shamgar-Handelman, L., and D. Handelman. 1991. "Celebrations of Bureaucracy: Birthday Parties in Israeli Kindergartens." *Ethnology* 30 (4): 293–312.
Shavit, Y., and S. Sitton. 2004. *Staging and Stagers in Modern Jewish Palestine: The Creation of Festive Lore in a New Culture, 1882–1948*. Detroit: Wayne State University Press.
Shchori-Rubin, Z. 2002. "Hebrew Kindergarten Teachers during the Period of the First and Second Aliya." [In Hebrew.] *Dor Ledor: Anthologies of Research and Documentation of the History of Jewish Education in Israel and in the Diaspora* 19:129–39.
Shchori-Rubin, Z. 2015. "The Story of the Kindergarten in the Land of Israel." [In Hebrew.] *Cathedra* 153 (Tishrei): 170–5.
Shenhav, Y. 2018. "A Heaven Empty of Angels: The Debate on Increasing Religiosity under the Canopy of Protestant Ethics." [In Hebrew.] *Soziologia Israelit* 19 (2): 1–22.
Shoham, H. 2014a. "Religion, Secularity and Tradition in Public Thought in Israel." [In Hebrew.] *Studies on the Resurrection of Israel* 24:29–58.
Shoham, H. 2014b. *Let's Celebrate a Holiday: Holidays and Civil Culture in Israel*. [In Hebrew.] Jerusalem: Israel Institute for Democracy.
Steinberger, P. 2013. "We Thought of a Plan in a Land of Israel Ambience—Ohel Yaakov Kindergartens: The First Religious-Zionist Network of Kindergartens in the Land of Israel, 1933–1978." [In Hebrew.] *Dor Ledor: Anthologies of Research and Documentation of the History of Jewish Education in Israel and in the Diaspora* 44:285–325.
Wolf, G. 2019. "Not on Sociology Alone Will Judaism Live." [In Hebrew.] *Hashiloach* 18:191–202.
Yaffe, O. 2004. "Being an Ultra-Orthodox Girl: Practices of Socialization, Pedagogical Discourse and Structuring the Self." [In Hebrew.] PhD diss., Hebrew University of Jerusalem.
Yaffe, O., and T. Rapoport. 2013. "On Education and Secularity—Kabbalat Shabbat in the Non-religious Kindergarten in Israel." In *A Close-Up Look at the Class and the School: Ethnographic Studies on Education*, edited by B. Alpert and S. Shlasky, 231–71. [In Hebrew.] Tel Aviv: MOFET Institute (Hebrew).

10

Language-Conducive Strategies in Young Learners' Constructivist Hebrew Classrooms

Margalit Kavenstock and Mila Schwartz

Hebrew is a curricular cornerstone in the early childhood (EC) Jewish classroom. This chapter analyzes teachers' language-conducive strategies implemented to create a constructivist learning environment in Hebrew language teaching. It gives voice to four EC teachers who teach children aged four through six in three Jewish day schools in New York City that offer full-day programs for ages two through middle and high school.

The chapter begins by describing the current status of Hebrew in Jewish day schools in the United States and then briefly introduces three main theoretical concepts: a constructivist approach to additional language (hereafter L2) teaching and learning, Gass and Mackey's (2007) input-interaction-output hypothesis, and language-conducive strategies (Schwartz 2018). These theoretical underpinnings are then illustrated through data obtained from examples of teaching Hebrew as L2 at three EC settings in New York City. The chapter closes with conclusions and field implications of this study.

By exploring how EC teachers create a constructivist learning context in their Hebrew classroom, what language-conducive strategies they apply, and how they reflect on these strategies, we hope to give EC Hebrew teachers a voice and a professional horizon to strive for, as well as to open up an important discussion on the quality of Hebrew teaching for young learners in the United States, an area that has largely not been explored in prior research.

Theoretical Background

Current Status of Hebrew in Jewish Day Schools in the United States

Contemporary research of Hebrew in Jewish day schools largely addresses kindergarten as part of the lower elementary school and ignores younger children learning on the same campus. Therefore, we have chosen to present here representative conclusions from the report "Hebrew for What? Hebrew at the Heart of Jewish Day Schools" (Pomson and Wertheimer 2017), "Hebrew Learning Ideologies and the Reconceptualization of American Judaism" (Avni 2016), and "Becoming Connected to Israel through Hebrew: Promising New Evidence" (Pomson and Ringvald 2021). Although not specifically addressing early childhood education (ECE), each one gives a different perspective on the position of contemporary Hebrew in Jewish education in the United States.

Pomson and Wertheimer (2017, 50) state:

> Hebrew unquestionably remains a pre-eminent component of current day school education, both for existential and functional reasons. Hebrew is not a heritage language as well as it is not a foreign language but rather a language of "social significance" associated with the Jewish community and its emotional and cultural values.

Avni (2016) states that increasingly American Jewish educators see in Modern Hebrew (also known as Israeli Hebrew) an important vehicle through which American Jews can build and strengthen ties with the land of Israel, Israeli society, and Israeli Jews. Therefore, many day schools, as well as informal programs, focus on the acquisition of Modern Hebrew.

Pomson and Ringvald (2021), in their research on young Hebrew learners in a summer camp program, note that "when children study Hebrew, they *become* [original emphasis] connected to Israel. Hebrew 'opens a window' onto Israeli culture and values. Hebrew helps cultivate an intimate relationship with Israel."

In the past decade, Jewish day schools have been rethinking the goals and quality of Hebrew teaching. Hebrew teachers in many schools had not learned how to teach an additional language, as well as lacking academic training for teaching children aged three through six. With the establishment of the Hebrew School at Middlebury College, in 2008, the process of academization of Hebrew and training teachers gained momentum, although the field of teaching Hebrew in ECE remains relatively marginal in terms of both training and research.

Constructivism and L2 Teaching

Constructivism has a wide range of implications for both research and pedagogical practice. Within the social constructivist perspective, the focus of knowledge is not on the teacher but rather on the learners and how they construct knowledge on their own while the teacher facilitates and monitors learners' development. According to Lowenthal and Muth (2008), social constructivists suppose that learning occurs through construction of meaning in social interaction within cultures and through language. Social constructivism in the classroom is rooted in Vygotsky's (1978) sociocultural theory, which views the child as first doing things in a social context, helped in various ways by other people (parents, teachers, peers) and language, and eventually shifting away from reliance on others to independent thinking and action.

Whenever the child is supported by other people in constructing his or her learning, it happens within a "zone of proximal development" (ZPD), defined by Vygotsky as "the distance between the actual developmental level as determined by independent problem solving and the level of potential development as determined through problem solving under adult guidance or in cooperation with more capable peers" (1978, 86).

Fromkin and Rodman (1993) stated that each individual speaker constructs his or her own understanding of L2, which, in turn, will be modified and evaluated by comparison with other speakers of the language. Nelson (1996), focusing on language acquisition in EC, emphasized the key role of interaction in the language-learning process. Thus, learning a foreign language in a constructivist point of view is an individual construction of meaning that is interrelated with collaboration and interaction with a native speaker or the teacher.

Constructivism is based on five core principles: learner centeredness, individualization and autonomy of learning, social interaction as learning is mediation, process-related awareness, and holistic language experience (Brooks and Brooks 1999). These principles should be reflected in classroom practice and are applicable to L2 learning (through all levels and skills). Brooks and Brooks (1999) and Kaufman and Brooks (1996) have identified some general characteristics that have been observed about teachers in constructivist classrooms, noting that they do the following:

1. Use raw data and primary sources, along with manipulative, interactive, and physical materials
2. When framing tasks, use cognitive terminology such as classify, analyze, predict, create, and so on
3. Allow student thinking to drive lessons, shift instructional strategies, or alter content, based on student responses
4. Inquire about students' understandings of concepts before sharing their own
5. Ask students open-ended questions and encourage them to ask others
6. Seek elaboration of students' initial responses

In the classroom, language teachers function not only as a source of knowledge but also as a model of children's linguistic behavior in L2 learning (Kozulin et al. 2003). They use elicitation as a scaffolding strategy, which encourages children's target language production and usage of its correct forms during natural conversational interaction with teachers and peers (Lightbown and Spada 2017). To elicit language production, the teacher uses the child's word and then develops verbal constructions to expand and extend his or her L2 production or offers the beginning of an utterance and asks the child to complete it.

The teacher scaffolding strategies presented here highlight the importance of the quality of teaching and teacher–child interaction during novel language learning. This factor plays a critical role in L2 learning, in particular in a preschool educational context, since the "teachers' starting point is the children's essential need to be understood, and regardless of the language they use" (Schwartz 2018, 3). It is notable as well that a substantial number of studies have focused on these scaffolding strategies in L2 teaching in secondary and high-school classrooms. However, knowledge on how teachers realize scaffolding in EC classrooms is still rather limited: Examples of studies that have been done include Gort and Pontier (2013) and Schwartz and Gorbatt (2017). This chapter aims to contribute to this knowledge.

Input-Interaction-Output Hypothesis

In the early 1980s, the research area of L2 learning was dominated by the comprehensible input hypothesis (Krashen 1984). Krashen claimed that "we acquire language in only one way: when we understand messages in that language, when we receive comprehensible input" (61). Later, following her studies of French immersion students, Swain found that even in a case of massive longitudinal L2 input, L2 French learners in Canada showed unexpectedly low speaking and writing abilities. In this regard, Swain (2005) asserted that "output," meaning an act of target language production, is an action that is crucial for learning a novel language. Furthermore, VanPatten (2003) claimed that substantial exposure to input has a critical role in the way learners create linguistic systems that serves as the basis for acquisition and output in L2 with communicative intent.

Later, Gass, and Mackey (2007) analyzed previous research, which resulted in their emphasizing the centrality of interaction in L2 learning. They proposed the input-interaction-output hypothesis to describe the L2 development process. Communication held in L2 engenders negotiation of meaning that helps L2 users become attentive to how effective they are in the attempt to convey messages. This attentiveness is critical to the learning process in an interaction, as it may lead the learner to reformulate inaccurate or unclear messages. In addition, classroom interactions provide an opportunity for the natural occurrence of repetitions, imitations, comprehension checks, receipt of feedback, and peer modeling.

Language-Conducive Strategies

Young children's willingness to communicate in a novel language that is not a language of their close environment and is not a necessary language for their well-being and security depends to a large extent on "what happens in the classroom" (Mihaljević Djigunović and Nikolov 2019, 516). Specifically, this willingness is related to the extent to which teachers are motivated to create a low-anxiety atmosphere leading to self-confidence and L2 production without fear or mental barriers (Mihaljević Djigunović and Nikolov 2019; Schwartz 2018).

Our focus in this study is to analyze how teachers use classroom interactions to apply scaffolding strategies conducive to production, namely language-conducive strategies (Schwartz 2018). These strategies have been defined as specific tactics elaborated "to enhance children's willingness to communicate" (16) in a novel language. They include diverse elicitation techniques: use of body movement, creating language areas, peer language modeling and learning and teacher modeling, and encouraging parental engagement (Schwartz 2020).

Research Methodology

Sociocultural Background of the Target Educational Settings

School 1

School 1 is a progressive Montessori Yeshiva Day School, founded in 2006 and catering to 520 students from the age of two through ninth grade. The students come from varied religious and socioeconomic backgrounds and are encouraged to be curious, to embrace one another's differences, and to be engaged in respectful dialogue. The Hebrew immersion program begins at age two and continues through middle school. Students learn in multiage groups. The classroom described in this chapter consists of children aged five through seven.

The school fosters a co-teaching model of "one teacher-one language": each classroom has one native English-speaking teacher and one native Hebrew-speaking teacher present all day long. Each of them is responsible for her own language delivery. The Hebrew teacher communicates with the children only in Hebrew and in various daily contexts. Learning units are built according to the proficiency approach, combined with Montessori, and incorporate the children's interest areas and ideas. Teachers use "Chalav u'Dvash—Hebrew for Pre-schoolers"—a program created by the Jewish Agency for Israel in 2006 for teaching Hebrew to young children in the diaspora, as a toolbox to help them enrich their various activities. Over the years, children are exposed to substantial authentic Israeli culture. By the end of second grade, they usually reach the intermediate-middle level in listening, intermediate-low level in speaking, and beginner level in reading and writing.

School 2

School 2 is a pluralistic and egalitarian school, founded in 1983, which caters to about 950 students from nursery through high school. The students come from diverse Jewish backgrounds. The educational approach is based on respect for the students, cultivates their curiosity and imagination, encourages creative expression, appreciates their initiative, and fosters critical thinking skills. The EC center promotes active, living use of Hebrew, enabling children (according to their age and language level) to converse with each other and with teachers in Hebrew. The school fosters the co-teaching model, and the Hebrew teacher is expected to communicate with the children in Hebrew all day long in various contexts. They also use the "Chalav u'Dvash—Hebrew for Pre-schoolers." The classroom described in this chapter consists of children from four and one-half through six years old.

School 3

School 3 is a Modern Orthodox Jewish day school founded more than ninety years ago. It caters to about two thousand students from nursery school through high school. One of its fundamental principles is *"Ivrit B'Ivrit"* (Hebrew in Hebrew). This means that in addition to a Hebrew language class, Jewish studies classes are conducted completely in Hebrew, implemented gradually from kindergarten. From age three, the morning program is in English and the afternoon program is increasingly in Hebrew. The daily afternoon program includes Jewish studies given by the head teacher mostly in English in nursery and pre-kindergarten and much in Hebrew in kindergarten, with Hebrew letters being introduced as well. By the end of kindergarten most of the children can identify and name the Hebrew letters as well as say some words that begin with each letter. In the three- and four-year-old groups, a Hebrew lesson is given by a special teacher for twenty minutes twice a week. Daily Hebrew delivery efforts are continued and supported by the Jewish studies teachers (who speak Hebrew) and their assistant teachers, who are native Israeli-Hebrew speakers, by repeating activities and tasks that the children have done with the Hebrew teachers. The class described in this chapter consists of children aged four and five. The Hebrew program is based on the Jewish calendar, combined with the "Chalav u'Dvash—Hebrew for Pre-schoolers" program as a toolbox for communicative, playful activities.

Participants

Participants were four individuals who at the time of the study taught Hebrew at one of the target schools. They are referred to here as N, R, J, and S, and their experience at the time of the study is described in the present tense, as are the descriptions of the target schools.

N (School 1)

N is a Hebrew native speaker and a teacher who has been teaching at the school for nine years. She earned her BA and MA in art from Adelphi University in the United States. She holds a New York State Permanent Certification for Art Education for K-12 and is certified in the Early Language Oral Proficiency Assessment and in the Responsive Classroom Management Approach. She has taught K-8 art, and since 2009 she has been teaching Hebrew in the early years. N serves as a Hebrew teacher for a group of five- to seven-year-olds and as the Hebrew program coordinator for the EC department of the school, which involves developing learning units and guiding teachers.

R (School 2)

R is a Hebrew native speaker and a teacher, born and raised in Israel. She earned her BA and teaching certificate from Wingate Institute in Israel and her MA in traditional Chinese medicine from ACTCM College in San Francisco. R was a kindergarten teacher in Israel. After moving to the United States, she taught Hebrew in elementary schools in California and New York. She started teaching at the elementary school of School 2 ten years ago and is in her fourth year as a kindergarten teacher. R has attended informal courses for teaching Hebrew to preschoolers. She is present in class all day and communicates with the children in Hebrew only.

J (School 2)

J has been the Hebrew coordinator of the EC department (ages two through six) at School 2 for five years. She is originally from South Africa and was raised and earned her academic degrees in Israel: a BA in special education from Tel Aviv University and an MA in criminology from the Hebrew University of Jerusalem. J worked in Israel as a teacher and special education coordinator at a middle school. She has served as a special education and Hebrew teaching coordinator in Jewish schools in Connecticut for twenty-one years.

S (School 3)

S is a Hebrew native speaker and a teacher, born in Israel, who served in that capacity during her military service. She earned her teaching degree from Levinsky College of Education in Israel and a BA in interdisciplinary studies from Grand Canyon University in the United States. She completed the Instructional Coaching Collaborate Course at Torah Umesorah in the United States and received various informal training on teaching through play. S worked for eleven years as a Hebrew teacher and coordinator at a Jewish day school in Dallas, Texas. After moving to New York twelve years ago, she started working at School 3, where in addition to being the Hebrew teacher in the kindergarten class, she is the Hebrew coordinator and teacher in seven classes of four-year-olds.

Research Design, Data Collection, and Analysis

A qualitative approach to data collection and analysis was implemented for this study. The first author collected and documented data during 2017–19 in three ECE settings for teaching Hebrew as L2 in New York City. She was familiar with the teachers and had observed their classroom practices in Hebrew (L2) teaching. She received permission from the school administration to take photos and videos, according to the school's rules, for the purpose of analyzing the observations.

The data was collected by means of ethnographic tools: semi-structured interviews with teachers, classroom observations, and field notes. This triangulation of data sources permitted the authors to enhance the credibility of their interpretations of the Hebrew language teachers' strategies and to reduce observer or interviewer bias (Lincoln and Guba 1985).

Classroom Observations and Field Notes

The teachers were informed that the purpose of the study was to examine characteristics of their classroom strategies in Hebrew (L2) delivery. They were asked to identify a time for observation that would include diverse daily routine activities (such as circle time, some structured and planned teacher-led activities within small groups) and some unplanned and unstructured activities (such as free play, games, and other activities during leisure time). Two observational sessions were conducted in each classroom for two to three hours per observation day, with detailed field notes.

The field notes were transcribed to capture how a constructivist learning environment was created and what language-conducive strategies had been implicated. In addition, the transcribed teachers' reflections were used to validate the observed classroom strategies. In the following section, results will be presented, followed by discussion and theoretical conceptualization.

Semi-structured Interviews

The first author conducted one semi-structured interview with each teacher individually through a forty-five-minute Zoom meeting in Hebrew. The goal was to examine how the teachers described their approaches toward Hebrew language teaching in the early years as well as their reflections on the language-conducive strategies observed during the study. They were asked about the rationale behind the observed strategies, the link between their classroom practices and their language and pedagogical beliefs, and the children's engagement in Hebrew classroom activities. The teachers were also asked about their background data (i.e., education, professional experience in Hebrew language teaching, the language model implemented in their early educational setting).

Results and Discussion

Constructivist Learning Environment

In general, the classroom observations, supported by the interviews, showed implementation of the central concept of the constructivist learning environment as a child-centered approach. In particular, the teachers implemented a child-centered approach by providing autonomy for young learners and supporting their innovativeness and investment, thereby creating an "agency-rich environment" (van Lier 2010, 5). J and N stated the following in their interviews:

> J: The school's philosophy is to give children a choice and personal creation. We do not work with stencils and ready-made things. Children receive guidance and a selection of materials and each child creates for himself. The same goes for games.
> N: I believe that a child should be given a situation in which he will have to use the language. My philosophy is that the child should feel ownership of his abilities. That he will decide how to reach the goal or how to win the game.

According to van Lier (2010), agency is a key concept in learning that incorporates such aspects as a learner's autonomy, motivation, and investment. Thus, the teachers enhanced children's agency by giving space for their choices and creativity, as expressed by S:

> The child feels that he or she is a part of the learning process. It is not dictated to him. He can create for himself. Many times, they surprise me because they do not always act the way I expected them to. They invent different things. Thus, the

child feels a wonderful feeling that he/she is capable of doing something in a new language.

She also added that children's openness to Hebrew as L2 is largely derived from age-appropriate playful and nonstructured activities, which foster positive emotions:

> I love that the kids are active and happy. For a child to want to learn, he needs to experience joy and the ability to create something. Many times, they do not feel they are learning.

This point of view is aligned with Nikolov's (1999) study that examined motivations for L2 learning among six- to fourteen-year-old children and concluded that the following was necessary for young learners: "classes must be fun and the teacher is in focus." Importantly, in our study, it was observed that the teachers embedded Hebrew learning in a thoughtful play- and creativity-supportive environment where children's positive emotional feedback made "the events interesting, easy to memorize and full of passion" (Taeschner, Gheorghiu, and Colibaba 2013, 226).

Language-Conducive Strategies

The following language-conducive strategies were observed in the classroom and also addressed by the teachers during the interviews: scaffolding by means of diverse elicitation techniques, including drawing on multimodalities; and teachers' and peers' modeling and learning (Schwartz 2020; Schwartz, Deeb, and Dubiner 2020).

Elicitation is a language-conducive strategy that promotes children's L2 production and usage of its correct forms during classroom interaction with teachers and peers (Lightbown and Spada 2017; Schwartz 2020). It can be in the form of diverse affordances/clues such as verbal stimuli (questioning, false statements, word beginning syllable, and utterance beginning) and nonverbal stimuli (pictures/photography, picture books, drawing, digital images), as well as a combination of both ways of stimulation.

The teachers in the present study had diverse and creative ways of eliciting Hebrew language production.

Creating Visual Images

R stated that "illustrated cards with written words are a visual stimulus to the child and I strongly believe in that."

Constructing a Model of a Street

N's class made a street out of empty cardboard boxes, naming all relevant objects in Hebrew:

> N: In the unit "Our Neighborhood," the children already had previous vocabulary, but the first thing we did was to go out, walk in the neighborhood, and identify

places that the children know, shops, restaurants, and so on. The children then created in class a map of the neighborhood. I made a blank map in advance and the children decided for themselves on the names of the streets, what would be where. Then, through a game a child instructs [in Hebrew] his friend how to get for example from school to the playground.

Creating Comics

Figure 10.1 is an example of a comic made by N based on her students' prompts. She stated:

I am constantly looking for ways to encourage the children to speak, so I create situations in which they participate and take ownership of the activity. That way, most of the activity will come from them and not from me. I asked the children what would they like me to draw and I drew the comic on the computer. They told me what each character was saying as well as what to draw where and why. They guided me. For example: We learned about the summer and they decided that they want a scene on the beach. They told me who and what to draw, who/what to draw next to whom or what, and what the characters are saying etc. It worked beautifully. Together we have created whole worlds using language in the most natural way without noticing that we speak and think in Hebrew. This is how they create the situation and I write what they say. The main thing is their speech. The girl who referred to this comic was 6 years old.

Figure 10.1 Example of creating comics.

Comics' images act in accordance with Vygotsky's (1978) principle of semiotic mediation. Their visual stimuli are converted to verbal responses. This occurs by transmitting information from the visual modality to the verbal modality, resulting in the target language productive use by stimulating its recall and retrieval. This is because comics, as a visual clue, provide a form of "mnemonic" strength in language production (Darrow 2012; Paivio 2014).

Combining Visual Stimulation with Body Enactment

S: I try ... to activate the child, both verbally and motorically.
Let the child have some tangible memory of the learning experience.

The techniques of L2 elicitation described here draw on a multimodal way to conduce L2 production. Just as neuroimaging research with adult populations has shown (Nyberg, Persson, and Nilsson 2002), children's retention and retrieval of words, collocations as word associations, and utterances in L2 can be supported by visual information, gestural elements, and body enactment (Tellier 2008). In addition to visual and gestural reinforcement of the learning materials in L2, the teachers in the present study were frequently observed activating motor modality by a strategy such as total physical response (TPR). Initially developed by Asher (1969) for improving L2 understanding and listening skills by means of listen-and-do motor acts, TPR included a sequence of simple instructions such as "stand up," "walk," and "jump." Later, this strategy was applied for conducing L2 production even among young language learners (Rodas Reinbach 2011).

In their interviews, the teachers in this study reflected on body enactment, dancing, and movement by means of TPR as a developmentally appropriate strategy influencing young children's motivation to participate in activities conducted in Hebrew (Bredekamp and Copple 1997). Interestingly, the teachers' modeling of body enactment as an elicitation strategy was imitated by the children, as in the following example:

R: There is a lovely girl, who really likes to learn Hebrew. What amazed me was that when I handed her the magic wand she said to the children: "Clouds and rain" ... The girl did not remember the word "rain" in Hebrew so she showed them rain with her fingers, and they followed. This is one of the beautiful stories of how a child, new to Hebrew, does a variation of what the teacher had taught.

Teacher and Peer Modeling and Learning

As L2 is mediated through social interaction (Gass and Mackey 2007), class observations indicated how children frequently repeated their teachers and peers as Hebrew language models. For example, it was observed that whenever a novice-level child joined the class and did not know the names of the colors in Hebrew, the student still showed an interest in active engagement in color-naming games. In one case, it was evident that a boy used game accessories to practice color names by means of self-talk aside from the peer group and after repeating the colors for a number of times, he seemed secure enough to join with the other children. Within the L2 learning context, Saville-Troike (1988) found that children used self-talk deliberately during a silent period in L2 learning to repeat utterances made by others and to recall and practice new linguistic forms in L2.

In addition, the teachers reported on encouraging peer modeling and learning as a constructivist strategy in L2 teaching. They noted that children drew on native Hebrew speakers as language experts: "One of the children speaks Hebrew and he gave instructions in a natural and authentic language" (R).

In the context of peer interaction during L2 learning in the classroom, Blum-Kulka and Snow (2004) distinguished between two types of peers: novice L2 learners and L2 experts. The latter are at a more advanced stage of competence and can play the role of L2 "teachers." Through their interaction with L2 experts, the novices develop linguistic, cultural, and communicative competence in L2.

Since language learning is deeply embedded within classroom social interactions between peers, as previously described, such activities as role-playing the teacher permitted children "to feel socially comfortable in a new language" and as a result to experience Hebrew productive use:

> R: I really like that they participate in role-play games. I encourage them to be "the teacher." I'm just the starting point and then I give them the baton, for example the game "King David says" … to me this is the happiest part when the child is King David or the restaurant manager. It's the creative part that comes out of the child and that's how it really is within the personal experience [with the Hebrew language].

In this context, Blum-Kulka and Snow (2004, 298) stressed that peers as language "teachers" create the possibility of an equal participant structure, whereas teacher–child interaction is asymmetric and provides less opportunity for reciprocal exchanges.

Conclusions and Field Implications

The set of strategies developed and implemented by the teachers was intended to cultivate positive emotions toward Hebrew and to increase a willingness to use it. There was not one sole strategy that characterized the teachers' work but a combination of language-conducive strategies. This interplay and conjoint implementation of strategies has a higher chance of making an impact. It was evident that the participants were influenced by their previous professional experience as teachers of art, music, and physical education. This experience was expressed in a multimodal approach toward L2 teaching that draws on the activation of visual modality with body enactment, dancing, and movement to enhance L2 retention and production.

In this study we found that the motivation and commitment of the teachers to teach Hebrew along with their recognition of the need to create a developmentally appropriate learning environment using a multisensory approach stimulated children's willingness to use Hebrew. The examples provided here demonstrated the relationship between the chosen strategy type and the output in Hebrew. Activities such as sociodramatic play and other social games in which children took an active part both as facilitators and "teacher models" and as participants promoted children's engagement in productive Hebrew use.

All three teachers had no formal education in language teaching but did have significant knowledge and experience working in other professions. Priestley et al. (2012) suggest that teachers such as this might have a wider repertoire of maneuvers available when faced with the challenges and ambiguities of a teacher's day-to-day work. From a holistic perspective, this point may contribute to the future professional development of Hebrew teachers and to their contribution as change agents.

It is noteworthy that the participating teachers did not draw on principles of the constructivist approach and did not mention this approach during their reflections. For instance, the children's voices were not heard in the teachers' reflections, although they stressed the central role of the learners in the choice of classroom activities and in taking "ownership of their activity." This can be accounted for in the fact that these experienced teachers lacked systematic professional training in early L2 teaching. This clash between the teachers' impressive experience, dedication, and creativity and the lack of specific academic knowledge in early additional language teaching demands attention from policy makers and pedagogical leaders to consider programs such as the Middlebury Hebrew School academic degrees or teaching certificate accreditations.

We believe that this study will open the gate for Hebrew educators and policy makers in various preschool settings all over the Jewish world to explore, reflect, and improve Hebrew pedagogic practices for the benefit of children in Jewish settings in future generations.

References

Asher, J. J. 1969. "The Total Physical Response Approach to Second Language Learning." *Modern Language Journal* 53 (1): 3–17.

Avni, S. 2016. "Hebrew Learning Ideologies and the Reconceptualization of American Judaism: Language Debates in American Jewish Schooling in the Early 20th Century." *International Journal of the Sociology of Language* 2016 (237): 119–37. https://doi.org/10.1515/ijsl-2015-0038.

Blum-Kulka, S., and K. Snow. 2004. "Introduction: The Potential of Peer Talk." *Thematic Issue of Discourse Studies: Peer Talk and Pragmatic Development* 6 (3): 291–306.

Bredekamp, S., and C. Copple. 1997. *Developmentally Appropriate Practice in Early Childhood Programs*. Washington, DC: National Association for the Education of Young Children.

Brooks, J. G., and M. G. Brooks. 1999. *In Search of Understanding: The Case for Constructivist Classrooms*. Alexandria, VA: ASCD.

Darrow, D. J. 2012. "Visualizing Second Language Learning: A Microgenetic Case Study Using Pantomime Comics for Adult ESL Students." MA diss., University of Alaska Fairbanks.

Fromkin, V., and R. Rodman. 1993. *An Introduction to Language*, 5th ed. Fort Worth, TX: Harcourt Brace Jovanovich.

Gass, S. M., and A. Mackey. 2007. "Input, Interaction, and Output in Second Language Acquisition." In *Theories in Second Language Acquisition: An Introduction*, edited by B. VanPatten and J. Williams, 175–99. Mahwah, NJ: Lawrence Erlbaum.

Gort, M., and R. W. Pontier. 2013. "Exploring Bilingual Pedagogies in Dual Language Preschool Classrooms." *Language and Education* 27:223–45.

Kaufman, D., and J. G. Brooks. 1996. "Interdisciplinary Collaboration in Teacher Education: A Constructivist Approach." *TESOL Quarterly* 30 (2): 231–51.

Kozulin, A., B. Gindis, V. S. Ageyev, and S. M. Miller. 2003. "Introduction: Sociocultural Theory and Education." In *Vygotsky's Educational Theory in Cultural Context*, edited by A. Kozulin, B. Gindis, V. S. Ageyev, and S. M. Miller, 1–11. New York: Cambridge University Press.

Krashen, S. 1984. *Writing: Research, Theory and Applications*. Beverly Hills: Laredo.

Lightbown, P., and N. Spada. 2017. *How Languages are Learned*, 4th ed. Oxford: Oxford University Press.

Lincoln, Y. S., and E. G. Guba. 1985. *Naturalistic Inquiry*. London: Sage.

Lowenthal, P., and R. Muth. 2008. "Constructivism." In *Encyclopedia of the Social and Cultural Foundations of Education*, edited by E. F. Provenzo, Jr., 177–9. Thousand Oaks, CA: Sage.

Mihaljević Djigunović, J., and M. Nikolov. 2019. "Motivation of Young Language Learners." In *Palgrave Macmillan Handbook of Motivation for Language Learning*, edited by M. Lamb, K. Csizér, A. Henry, and S. Ryan, 515–34. Basingstoke, UK: Palgrave Macmillan.

Nelson, K. 1996. *Language in Cognitive Development: The Emergence of the Mediated Mind*. Cambridge: Cambridge University Press.

Nikolov, M. 1999. "'Why Do You Learn English?' 'Because the Teacher is Short.' A Study of Hungarian Children's Foreign Language Learning Motivation." *Language Teaching Research* 3 (1): 33–56.

Nyberg, L., J. Persson, and L. G. Nilsson. 2002. "Individual Differences in Memory Enhancement by Encoding Enactment: Relationships to Adult Age and Biological Factors." *Neuroscience and Biobehavioral Reviews* 26 (7): 835–9.

Paivio, A. 2014. *Mind and Its Evolution: A Dual Coding Theoretical Interpretation*. New York: Psychology.

Pomson, A., and V. Ringvald. 2021. "Becoming Connected to Israel through Hebrew: Promising New Evidence." eJewish Philanthropy. March 19, 2021. https://ejewishphilanthropy.com/becoming-connected-to-israel-through-hebrew-promising-new-evidence/.

Pomson, A., and J. Wertheimer. 2017. "Hebrew for What? Hebrew at the Heart of Jewish Day Schools." AVI CHAI Foundation. March 29, 2017. https://avichai.org/knowledge_base/hebrew-for-what-hebrew-at-the-heart-of-jewish-day-schools/.

Priestley, M., R. Edwards, A. Priestley, and K. Miller. 2012. "Teacher Agency in Curriculum Making: Agents of Change and Spaces for Manoeuvre." *Curriculum Inquiry* 43 (2): 191–214.

Rodas Reinbach, D. L. 2011. "Total Physical Response (TPR) Storytelling as a Strategy for Teaching English as a Foreign Language to Pre-school Children (Ages 4 to 5)." MA diss., Universidad de Cuenca, Ecuador.

Saville-Troike, M. 1988. "Private Speech: Evidence for Second Language Learning Strategies during the 'Silent' Period." *Journal of Child Language* 15 (3): 567–90.

Schwartz, M. 2018. "Preschool Bilingual Education: Agency in Interactions between Children, Teachers, and Parents." In *Preschool Bilingual Education: Agency in Interactions between Children, Teachers, and Parents*, edited by M. Schwartz, 1–24. Dordrecht, Netherlands: Springer.

Schwartz, M. 2020. "Language-Conducive Strategies in Early Language Education: A Conceptual Framework." In *Handbook of Early Language Education*, edited by M. Schwartz, 194–217. Dordrecht, Netherlands: Springer.

Schwartz, M., I. Deeb, and D. Dubiner. 2020. "'When They Act, They Speak More': Strategies That Encourage Language Production in a Bilingual Preschool." *International Journal of Bilingual Education and Bilingualism* 25 (3): 800. doi:10.1080/1 3670050.2020.1719029.

Schwartz, M., and N. Gorbatt. 2017. "'There Is No Need in Translation: She Understands': Teachers' Mediation Strategies in Preschool Bilingual Classroom." *Modern Language Journal* 101 (1): 143–62.

Swain, M. 2005. "The Output Hypothesis: Theory and Research." In *Handbook of Research in Second Language Teaching and Learning*, edited E. Hinkel, 471–83. Mahwah, NJ: Lawrence Erlbaum.

Taeschner, T., I. Gheorghiu, and A. Colibaba. 2013. "The Narrative Format for Learning and Teaching Languages to Children and Adults." *Synergy* 2:223–35.

Tellier, M. 2008. "The Effect of Gestures on Second Language Memorisation by Young Children." *Gesture* 8:219–35.

Van Lier, L. 2010. "The Ecology of Language Learning: Practice to Theory, Theory to Practice." *Procedia, Social and Behavioural Sciences* 3:2–6.

VanPatten, B. 2003. *From Input to Output: A Teacher's Guide to Second Language Acquisition*. New York: McGraw-Hill.

Vygotsky, L. S. 1978. *Mind in Society*. Cambridge, MA: Harvard University Press.

11

Enhancing Spiritual Awareness and Development in Early Childhood Jewish Settings

Michael Shire and Deborah Schein

Spiritual awareness and development has been an underdeveloped area of inquiry or practice in Jewish education, where the focus has tended to be on the acquisition of skills and accumulation of knowledge (Kress 2013). Yet children do experience a rich, nonverbal inner life that, properly nurtured, can result in spiritual awareness. Having the ability to tap into their spiritual capacity enables children to explore their spiritual selves and prepare themselves for Jewish religious experience (Berryman 2013).

In the past several decades, children's spirituality has come to the fore of psychological and sociological studies in religion and secular educational systems (Fowler 1981; Hay and Nye 2006). Yet the Jewish community often overlooks this aspect of children's identity and desire to make meaning in their lives. Working with children and their families during early childhood (EC) is a crucial foundational stage in the development of spiritual awareness and the cultivation of religious ritual, symbol, language, and experience (Berryman 2013, 33–4).

This chapter presents two alternatives for enhancing children's spirituality in the context of early childhood Jewish education (ECJE). The first is Torah Godly Play, a distinctive methodology to tell stories, foster wondering questions, and create community while encouraging imagination, spiritual growth, and religious learning. Torah Godly Play is an adaptation for Jewish settings of Godly Play, developed by the Rev. Jerome Berryman to enhance the spiritual development of children through the telling of sacred stories. Torah Godly Play, devised by chapter coauthor Michael Shire, is now used extensively in Jewish EC, day school, and congregational education settings. Teachers have been trained in the methodology in the United States over the past ten years in all Jewish denominational settings. Generally, Torah Godly Play is focused on EC and elementary-age children, although its use is now extending to adolescents and senior life facilities. Drawing upon the sacred stories of the Bible, Torah Godly Play invites children into the narrative while leaving room for wonder, creativity, and imagination as they build their own religious language to express that searching as well as conceptions of the presence of the Divine in their lives and expressions of Jewish religious and cultural symbols, rituals, and liturgy. The chapter will first examine the history and theoretical point of view of Torah Godly Play, illuminating its roots in the Godly Play method and the faith development school and concept of relational consciousness as a construct of spiritual awareness. Then, it will present examples of Torah Godly Play sessions and discuss the implications of Torah Godly Play for ECJE.

During Torah Godly Play, the storyteller is adept at creating an interaction between the child, the environment, and the story, which leads the child to contemplate the story in terms of religion and spirituality. Certain teachers naturally have this skill. However, many educators do not have the language or framework to recognize spiritual moments (Schein 2018).

As the second perspective on enhancing children's spirituality in ECJE, this chapter presents findings and a discussion regarding the spiritual moments that emerged for a group of EC educators interviewed for a social constructivist grounded theory study of spiritual development of young children. Five distinct moments emerged, which are described here as spiritual moments in time, in space, in and with nature, and in relationships, and spiritual moments beyond the self through children's asking and exploring big, important questions. The chapter will conclude with some ideas and reflections for future research in spiritual development and spiritual awareness as fundamental for human well-being.

Torah Godly Play

Berryman and the Development of Godly Play

Rev. Jerome Berryman (1991) began developing Godly Play with his wife Thea while he was working as a Christian chaplain with terminally ill children. His work offered him an understanding of what children need at the end of life, and he began to recognize the essential questions and immersion in stories of meaning that provided them deepening levels of understanding and awareness of their condition. Berryman experienced a horizontal relationship with the children and their families as their search for understanding in the face of serious illness was directed by the children themselves. His chaplaincy work highlighted their questions of meaning and purpose and search for God's presence, alongside the guiding and sponsoring presence of adults.

Godly Play became a practice dealing with the depth and closeness of the nature of children and a sacred story and the relationship between the two. Discerning purpose for life is owned by the children themselves as they construct a narrative of meaning offering them an ability to express and develop emotional responses to their own situations. Berryman found that this was a powerful element in a community of children and shared by all. To this end, his development of the methodology of Godly Play sought to actively cultivate spiritual awareness, incorporating the essential element of open-ended wondering questions, a sacred story, and response time in a community of children.

The Influence of Maria Montessori and Sofia Cavaletti and Implications for ECJE

Having studied and interned as an educator with Sofia Cavaletti in Italy, Berryman and his wife absorbed the approach to EC and pedagogy espoused by Cavaletti's teacher,

Maria Montessori (Berryman 2013). Godly Play is, therefore, very much influenced by the pedagogical concepts that place the child at the center of their own discovery inside a highly structured, prepared environment. As in Montessori learning, combining intentionality for aesthetics with an understanding of the role of the natural world on the visual and tactile senses, Godly Play refines an approach to its educational materials that is carefully considered and highly developed. Artifacts used for telling stories are constructed of natural materials handled by adults and children alike with care and appreciation as they come to symbolize the workings of the imagination in sacred story.

Montessori's (2004) concept of the prepared environment influences Godly Play with its open access classroom with biblical stories in material form available on open shelving at children's height. There is a large empty space in the center prepared for a circle of children to experience one of the sacred stories. The children are consciously prepared to enter this space by a doorkeeper who individually invites each child to enter the classroom after pausing to consider what it means to "be ready for a story." The circle of children, with a storyteller in front of them, focus their vision on the focal shelf behind the storyteller. There is an explicit intention for order and concentration in this prepared environment, leaving room for creativity and the imagination to be foregrounded in the sensorial responses of the children. This learning takes seriously children's choices of how to retrieve materials, how to return them, how to play with them, how to speak, and how to be silent.

Cavaletti introduced the notion of sacred story into the Montessori classroom through material elements inviting children to enter the story through their imagination and play (Hyde 2004). Accordingly, the inner nonverbal dimensions of spiritual awareness are overlaid with the linguistic canon of sacred stories. This combination of inner implicit religiosity with an explicit religiosity of symbol, story, and ritual reflects Rosenak's (1987) call for a holistic approach to Jewish education. It is an approach that can integrate the formation of spiritual awareness in the child with the religious language, symbolic understanding, and ritual performance of the particularism of religious Judaism.

Holtz (2003) has outlined a series of orientations for reading Jewish texts in educational settings. The personalized orientation comes closest to, though is not identical with, this spiritually constructed approach to participating in Torah Godly Play. It considers the reader's response as the key to drawing out meaning even in the youngest child, allowing the child to see sacred narrative as a whole without the need to analyze or apply it. This is similar to the ways in which the story at the center of Torah Godly Play practice empowers and enhances the meaning making of the child.

The Faith Development School

Berryman was also one of the school of thinkers who originated the theory of faith development in the 1980s (Fowler, Keen, and Berryman 1978). Leading this developmental approach was Fowler (1981), whose ongoing contribution lies in the notion of the spiritual as a component of the psychology of human meaning and its growth in the individual. Fowler understood the search for meaning to be a universal human innate capacity that incorporates cognitive, moral, social, and emotional learning in a composite concept of faith. However, for Fowler (1981), faith is not acted out as a static noun but rather as a dynamic lifelong process of change and growth in faith stages mediated by cultural contexts, symbolic constructs, and language.

In Godly Play, this quest is captured in its adoption of religious language to express emerging nonverbal meaning in the child. As such the careful use of language in the scripts of the sacred stories used by adults is highly intentional. Though Fowler's work spawned a push for universal spiritual attributes in assuming spiritual awareness is a universal human characteristic exclusive of religion, this was not his position, which was that religious experience, language about God, and symbolic function are significant indicators of spiritual awareness in religious experience. This is in tune with Godly Play's attempt to scaffold the development of the inner operations of the child but not repress or suppress the natural and unboundaried expressions of ultimate meanings.

Relational Consciousness as a Construct of Spiritual Awareness

The work of Hay and Nye (2006) gave evidence of this suppression in religious education classrooms as part of a study to investigate the nature of children's spirituality. In ascertaining that there is a clear consciousness at work in the lives of young children that is within and beyond the self, they posited that this is driven in relationship to exposure to symbol, ritual, and language. Hay and Nye determined that this relational consciousness is an innate yet fragile human activity prone to be suppressed by unfiltered adult experience and absorption of theological language without personal meaning. It is subject to elimination in the individual through embarrassment or peer pressure, a phenomenon that is seen regularly in religious education as children mature beyond childhood years.

Hay and Nye's (2006) understanding of relational consciousness as the special awareness that children hold in relation to themselves, to the other, to the world, and to God is a fundamental core of their faith expression. This is evident in each child's spiritual signature, which emerges to express and refine their relational consciousness. This is demonstrated in Godly Play classrooms, where the work with children demonstrates their capacity to exhibit different ways of knowing, not just intellectually, but also from their self, their experience of the world, and their experience of God's presence. There is also the presence of "flow," as described by Csikszentmihalyi (2008), as creativity and imagination enhance ways of knowing in the children.

Torah Godly Play Adaptation

Godly Play was adapted to Torah Godly Play, for Jewish settings, using the same fundamental principles of spiritual development but drawing on Jewish story, ritual, and symbol in its design. As Jewish education in the twenty-first century seeks to expand its goals beyond subject-specific domains and to incorporate social, emotional, and spiritual learning into the intentional outcomes of its practice, Torah Godly Play offers a spiritual pedagogy of teaching Torah (the holy scroll containing the Five Books of Moses). Shire learned the practice directly from Berryman and designed the adaptation for Jewish educational settings first in the UK in the 1990s and then in Boston in 2011. Since that time more than 250 educators have been trained in the practice, and it has been incorporated in Jewish educational settings particularly on the East Coast of the United States. A book of scripts for Jewish educational settings has been produced with a second one in development. Certain specific adaptations have also been made to the sensory materials for the telling of stories.

As a feature of ECJE, Torah Godly Play as an adaptation of the Godly Play methodology focuses on deepening the spiritual awareness of children in Jewish settings. It invites children to form their religious language and experience through imaginative and creative experience of biblical narratives. As a pedagogy of religious formation, it seeks to enhance the role of ritual and symbol, language for God's presence, and cultural traditions in Judaism. It is attentive to the wonderings of the child, listening for their spiritual signatures and providing creative means to develop their ways of knowing in religious experience. Not merely a means to transmit knowledge of Jewish biblical narrative, it also acts as liturgical action replicating the sacred act of reading and rereading Torah as a deepening practice of meaning making.

As described regarding Godly Play, the Torah Godly Play method requires a unique approach to storytelling coupled with artifacts—the storytelling circle; the doorkeeper; the storyteller inviting children into a story followed by opportunities for wondering, exploration, and creativity; and closing the circle. It is designed intentionally in all aspects for explicit and implicit religiosity. It enables the very youngest children to make these sacred stories their own and live within them as they imagine their own notions of God, commitment, promise, joy, sadness, and love. Artifacts and objects for telling stories are carefully and intentionally designed for maximum spiritual resonance, using wood, stone, cloth, and sand. Torah Godly Play adapts Godly Play's innovative approach to religious education that seeks not so much to tell stories of faith in order for children to know them as to act as a spiritual activity of finding meaning, identity, and God. The pedagogical ideal of this approach is that, from the earliest age, children are invited to experience and become increasingly aware of the spiritual call within sacred stories and of their own deep response as naturally afforded by religious narrative.

An Example from a Torah Godly Play Classroom: The Story of Noah

When we work with children in Torah Godly Play, we are seeking to cultivate the inner dispositions in the child; the fostering of relationship-building between self, other, the world, and God; and the social nurturing that comes from working with other children and adults in the Jewish classroom. This case study derives from a Conservative synagogue EC center in Washington, DC, where the teacher acted as participant observer, taking notes on children's responses while also acting as the storyteller in the classroom.[1] The classes described here include a number of Torah Godly Play stories, including Noah, Jacob, the Exodus, and the giving of the Ten Commandments. The classroom experience of the Noah story, described in this section in the present tense, was taught in 2019, and the notes were provided to Shire for write-up and analysis. The classroom experiences of the other stories, discussed in the present tense in the following section, were taught by Shire in several Jewish congregational and day schools in Boston.

A group of four- to six-year-olds meet in a Torah Godly play classroom with a storyteller, who prepares them for the story of Noah. In front of them lies an underlay of felt with wooden carvings of animals, Noah and his family, and a dove on it. There is also a representation of an ark in which the wooden pieces will go. The storyteller, looking down at the pieces in front of her, describes the beginning of the narrative: How God decided to send the flood to make the world new again and how God chose a good family to build an ark in which to collect creatures of every kind. As she describes the waters rising, she lifts the ark above the heads of the children and describes God's actions in protecting the creatures in the ark. When the storyteller brings the ark down, she sends out the dove in her palm to search for dry land to make a home. As all the creatures emerge from the ark, the storyteller arcs her hand over the scene to represent the rainbow as a sign of God's promise that God would never again send such a flood. At the end of the telling, the storyteller finally raises her eyes to look at the children and invites them to wonder about the story they have heard. She starts with, "I wonder which part of the story you liked the best?"

Becoming intrigued with the motion of the story, Marcus (one of the children) recalls the ways in which the ark first rose and then steadily came down as the waters went down. He likes this movement that God makes in the story. His wondering focuses on the movement of the ark in relation to God's actions upon the creatures. His attention has been drawn by the continuous narrative of the story from beginning to end with careful listening and focus on the objects in the story. He uses the language of the storyteller to describe what God is doing to the ark.

Meanwhile, David, who loves counting, wonders about the number of days Noah waits to send out the dove each time. His love of numbers is stimulated by this part of the story. Edward says, "My favorite part was when God made the flood because then the boat went up and sailed to another island," extending his vision of the story, and Josh remarks on "when it was the flood and the earth turned into one giant ocean." The children's imaginations have been stimulated through the methodology of the telling, enabling them to wonder for themselves.

When the storyteller asks, "I wonder which part of the story was the most important," Lizzie says, "God decided not to wash away the world again because He didn't know He was just getting everyone to die." Edward says, "God didn't notice He was breaking houses down." We hear that the children understand God is learning something as they are and wondering about God's role in a story involving death and destruction. God is readily present for them, and they are beginning to form a concept of what this God language really means to them. Edward asks the storyteller, "You said that God had promised that He would not destroy the world again. Well, why would He? Because God's nice, not mean."

Then the children wonder together about the role of human beings in this story:

Lizzie:	God never wanted to send a flood again.
Harvey:	Because God promised and that means He won't do it again, that's what makes it so important.
Ari:	But what about the bad guys? The flood washed away all the bad guys.

Harvey:	And the bad guys turned into good guys. But some people are still bad guys.
Eitan:	First Noah was a bad guy, then he was a good guy.
Storyteller:	How did he become a good guy?
Eitan:	Magic!
Storyteller:	Did someone say something to him?
Eitan:	They said, "Try to be a good guy!"

Relating to each other's responses, they have a deep understanding of the moral questions in the story and cannot quite resolve the troubling questions of theodicy. Typically, they turn quickly to their world of fantasy, but the storyteller is listening for the essential spiritual questions and probes Eitan's wonderings a little deeper.

The storyteller asks, "I wonder which part of the story we could leave out and still have all the story we need?" "The dove flying," says Nina. Greg says, "The animals coming into the boat—we just need Noah and his family." The storyteller thinks to herself and asks, "I wonder why we have to have every single kind of animal in the boat?" She, too, has space to wonder with the children, emphasizing this equal and horizontal relationship for a search for meaning.

The wondering deepens as the storyteller asks, "I wonder where you are in the story or which part was especially about you?" Simon responds, clearly and definitively, "I was Noah!" The storyteller asks, "How did you build your ark?" Simon responds, "I used woodblocks and a hammer." Eitan says, "I was in my mummy's tummy because we weren't alive." Bess says, "I was the cow." "How did it feel to be a cow on the ark?" asks the storyteller. "I was cold so I snuggled up with my mom." "Could you feel the water moving the ark?" "Yeah and I was not comfortable with that, so I started mooing." The story becomes part of their own experience, giving it a reality in their own lives while still affecting their extended imaginations.

As the wondering time concludes and the storyteller puts all the wooden pieces back into the wicker basket, each creature is named and removed gently from the center of the circle. Now the storyteller invites the children to choose a creative exploration of their wonderings. Some go to the story itself and play with its telling one more time. Some take up art materials for drawing or making a collage and some look in picture books for other good stories. The storyteller sits quietly by the focal shelf. After this time is concluded, the children return to the circle and the storyteller invites them to say what they worked on:

Ari:	I made the waves and the animals on the bridge and the windows … God is dropping marbles in the water—it's called waves.
Ellie:	I made animals of every kind. Before the flood.
Noah:	I drew the sun and the ark, water and dry land. The brown circle is the ark. The animals are inside. The other brown circle is the dry land. The water covered the sun. The water went everywhere. Then there was a new sun.

Their work remains in the classroom, and they can return to the wonderings contained in their work each time they come back to the Torah Godly Play classroom, but they also respond to their parents or siblings who ask in the corridor or in the car, "What did you wonder about today?"

Implications of Torah Godly Play for ECJE

The development of spiritual awareness for EC years in Jewish educational settings is dependent on three dimensions of constructivist education: the trust that children have the ability to cultivate dispositions conducive to implicit and explicit religiosity; the nurturing of relational consciousness as children come to greater awareness of their spiritual signatures; and the nurturing of collaborative and loving relationships in a community of children guided and sponsored by loving adults (Shire 2019).

Children in Torah Godly Play cultivate the dispositions of concentration and focus, quietude and contemplation in focusing on a sacred story, and participating in expressive exploration, all required for implicit religiosity. They work on their creative imaginations and emerging concepts of religious language, symbol, and ritual through the wondering opportunities and reflection on experience, all of which are required for explicit religiosity. Participating in a loving, nurturing practice of habituation with deepening capacity offers the children an authorship of their own making. This combination of implicit and explicit religiosity is key to even the youngest children beginning to form their own foundational synthesis of meaning making within a religious tradition. As Josh (age four) wonders about biblical Jacob wrestling with an angel, he remarks, "He came to know that he was a new person."

A heightened experience of biblical narrative is a special feature of Torah Godly Play, and it is the focus on children's spiritual signatures that nurtures their relational consciousness. The child is recognized for who she is in her searching and wondering as she comes to learn new ways of knowing. Gabriella (age six) responds to her favorite part of the Exodus story: "I like how Moses told Pharoah to let the people go in a nice way. Moses said it in a really kind voice and so Pharoah let them go." Her kindness in the classroom is palpable and stands out in her relationships with fellow children and adults alike. John (age five) has a fascination with science and responds to God's gift of the sixth day of Creation in forming human beings: "Well actually things were made before God made human beings. It is actually weird because God made everything else afterwards and yet God made the first person at the beginning." Their wonderings reflect their own spiritual identities in new ways of coming to know self and sacred story.

Adults in the Torah Godly Play classroom nurture and stimulate the imaginative wonderings of the children, as well as removing themselves as far as possible to promote a collaborative community of children. This is a fine balance for spiritual support and the emergence of an open and natural intimate knowing of the child. Dimitri (age six) has been exceptionally quiet and retiring in his Torah Godly Play classroom. Yet something in the story of Moses's ascent of Mt. Sinai to receive the Ten Commandments has stimulated him to excited and joyous realization. "Moses had courage when he said, 'Let my People go' and he had courage when he went up the mountain. My father is brave too when he went to serve his country. He taught us the best way to live just like Moses did." Dimitri and a new friend choose to work together on a paper-mache mountain during their creative exploration. The storyteller is watery-eyed, and Dimitri is known in a new way.

This fostering of love continues throughout the experience in which we honor the child in her own creative capacities enhancing the community of children in their own deliberation and collaboration. The children develop deep relationships that grow outward to the adults in the classroom as well as providing an opportunity to see beyond the classroom to the wider world and the Divine presence. Torah Godly Play models this search for the Divine presence as biblical figures come close to God and through that closeness find resolution to life's challenges and actions on behalf of themselves and others.

As we seek to enhance spiritual awareness in EC, we work with children to stimulate their imaginative creativity through sacred narrative and spiritual practice involving Jewish symbols, ritual, and language. In doing so, we enable them to become authors of their own search for meaning and foundational concepts of God, human purpose, moral action, death, and a range of emotional reactions to life experiences. The nature of play as a structured and yet non-goal-oriented activity is ideal for this kind of spiritual knowing and wondering in a new way. It is available and accessible to the youngest learners and a foundational means to build self and awareness of the other on a lifelong journey of playful growth and depth.

A Research Study on Spiritual Moments for Young Children

Coauthor Deborah Schein (2012) conducted a research study in which EC professionals were interviewed on the topic of spiritual development of children from birth to age five. Participants were recruited from a variety of EC educational backgrounds, including Montessori, Waldorf, Reggio Emilia, play-based, and nature educators. There was gender, religious, and racial diversity among the participants. They all had been directly involved as ECE teachers during their careers and had shown a commitment to the process of spiritual development. A few of the participants were Jewish, although the study focused on spiritual development for all children and did not delve into religion or thoughts and reflections about God. The goal of this study was to find commonality of spiritual development for all children.

Data collection included hour-long initial and follow-up interviews, which were audio-recorded, transcribed, and member-checked. The interview questions related to the nature of the spiritual development of young children from birth. In addition, three educators working in classrooms at that time kept spirituality journals for a period of four weeks. Data analysis included open, axial, and selective coding as well as bracketing (Strauss and Corbin 2015). The findings revealed a definition of spiritual development and the educators' description of a concept referred to as "spiritual moments." (The definition used by the researcher of a "moment" as "a comparatively brief period of time" was from Merriam-Webster Dictionary: https://www.merriam-webster.com/dictionary/moment.)

Conversations with Educators about Spiritual Moments

Spiritual moments is a concept that emerged when participants in this study were asked: What kinds of learning activities and experiences foster a child's spiritual development? Each participant mentioned experiences and spiritual moments. One participant said that such moments happen quickly in the eye contact and physical contact between self and child or child and nature. After data analysis, spiritual moments in five distinct spheres emerged: in time, in space, in and with nature, in relationships, and regarding big questions that help to make one feel part of something bigger than oneself. These spiritual moments sustain a child's spiritual development, nurture spiritual awareness, and prepare a child for engagement in spiritual pedagogies, such as Torah Godly Play.

Spiritual Moments in Time

Participants spoke about quiet, calm moments as spiritual moments in time. They reported that children need extended time to play or to explore on their own and with other children. They saw spiritual moments in set routines and when order exists in a child's life. One participant shared that children require "slow time during the day, where the need to stay on schedule or accomplish certain tasks is suspended … open-ended time to play—or just be."

Another participant shared a new interpretation for the word "boredom," a word common in the vocabularies of contemporary American children: "I had a friend who [said to] children … who complained that they were bored … 'Oh how wonderful—A time to ponder!'"

Spiritual Moments in Space

Participants spoke about the need for children to explore and interact in beautiful spaces in order for them to experience spiritual moments. Such moments required the environment to be pleasing, intentional, and contain a sense of awe, caring, and responsibility. Terms such as the aesthetics, beauty, intentionality, and perspective were often used when participants spoke about spiritual moments in space. For example, one participant said, "I was thinking about … beauty in a classroom … The result is a calming, pleasing and settled atmosphere."

Another participant said,

> I tend to talk about the importance of paying attention to aesthetics, explaining that aesthetics is a branch of philosophy and is the study of beauty in the world. Eventually, we explore the impact of light and color on mood and behavior, the impact of smell and sound, the importance of paying attention to visual patterns for brain development [Piaget schema theory], and how this all relates to aesthetics and tending to care of the soul.

Coming from a place of discontent, this educator shared these words:

Typically, we American EC educators have tried to fill the environment with scientific explanations when, quite frankly, I think we should be creating environments that could be producing questions, wonderment, and curiosity about the world rather than answers to things ... to teach children their colors appeals to the lowest part of brain development, not to mention a real lack of spiritual development or cognitive development. You reduce it to a name of a particular kind of color that robs it all of the other possibilities.

Spiritual Moments in and with Nature

Participants spoke often of spiritual moments in nature (being outdoors) and with nature (bringing nature indoors) as space and time for children to be interactive with the natural world, where they can develop a respect for changes in the world within oneself, and others. Educators mentioned words such as "awe," "caring," and "responsibility for the earth." Participants also mentioned how nature brings out children's ability to be more responsible, kind, and caring. One participant shared, "Sometimes I think that nature is the most perfect toy. It is interactive, it changes all the time ... I think nature can help with that sense of awe, and caring."

Another said,

> I feel strongly about [children] having close contact with nature. They need to be immersed in ... that pile of leaves and the sand on the beach. Their involvement in nature should also include their being active in the caring of ... the natural world around them. This is one of the strongest ways to support spiritual development because there is that sense of beauty and mystery and that oneness in the natural world.

Participants also spoke about how nature can impact other areas of human development that are sometimes related to spirituality such as ethics, kindness, caring, and responsibility. Today, there is a plethora of research in nature education that supports the important role nature plays in human development, including spiritual development (Sobel 2004).

Spiritual Moments in Relationships

According to the participants, spiritual moments in relationships lead to the emergence of kindness, respect, and empathy. One participant defined spiritual moments in relationships as "empathy, displays of kindness, and feelings of harmony." She said, "When I see a child doing something counter to what would be self-serving [such as] handing a toy they wanted to use to someone else to use first—that is a spiritual moment." She added:

> When I see a child spontaneously comfort another, or attempt to bring a child on the fringe of an activity into the group, those are spiritual moments ... This attentiveness to the interrelatedness of all living beings is an element that I could connect to spiritual development.

Two participants shared their ideas about creating sacred space for spiritual moments to occur in relationships between teacher and student. One said, "We create sacred space when we sit on the sofa with our arm around the child to read a book and listen to their comments." The other participant said:

> When we take the time every school day to engage in personal conversation with each student, ask them to tell us what they were thinking when they drew a picture, or when we put a band-aid on a scratch that we can barely see. If we respond to every student in that way, I believe we are beginning to create sacred space.

Spiritual Moments beyond the Self through Children's Asking and Exploring Big, Important Questions

Participants defined these moments as filled with a myriad of big important questions children ask about life and existence and a deep desire to explore and learn about the world. Participants offered examples of what it means to go beyond oneself. One said, "When a child discusses what they think became of our dead fish, or their pet, these can be spiritual moments." The child is offering their inner beliefs on how the world works.

Another participant stated:

> I think that children ... even though they are young ... there is something beyond themselves that can be bigger than themselves. Sort of a sense of wonder ... How did it all get put there? Why does the world look and function the way that it does?

Implications of Spiritual Moments for ECJE

Although spiritual moments were researched without reference to God and religion, it is possible to explore the implications of spiritual moments for ECJE. The Jewish calendar as a basis for classroom life offers many opportunities for spiritual moments in time. Shabbat (Sabbath) provides the focal point of the week, and the holidays mark historical time and the passage of a year. Because of children's absorbent minds, these qualities of time make an impression on young children and become internalized. These experiences help the child to develop an ability to know oneself as a spiritually Jewish person.

Just as spiritual moments in space are reflected in Torah Godly Play through Montessori's concept of the prepared environment, so too are they reflected in a Jewish home, synagogue, classroom, and outdoor space. The focus is on the child's experiencing wonder, awe, caring, and responsibility through open-ended play in the midst of Jewish culture, practices, beliefs, and language. Furthermore, spiritual moments in space can be enhanced through the sharing of blessings or prayers that focus one's attention on wonders of creation in nature. Examples for this include the blessings that are traditionally said when a person sees lightning, hears thunder, sees a rainbow, and so on.

Spiritual moments in and with nature have the potential of connecting young Jewish children to Jewish holidays. For example, Rosh Hashanah (Jewish New Year) is referred to as the birthday of the earth, Sukkot (one of the three biblical holidays celebrated by building huts) is about harvesting food, and so on. Again, the use of prayers and blessings connected to specific holidays can enhance and help to identify Jewish moments with nature.

Participants in the study spoke about spiritual moments in relationships as leading to empathy. Empathy may provide a foundation for Jewish relational values such as *tikkun olam* (repairing the world) and hospitality based on selected biblical stories (e.g., Abraham and Sarah). With empathy for ourselves and others we are capable of becoming kinder and more compassionate human beings.

The concept of spiritual moments beyond oneself through big questions has roots in Judaism. Judaism is filled with questions, debate, and delight in analyzing words. For young children, questions emerge from hands-on experiences and open-ended time to play, especially time in nature, with friends, and with a grown-up to offer language and love. One of the greatest values of Torah Godly Play is that it offers children a rich opportunity to explore their own questions about God, Bible stories, and Judaism, alone or with friends. Spiritual moments through big questions extend the opportunity for such exploration into everyday life.

Conclusion

The two perspectives described in this chapter strive to explore different aspects for enhancing spiritual awareness and development in ECJE. One is through a rich pedagogy of guided, non-goal-oriented play experiences focusing on specific biblical stories. The other suggests building pedagogic opportunities for tapping into young children's natural sense of joy and awe with the world around them. One enhances spiritual development through the specific content that the teacher brings to the educational context and the other through natural occurrences in the classroom context. Both strive to help the child to construct meaning through interaction with others and one's surroundings, connecting to self, other, life, nature, and Jewish tradition.

Spiritual development as reflected in spiritual moments and spiritual awareness reflected in Torah Godly Play can work together to provide substantial benefits for children in ECJE. Research in spirituality and neuroscience, spearheaded by Miller (2021), has demonstrated that both spirituality and religion provide links to human well-being. Although that study pertained to adolescents, Miller reports, "Our brains are wired to perceive and receive that which uplifts, illuminates, and heals" (10). For the young child, this can mean that spiritual development and spiritual awareness can lead to "grit, resiliency, optimism, tenacity, and creativity ... All we need to do is choose to engage it" (10, 9). Research is needed to understand more fully how parents and educators might foster both spiritual development and spiritual awareness in children, how these two concepts might further complement and combine to strengthen spirituality in children in ECJE, and how ideas of God and religion become part of a young child's consciousness.

Note

1. With thanks and appreciation to educator Wilhelmina Gottschalk for her contribution.

References

Berryman, J. 1991. *Godly Play: An Imaginative Approach to Religious Education*. Minneapolis, MN: Augsburg.
Berryman, J. 2013. *The Spiritual Guidance of Children: Montessori, Godly Play, and the Future*. New York: Morehouse.
Csikszentmihalyi, M. 2008. *Flow: The Psychology of Optimal Experience*, 1st ed. New York: HarperCollins.
Fowler, J. 1981. *Stages of Faith: The Psychology of Human Meaning*. San Francisco, CA: Harper and Row.
Fowler, J. W., S. Keen, and J. Berryman. 1978. *Life Maps: Conversations on the Journey of Faith*. Waco, TX: Word.
Hay, D., and R. Nye. 2006. *The Spirit of the Child*, rev. ed. London: Fount.
Holtz, B. 2003. *Textual Inquiry: Teaching the Bible in Theory and in Practice*. New York: Jewish Theological Seminary of America.
Hyde, B. 2004. "Children's Spirituality and 'The Good Shepherd Experience.'" *Religious Education* 99 (2): 137–50. https://doi.org/10.1080/00344080490433710.
Kress, J. S., ed. 2013. *Growing Jewish Mind, Growing Jewish Souls: Promoting Spiritual, Social, and Emotional Growth in Jewish Education*. Cincinnati, OH: URJ.
Miller, L. 2021. *The Awakened Brain: The New Science of Spirituality and Our Quest for an Inspired Life*. New York: Random House.
Montessori, M. 2004. *The Discovery of the Child*. New Delhi, India: Aakar.
Rosenak, M. 1987. *Commandments and Concerns: Jewish Religious Education in Secular Society*. Philadelphia, PA: Jewish Publication Society.
Schein, D. 2012. "Early Childhood Educators' Perceptions of Spiritual Development in Young Children: A Social Constructivist Grounded Theory Study." PhD diss., Walden University, Minneapolis.
Schein, D. 2018. *Inspiring Wonder, Awe, and Empathy: Spiritual Development for Children*. Saint Paul, MN: Redleaf.
Shire, M. 2019. "Torah Godly Play: An Innovative Approach to Religious Education for Shlemut." *Gleanings: A Dialogue on Jewish Education from the Leadership Commons at the William Davidson Graduate School of Jewish Education* 6 (2). Accessed April 29, 2021. https://www.jtsa.edu/torah-godly-play-an-innovative-approach.
Sobel, D. 2004. *Place-Based Education: Connecting Classrooms and Communities*. Great Barrington, MA: Orion Society.
Strauss, A., and J. Corbin. 2015. *Techniques and Procedures for Developing Grounded Theory*, 4th ed. Thousand Oaks, CA: Sage.

Part Four

Continuing the Work

12

Leadership in Early Childhood Jewish Education in the United States

Lyndall Miller

חד אמר דור לפי פרנס וחד אמר פרנס לפי דורו

One says: The level of the generation follows the level of the leader; and one says: The level of the leader follows the level of his generation.
—Talmud Bavli, Arakhim 17a

The success of an educational enterprise depends on the interaction between the school community and its leaders (Hoffman 2016; MacDonald 2016; Northouse 2015). In the above quote from the Talmud (a body of Jewish civil and ceremonial law and legend), one sage argues that a generation will follow a leader, while another states that the leader follows the generation. If we want progress in an educational endeavor, we must seek those leaders who can inspire the generation.

While we can identify transformational leaders in Jewish tradition, from Abraham to Moses and Abraham Joshua Heschel to Erica Brown, we have been less successful in the elucidation of the capacities of those who can lead transformative change. The study of leadership itself, as opposed to identifying specific leaders, has only been underway for about the past one hundred years (Hoffman 2016; Northouse 2015; Starratt 2016). However, scholars have still not reached a universal consensus as to what "leadership" means (Northouse 2015).

Yet, as *Pirkei Avot* (a compilation of the ethical teachings and maxims from Rabbinic Jewish tradition) tells us in verse 2:21, "You are not required to finish the work, but neither are you free to desist from it." The study information reported in this chapter is from the author's (Miller 2020) doctoral dissertation, which was designed to "continue the work"—to discover useful leadership capacities in early childhood education (ECE) in a Jewish context. Current advances in the general field of ECE were used, because of an absence of such research in early childhood Jewish education (ECJE). These ideas were then reviewed as they emerged in coded interviews with seven regional and national leaders in the ECJE field and explored for their possible expression within the Jewish context. This process revealed interesting areas of further study in the special field of Jewish EC leadership as it could be conceived and advanced whether it be in the United States or in Israel. This research could also allow other strongly culturally based early childhood (EC) programs to consider the expression of these leadership capacities within their own contexts.

Leadership in the General Field of ECE

Even though this study of ECJE capacities could not be based on current studies of leadership in Jewish EC settings due to lack of research, the general field of leadership in ECE has received serious attention. More than fifty recent studies (primarily completed since 2008) were reviewed. The Atlas.ti 8 coding program for qualitative data analysis and research was used to code the theories and research to detect any consistencies or dramatic differences. In general, the studies and theories were rich and yet in great consonance with each other in terms of essential elements of EC leadership (Abel, Talan, and Masterson 2017; Goffin and Washington 2019; MacDonald 2016). (The reader will note that the coding resulted primarily in information on visionary rather than administrative leadership. For this study, the administrative aspects, such as budget creation, hiring and firing, etc., were dependent on the development of the leader's vision. However, more study on administrative aspects of leadership is certainly indicated.)

The following eight leadership capacities surfaced from the coding of the literature on current ECE leadership theory and research:

1. The capacity to develop self-awareness, reflection, and personal mastery throughout the lifespan (Beaudin 2017; Collay 2014; Colmer 2017; Nicholoson and Kroll 2014)
2. The capacity to acquire and employ deep knowledge of human development in cultural contexts and theories of pedagogy (Brown and Manning 2000; Kostelnik and Grady 2009)
3. The capacity to develop trust and actively support relationships (Colmer 2017; Nicholson et al. 2020; Rodd 2013)
4. The capacity to engage in mentorship, both as a mentor and as a mentee (Rodd 2013; Seemiller and Priest 2017)
5. The capacity to promote dialogue, collaboration, and shared leadership through teamwork (MacDonald 2016; Rodd 2013; Sims et al. 2015)
6. The capacity to discover and manage opportunities for change (Bella 2016; Nicholson et al. 2020; Stamopoulos 2012)
7. The capacity to develop school culture as a community in part through the co-creation of its vision (MacDonald 2016; Nicholson et al. 2020; Sims et al. 2015)
8. The capacity to engage in advocacy and social justice work (Abel, Talan, and Masterson 2017; Bella 2016; Nicholson et al. 2020)

These capacities appeared quite consistently throughout numerous ECE studies. Therefore, they provided a useful platform from which to view expectations for leaders in ECJE, which is the focus of this chapter.

Methodology

To understand how these capacities related to essential ECJE leadership capacities, seven American leaders in the field were engaged as study participants. Those interviewed were chosen because of their roles as directors of large regional or national programs aimed at transforming the field of ECJE during approximately the past ten years. Four participants had held positions in three institutions prominent in Jewish life in the United States: Jewish Community Center Association of North America (JCCA), Early Childhood Educators of Reform Judaism, and the United Synagogue of Conservative Judaism. Three other participants had established new initiatives with major support from Jewish philanthropic organizations. All of the participants had published writings on various aspects of ECJE, spoken at multiple conferences, and earned multiple awards. All but one was still working in ECJE or a closely related field at the time of the study. One participant identified as male and the others as female. The median age was in the early sixties.

There were other prominent leaders in ECJE who could have been interviewed and who should be in the future, based on the results of this research, both in order to obtain the input of younger leaders and to not rely so heavily on only those who identify as female. These seven participants were chosen because of the variety of experience they offered in terms of the organizations they represented—specifically federations, JCCAs, funded initiatives, and Reform and Conservative Jewish denominations—and the varied geographic areas they worked in (the West Coast, the East Coast, and the Midwest). The number of participants was limited to seven due to logistical limits of the study (i.e., the number who could be interviewed within the time allotted for such a pilot study).

Each participant was interviewed from one to two hours using a semi-clinical interview approach, with the responses coded and grouped using Atlas.ti 8. The interview explored the leadership capacities essential for success, the effect of the Jewish context, the participant's definition of success, and what the participant thought the field of ECJE should offer for the ongoing development of these specific leadership capacities. The following open-ended, nonjudgmental questions were used to guide the discussion, followed by additional probing questions as appropriate to discover any resonance with the capacities in the literature review, looking for consonant and divergent responses:

1. What do you feel are the most important capacities for a leader in ECJE?
2. In what ways does Jewish life and culture affect what leaders do in our field? What do they not do?
3. How would you define success in a leadership program for Jewish EC educators?
4. What do you feel we offer leaders in our field today? What should we be offering?

All interviews were transcribed and returned to the respondents to check for accuracy. The transcriptions were then coded using Atlas.ti 8. Interviews were first analyzed for emergent categories and then recoded applying the capacities from the literature review.

The respondents were not prompted about the specific capacities that were found in the literature. Rather, they were asked what they thought was essential for leaders in Jewish schools for young children and the possible advantages and disadvantages of the Jewish context. However, their responses were found to align surprisingly well with capacities discussed in the general ECE literature reviewed.

Findings

While the consonance between the capacities noted in the general field of ECE and those in ECJE was clear, an overall difference seemed to be produced by the Jewish context. Each capacity identified by the participants emphasized a relationship to Jewish life and learning. The following eight capacities were identified by the participants.

The Capacity for Self-Awareness and Personal Mastery, as well as Reflection on One's Identity as an EC Jewish Educator

For these leaders, self-awareness and reflective practice included an understanding of one's personal relationship with Judaism and the construction of a Jewish leadership identity. Building self-awareness through reflection required continuous attention to one's own developing beliefs. The interviews revealed how the participants strongly emphasized the interrelationship between self-awareness, reflective practice, and personal mastery within a Jewish framework. A sentiment expressed by all of the participants is reflected in this statement from a participant who managed a large national network of programs:

> So there's no question that I think the biggest one is, knowing who you are, understanding who you are and what you believe. What you believe Jewishly, whatever that is, who you are, what Judaism means to you and what that looks like and how you talk about it and how you show it, number one.

Participants disagreed as to whether someone who is not Jewish could develop this core sense of Judaism as a reference for all actions and interactions. Some felt it was not possible while others claimed that it was possible if the leader had an authentic, positive relationship with Judaism. This question about whether it is necessary to be Jewish to be an educator in a Jewish school was also a factor in other categories of capacities identified and will be addressed in the "Discussion" section at the end of the chapter.

Responses also indicated that one way self-knowledge was achieved was through text study, as expressed by one of the younger participants who is now prominent in the field in many arenas:

So, I think it's an on-going process of taking a text and asking what does it mean ... then go through these processes that I lead or that I'm a part of [a group in] looking at a text and saying what does the metaphor ... mean for ... this community of practice? ... And you take this external something, [you each] bring it into yourself and you wrestle with it and then something is left behind on you. And you think about it.

Engagement in text study meant that a leader could gain insight as well as knowledge into one's own leadership practice.

The Capacity for Acquiring a Knowledge of Human Development in Cultural Contexts and Theories of Pedagogy, Including Jewish Learning and Jewish Learning Processes

Participants focused on text study, which involves the exploration and discussion of Jewish sacred literature. This kind of active learning, according to the participants, involved constructing and reconstructing self-understanding through reflection and dialogue with others. One respondent commented that leaders need to make use of every "opportunity for people to grow Jewishly and their work to understand the traditions and texts to use them for wisdom, to thread them through the work that they do." These processes of exploring and applying ideas that emerge from text study appeared again in the next capacity.

It was not within the purview of this study to ascertain the level or type of Jewish knowledge that should be considered "sufficient," but there were clearly varied opinions on this issue. An example of one of these opinions was in the following:

In terms of Jewish knowledge, you can't help but think if you're going to start your Jewish learning at the same time you're starting your leadership in education, it's going to be thin. And how thin that is or how given the [variety of the Jewish] world—what does it mean to be Jewish-ly knowledgeable? I'm not looking for somebody to have an advanced degree in Jewish studies.

An associated approach was considered in which Jewish knowledge is acquired (i.e., Jewish learning processes) through direct, immersive experiences. One participant stated:

I mean, providing experiences for people, that if you provide experiences for people that move them in the ways we've just talked about, move them Jewishly, move them about children and families, give them opportunities to see and experience the world and nature. Things that ... inspire them and create wonder and create awakenings and gratitude or hope ... So that, if you can see by the end of the time with these people that they have captured that as part of who they are and will be able to provide that as a leader to other people, that is a goal.

Two participants raised the possible difficulties in having leaders in place who were not Jewish. The other five participants expressed that they felt learning and highly intentional experiences could provide the necessary Jewish knowledge. Questions remained regarding the level of Jewish knowledge that should be required of ECJE leaders, gained either through active learning or through immersive experiences or both.

The Capacity to Build and Support Relationships by Promoting Jewish Values

Every participant spoke about the necessity of having the ability to develop relationships within the context of the school. Trust was at the foundation of these relationships, even in situations where there may not be agreement. Indeed, building trusting relationships required including in a safe way those who had different perspectives. One of the participants, who worked intensively with lay and professional ECJE leaders, was clear about the need for trust in all relationships in an institutional program:

> If you do not trust someone or if you don't feel like you're building trust with someone, it's very hard to respect them and have them respect you. And I don't think our world pays enough attention to what it takes to build that trust … I start with various simple exercises of questions to ask one another and they're very deep and they're very intentional … And it's something as basic as, you know, talking about their values from their childhood, their experience, things that are near and dear to them that nobody ever takes the time to ask them. That's how you build trust.

Judaism was seen as a platform that supports the development of this foundational trust, with relationships fostered by referencing Jewish values. Text study and shared learning was a primary vehicle for transmitting these values and for reinforcing relational perspectives. As stated by one of the oldest and most experienced participants,

> Understanding—and this is what I came to understand—that ideas within Judaism are not transferable by just having a list of words that you teach like these are their values, these 10 words like isolated de-contextualized words [are] not values, but values and Judaism [as] invented in the text. So, learning how to learn was an experience that most people and certainly not a lot of women had where … what we were doing was giving people the experience of Jewish learning and the opportunity to learn not just values, but to explore in a deep way [with others] how they become your own values and how that exercise in learning text is transforming.

The question about the identity of the educator in a Jewish school arose in this context again, with some expressing that all people could engage in acquiring these values and others concerned that they would not be as relevant to those who did not identify as Jewish.

The Capacity for Mentoring as an Aspect of Jewish Tradition

The participants recognized the power of mentoring in their career trajectories. Each noted that being recognized by others allowed them to understand their own abilities and that the mentors supported them as they moved forward. They were also explicit about the power of mentoring for creating potential future leaders:

> If you're going to be a leader, you need to train leaders around you ... it can't be about you. So, when I depart this part of my life or my life, there are going to be a whole bunch of people who can do what I'm doing around me ... some would be more apt to do certain things than others, but you have to be—you have to just keep ... the *dor l'dor* [generation to generation] thing, whoever made that up, pretty smart.

This quote emphasizes the idea of advancing students to become mentors and teachers—passing learning from one generation to another and "raising up many disciples" (Pirkei Avot 1:1).

The Capacity to Support Dialogue, Collaboration, and Shared Leadership/Teamwork in Consonance with Jewish Processes of Text Study

Dialogue and collaboration were frequently mentioned, along with teamwork. The word "team," for these leaders, implied a group involved in dialogue that resulted in ideas that were discussed, fine-tuned, implemented, and then evaluated. All of the participants had made use of leadership teams based on dialogue and collaboration in their work. The practice of dialogue in Jewish schools for this capacity was, like for the others, supported by Jewish text study, which requires an approach to life that emerges from study, dialogue, and shared meaning making. This position was expressed well by one of the younger participants:

> I think it's an on-going process of taking a text and asking what does it mean to them in real time ... I think the process of text study which is something I see a lot in professional development for Jewish early [education] leaders.

Based on responses from all of those interviewed, a leader of a program must provide the time and opportunities necessary for deep collaborative work. All of the participants indicated text study as a way to begin and continue useful conversations to engage in meaning-making, a position upheld by Jewish learning traditions.

The Capacity to Seek Out and Manage Change, Specifically Relating to Jewish Content

The term "institutional change" appeared more than a hundred times in the interviews. The participants spoke specifically about how schools need to be constantly seeking areas of growth, as well as being committed to a change process. The dialogue, collaboration, and teamwork discussed regarding previous capacities was also discussed as providing the formats in which these change processes can take place. Although the participants recognized difficulties, including conflict, loss, and unsettled morale, these problems, kept within certain bounds, were seen as necessary to growth. This kind of growth required a strong base in the previous capacities in order to avoid the superficial and to support transformation.

> Many times, a difficult conversation produces growth … when we create that place of trust and when we know how to have the difficult conversations … when the director and their supportive admin people are able to create that kind of an environment where everybody understands that we can grow one another and it's done positively because we know we're not complete … Then you can grow a place and change a place; otherwise it's very difficult. So for that you need self-awareness, you know what you need to know, where the other … ends and where you begin, what you're bringing to the conversation as much as you can and then to be able to have those [dialogues].

Remarks about change processes also related to forward movement in Jewish content and processes in schools. Change was seen as particularly essential in areas of Jewish curriculum. While the focus of the study was not on identifying what Jewish content should be, the need for creativity and development of Jewish ideas and their implementation were specifically mentioned.

> [How do staff members] have the support to understand that every holiday has some big ideas that take us to a [new] place, and the same with Torah [the holy scroll containing the Five Books of Moses] portions and the same with all the pieces that come with Judaism—what is it that we're trying to create here and then how do [we] go about that?

It was clear from the interviews that leaders need to be ready to have the difficult conversations, based on trust and supported by learning, to make the shifts needed to enhance the Jewish experiences provided by the schools.

The Capacity to Develop School Culture as a Jewish Community through the Co-creation of Vision

Every participant insisted that programs need to take on the functioning of a Jewish community. Two core functions identified were: using Jewish values to frame relationships and participating in ongoing learning and growth. A program, under a visionary leader, has to undertake the task of self-reflection, discovering/constructing the expression of core Jewish values, and developing the stance of its members in relationship to Jewish life. This vision in turn needs to be clearly expressed and used as a reference for future decision-making. The vision also needs to be periodically revisited for its responsiveness to changing conditions. As a goal, one respondent commented, "the program would have established … a community, not a cohort, but a community of people who trust each other, who push each other, who will continue to journey with each other for decades and be a voice and an advocate for the field."

Another important feature of organizational culture and visioning identified was the aspiration to include a wide variety of members in that community. Family members, institutional leaders, and lay leaders were considered essential partners in successful collaboration and change. As the person responsible for setting the culture of the program, the leader was seen as having to provide the space, the support, and the inspiration for vision development as a process.

Finally, all the participants expressed that the organizational culture of any program, along with including families and institutional leaders, must have a strong understanding of its relationship to its Jewish (and local) community. One respondent, in particular, stated that knowledge of sociology in general and the sociology of Jewish communities should be a requirement for leaders in the field.

The Capacity to Advocate for the Field and to Apply Jewish Values to Issues of Social Justice

The participants were dismayed by the challenges of the field of ECE at large. In particular, the lack of institutional understanding, financial support, and compensation of educators in the field were seen as socially unjust and possibly the result of discrimination against women, who make up the majority of EC educators. However, they expressed that this situation was even more egregious in Jewish EC programs, because these organizations operated under Jewish auspices, supposedly espousing Jewish values. They were deeply concerned by the fact that institutions often used EC program income to fund other functions, which put an undue burden on directors and detracted from their ability to use the capacities described here. They considered the situation an existential threat.

As advocates, they saw two ways to change this picture. One was to engage the institutional leadership in understanding and collaborating on the vision of the program, as previously mentioned. Another was to provide opportunities for directors to learn more about business skills appropriate for nonprofits so that they could understand institutional budgets and be better prepared to speak to institutional authorities using shared language (the managerial side of leadership).

However, another challenge to the field identified was the lack of serious learning opportunities for leaders and emerging leaders in ECJE, regarding any topic. While each of the participants had initiated such programs, they all expressed the great need for expanded options for the essential learning of content and processes of leadership. They asserted that these learning opportunities, whether through academic courses or professional development, must allow for emerging leaders to study Judaism, their own relationship to Judaism, and how they express it. They stated that there had been ways of moving forward with these challenges in the past through the work of national organizations of leaders in ECJE and that these organizations provided a wider pool of people who could engage in dialogue and collaboration. All of the participants were interested in renewing ways of connecting across programs and communities.

> I think some people might say being an advocate for the work for me it's like sharing it and multiplying it ... It's like we're linking arms together and we're

going to do this thing together. So ... will we ever make the kind of progress we need in the field? ... it would be helpful and it has been helpful to have other people to talk it out with and to say we're in this together ... if I would do a map of where there are strongholds of people who work together on developing their leadership. There's just so many holes and we haven't found a way to scale. And we haven't found a way to leverage the strengths and then blanket the other places to support them.

Beyond working together for the field, the participants expressed a need for programs to participate in current movements for social justice, from climate change to anti-racism and action against poverty. One leader specifically felt that social activism might be a uniting value for all of the Jewish EC programs.

Discussion

Table 12.1 presents the eight leadership capacities that emerged from the literature review of the general field of ECE juxtaposed to the eight that were found in the ECJE interviews. As mentioned previously, the similarities were striking.

Table 12.1 Comparison of Literature and Interview Leadership Capacities

Leadership Capacities from Literature Review	Leadership Capacities from Interviews
Develop self-awareness and personal mastery throughout the life span	Develop self-awareness, personal mastery, as well as reflection on one's identity as an EC Jewish educator
Acquire and employ deep knowledge of human development in cultural contexts and theories of pedagogy	Acquire a knowledge of human development in cultural contexts and theories of pedagogy, including Jewish learning and Jewish learning processes
Develop trust and actively support relationships	Build and support relationships by promoting Jewish values
Engage in mentorship, both as a mentor and as a mentee	Engage in mentoring as an aspect of Jewish tradition
Promote dialogue, collaboration, and shared leadership through teamwork	Support dialogue, collaboration, and shared leadership/teamwork in consonance with Jewish processes of text study
Discover and manage opportunities for change	Seek out and manage change, specifically relating to Jewish content
Develop school culture as a community in part through the co-creation of its vision	Develop school culture as a Jewish community through the co-creation of vision
Engage in advocacy and social justice work	Advocate for the field of ECJE and apply Jewish values to issues of social justice

Some of the findings from the interviews were surprising. This was due to how much an issue was emphasized—for example, the importance of text study and Jewish context—or how strongly participants disagreed with each other on an issue—for example, whether a non-Jewish educator should lead a Jewish school and what leadership capacities were most significant.

While text study has long been considered essential for Jewish education for adults, the emphasis placed on it by these ECJE leaders was unexpectedly pronounced. This kind of learning was seen by all as essential for self-understanding and reflection on core values and for learning how to engage in shared meaning-making as well as acquiring Jewish knowledge.

The understanding of the context of an ECJE program extended beyond the school and the institution to the specifics of the wider Jewish community. The need for sociological studies of the Jewish cultural needs (and general cultural needs) of the community in which a school finds itself influences the ways that leaders can meet families' needs. This emphasis was stronger than expected and represents a clearer understanding of the necessity of being responsive to social imperatives and disruptions.

A primary point of disagreement, as mentioned previously, was the appropriateness of a non-Jewish educator being a leader in a Jewish school. While all the participants recognized that there are non-Jewish educators in ECJE programs, the question arose as to whether these educators could truly inform the Jewish character of the program as a leader. For some participants, there was a sense of a necessary unmeasurable quality that came from a leader identifying as Jewish. As one participant said, "You had to be Jewish in your kishkes (guts)" in order to transmit Judaism to others in a holistic rather than a particularistic way. Other participants expressed that a real commitment to Jewish life and learning could enable those who did not identify as Jewish to become authentic ECJE leaders. Across the board, reflection and being "in dialogue" with being an educator in a Jewish school was seen to be essential. The participants whose position was that leaders of ECJE programs could be non-Jewish expressed that in some ways, educators coming into the field from non-Jewish backgrounds would be more likely to engage in those reflections.

Finally, how much different participants concentrated on expanding one leadership capacity over another (e.g., teamwork and dialogue over social action) was noteworthy. This difference may have been in response to their own experiences and contexts but also may represent individual leaders having expertise in only pieces of a whole. Therefore, the study suggests the usefulness in developing an approach to leadership in ECJE of conversations between leaders where all can share their experience.

Implications and Suggestions for Further Research

This study, while not an examination of actual leadership practices in ECJE, does provide a framework for understanding those practices and how they might be employed in the future through the views of a sample of the leaders in the field. It also suggests areas for future research. There are wonderings that arose throughout the consideration of the findings. These ideas provide areas of possible discussion with those who are prominent in the field as well as revisiting those leaders who were interviewed for this study:

1. What are the programs that allow for mentoring, professional development, and the support of learning communities in the field in terms of leadership? Do we have a view of the landscape?
2. What is currently being offered in terms of professional development and coursework in leadership in ECJE?
3. How can we allow for more educators to become leaders through collaborating with others to refine and develop their own ideas?
4. What Jewish learning experiences, particularly accessible and relevant text study, are we offering to educators, leaders, and emerging leaders in ECJE?
5. What is the relationship between the constructivist learning approach and Jewish experiential learning?
6. How do institutional and lay leaders understand how the content and processes inherent in Judaism affect the leadership in ECJE?
7. How can we keep our field viable by advocating for ourselves and by working for social justice for others who educate young children and families?

This study provided an opportunity to learn from some of the leaders of the field, who reflected on their own leadership journeys and considered the capacities that allowed them to build Jewish EC learning communities. It is essential to follow up with additional research that supports or challenges the framework offered here. If found useful, it could help build professional learning opportunities in leadership in ECJE or evaluate current efforts in both the United States and Israel. These capacities could certainly be further defined, clarified, and expanded, or explored in other cultural and global contexts. Let us continue to look for opportunities, formal and informal, to engage in this conversation in service to the field that so inspires us all.

References

Abel, M., T. Talan, and M. Masterson. 2017. "Whole Leadership: A Framework for Early Childhood Programs." McCormick Center for Early Childhood Leadership at National Louis University. March 22, 2017. https://mccormickcenter.nl.edu/library/whole-leadership-a-framework-for-early-childhood-programs/.

Beaudin, H. L. 2017. "Navigating the Changing Landscape of Early Education within a Preschool Setting." *Organizational Improvement Plan at Western University*, 6. June 9, 2017. http://ir.lib.uwo.ca/oip/6.

Bella, J. 2016. "A Critical Intersection: Administrative and Pedagogical Leadership." McCormick Center for Early Childhood Leadership at National Louis University. April

18, 2016. https://mccormickcenter.nl.edu/library/a-critical-intersection-administrative-and-pedagogical-leadership/.

Brown, M., and J. Manning. 2000. "Core Knowledge for Directors." In *Managing Quality in Young Children's Programs: The Leader's Role*, edited by M. Culkin, 78–96. New York: Teachers College.

Collay, M. 2014. "Developing Leadership Identity through Critical Reflection: Voice, Knowledge and Advocacy." *Reflective Practice* 15 (6): 780–92. https://doi.org/10.1080/14623943.2014.944136.

Colmer, K. 2017. "Collaborative Professional Learning: Contributing to the Growth of Leadership, Professional Identity and Professionalism." *European Early Childhood Education Research Journal* 25 (3): 436–49. https://doi.org/10.1080/1350293X.2017.1308167.

Goffin, S. T., and V. Washington. 2019. *Ready or Not: Leadership Choices in Early Care and Education*, 2nd ed. New York: Teachers College.

Hoffman, L. A., ed. 2016. *More Than Managing: The Relentless Pursuit of Effective Jewish Leadership*. Woodstock: Jewish Lights.

Kostelnik, M., and M. Grady. 2009. *Getting It Right from the Start: The Principal's Guide to Early Childhood Education*. Newbury Park, CA: Corwin.

MacDonald, S. 2016. *Inspiring Early Childhood Leadership: Eight Strategies to Ignite Passion and Transform Program Quality*. Lewisville, NC: Gryphon House.

Miller, L. 2020. "Voices from the Field: A Proposed Framework for Capacities in Jewish Early Childhood Education." EdD diss., Gratz College, Melrose Park, PN.

Nicholoson, J., and L. Kroll. 2014. "Developing Leadership for Early Childhood Professionals through Oral Inquiry: Strengthening Equity through Making Particulars Visible in Dilemmas of Practice." *Early Childhood Development and Care* 185 (1): 17–43. https://doi.org/10.1080/03004430.2014.903939.

Nicholson, J., K. Kuhl, H. Maniates, B. Lin, and S. Bonetti. 2020. "A Review of the Literature on Leadership in Early Childhood: Examining Epistemological Foundations and Considerations of Social Justice." *Early Child Development and Care* 190 (2): 91–122. https://doi.org/10.1080/03004430.2018.1455036.

Northouse, P. 2015. *Leadership: Theory and Practice*. Thousand Oaks, CA: Sage.

Rodd, J. 2013. *Leadership in Early Childhood*, 3rd ed. London: Open University Press.

Seemiller, C., and K. Priest. 2017. "Leadership Educator Journeys: Expanding a Model of Leadership Educator Professional Identity Development." *Journal of Leadership Education* 15 (2): 99–113. https://doi.org/1012806/V15/I2/R1.

Sims, M., R. Forrest, A. Semann, and C. Slattery. 2015. "Conceptions of Early Childhood Leadership: Driving the New Professionalism?" *International Journal of Leadership in Education* 18 (2): 149–66.

Stamopoulos, E. 2012. "Reframing Early Childhood Leadership." *Australasian Journal of Early Childhood* 37 (2): 41–8. https://doi.org/10.1177%2F183693911203700207.

Starratt, R. 2016. "Presence." In *The Jossey-Bass Reader on Educational Leadership*, edited by M. Grogan, 55–76. Hoboken, NJ: Jossey-Bass.

Conclusion

Sigal Achituv, Meir Muller, and Shelley T. Alexander

This book discusses many of the opportunities and challenges facing early childhood Jewish education (ECJE) in Israel and the United States. While educational contexts differ widely, insights provided in these chapters hopefully will strengthen both systems. In an effort to highlight some of the issues facing the field, we conclude with a discussion of how the opportunities and challenges explored in the chapters on core Jewish subjects align with at least one of the three contemporary critical lenses. We then provide suggested questions for future research.

The lens of multiculturalism is applied in a number of the core Jewish subject chapters with the following focal points. First, when Israeli religious educators teach Bible stories in a classroom, value conflicts can arise between liberal values of multiculturalism in contrast to the Bible view of the "other." The educator's personal and religious identity plays a crucial role in the interpretation of these stories for the children.

Second, the Israeli national educational program of Sifriyat Pijama uses stories as an agent of social change by shared reading and conversations in the home setting. It is attempting to create a national literary canon for young children and shaping a positive ethnic identity and common cultural knowledge. Exposure to a wide diversity of people, values, and cultural norms through the stories and conversations promotes a foundation for multicultural appreciation and knowledge.

Third, the early childhood (EC) classroom provides another aspect to the role of social and cultural agents toward a more diverse Israeli society as seen in the study on holiday celebrations and ceremonies in the *gan*. The analysis of these are implemented with a variety of approaches, from traditional to more open, and the rituals developed have historically caused reverberations by challenging conventional hegemony in the general society's attitudes toward Jewish holidays and ceremonies.

Finally, the study on leadership in the field of ECJE in the United States emphasizes many key capacities that pertain to creating a more diverse cultural educational context. They include: "the capacity to acquire and employ deep knowledge of human development in cultural contexts and theories of pedagogy, the capacity to discover and manage opportunities for change, the capacity to develop school culture as a community in part through the co-creation of its vision, and the capacity to engage in advocacy and social justice work" (pp. 197–202 in Chapter 12).

The lens of gender awareness is used to relate to the three core Jewish subjects of Bible stories, Sifriyat Pijama, and holiday celebrations and ceremonies. Similar to multiculturalism, the study exploring the telling of Bible stories in the Israeli gan indicates that value conflicts can challenge educators. Liberal views of feminism and gender roles contrast with the traditional role and status of women depicted in the Bible. The influence of the educator's personal ideology and religious identity are important factors in the telling and interpretation of the stories to the children.

The description of the book selection criteria for Sifriyat Pijama clearly indicates the program's concern for issues surrounding gender roles in providing children and their families with quality literature to nurture shared conversations and activities. The selection committee relates to such areas as the representation of gender roles, strong female protagonists, family structure, and social equity.

The study on holiday celebrations and ceremonies in Israeli *ganim* makes use of a spectrum as an analysis tool to make comparisons. At one end are those programs that have distinctly defined gender roles and social messages, while at the other end are those marked with open approaches and an absence of gender division of roles. Examples of secular programs are offered, which carry complex social messages as to the role of gender division, and sometimes these messages given in gan contradict those imparted in the home and even the educator's personal view.

Last, the lens of constructivism is employed in several chapters. For instance, here again, in the case of Israeli religious educators telling Bible stories, value conflicts can arise between dogmatic religious beliefs and allowing the child to construct his or her knowledge. The educator may often feel the challenge and responsibility to convey institutional ideology and personal values and beliefs while nurturing the child's independence and individual cognitive development as constructivist pedagogy requires. The content from which the children construct knowledge stems from what the educator chooses, intentionally or not, to highlight and emphasize.

Another chapter's study uses a spectrum of pedagogies to analyze holiday celebrations and ceremonies in Israeli ganim, defining one end of the scale as reliance on traditional methods and the other as constructivist in orientation. Here, the constructivist-oriented educators are found to design programs, celebrations, and ceremonies that bring together old traditions with new in a quest to explore deeper meanings and be particularly attentive to the needs of the child, the family, the gan staff, and the community.

Furthermore, teaching Hebrew is a main staple in some diaspora EC classrooms' curriculum, and this study examines the constructivist learning environment for the teaching of Hebrew. Findings indicate that three elements increased the learner's willingness to engage in Hebrew use: teacher motivation and commitment to this endeavor, creating a program that is developmentally appropriate, and a multisensory approach.

Emphasis on nurturing spiritual awareness in the ECJE constructivist classroom can be explored by the young child being guided through rich play experiences surrounding specific Bible stories or by tapping into wonder and awe of naturally occurring moments in the child's world. It is the child's ability to construct meaning and make connections to Jewish tradition, life, and nature that foster spiritual development.

These groupings of ways in which the content of the chapters relates to the three critical lenses lead to ideas for future investigation in addition to the research questions proposed by the authors.

Multiculturalism

1. How do Jewish programs in both Israel and the United States confront issues of inequity through pedagogy?
2. How are anti-Semitism/anti-Israel issues being discussed worldwide in the field of early childhood education (ECE)?
3. In what ways can researchers consider pedagogies of cultural sensitivity at the intersection of the Israeli-Jewish and Arab EC communities?
4. How is the phenomenon of migrant and immigrant populations in ECJE being researched?
5. In the United States what is the cultural impact of non-Jewish staff and students in both curriculum and pedagogy?

Gender Awareness

1. In what ways are female Jewish historical and contemporary figures highlighted in curriculum in Israel and the United States?
2. How do children in Jewish EC centers define gender roles within Jewish contexts?
3. What systems are in place to monitor issues of gender discrimination in EC Jewish schools?
4. Are social expectations for boys and girls different in EC classrooms, and can this lead to differing levels of engagement in Jewish life?
5. What is the role of male educators in EC Jewish schools in Israel and the United States?

Constructivism

1. How does a constructivist pedagogy affect children's application of ritual observance?
2. How does a constructivist pedagogy affect children's ability to memorize religious liturgies and texts?
3. In Israeli nonreligious teacher educator programs, how can constructivist pedagogy create positive change in teacher educators' attitudes to Judaism and tradition?
4. What are family perspectives of Jewish programs that use a constructivist pedagogy?
5. What short- and long-term effects are found after children leave constructivist ECJE centers and enter elementary schools?

In conclusion, we offer the following story from ancient Jewish sources to express the significant role of EC educators in bringing blessings to the community and the world: "In a time of drought, a great scholar successfully prayed for rain when others' prayers were not answered. He was asked: What are your good deeds that merit this result? He replied: I am a teacher of young children" (Taanit 24a).

This story reflects the traditional Jewish view concerning the importance and power of EC educators as they impact the life of one's community. This impact has been made evident with new appreciation for the care of the youngest members of our society emerging from the chaos of the pandemic. It is our hope that this book will provide a resource and inspiration for those who are working in the field of ECE in bringing blessings to the children and communities they serve.

Glossary

Abba shel Shabbat	Sabbath father
Agada	Jewish legend
Aliyah	Immigration to Israel
Ashkenazi/c	From Central and Eastern European Jewry
Bikurim	First harvested fruits, referred to as "First Fruits"
Brachot	Blessings
B'tzelem Elokim	In the image of God
Chabad	A Chassidic community with the majority of residence in Israel and the United States
Challah	Traditional Shabbat braided bread
Charoset	A Passover food symbolizing the mortar enslaved Jewish people used
Chazzan	Cantor
Cheder	All-boys Jewish school where only religious studies are taught
Dor l'dor	Generation to generation
Dreidel/s	Spinning top-like toy/spinning top-like toys
Ema shel Shabbat	Sabbath mother
Gabai	Prayer service proctor
Gan zorem	Flowing kindergarten
Gan/ganim	Pre-elementary school for children aged three to six/pre-elementary schools for children aged three to six
Ganenet/gananot	Preschool teacher/teachers
Gemilut chasidim	Acts of kindness
Haggadah	Passover text read at Passover dinner
Hallel	Liturgy praising of the Lord
Hanukkiah/Hanukkiot	Ritual candelabrum/candelabrums for Hanukkah
Haredi	Ultra-Orthodox
Havdalah	Ritual ceremony concluding the Sabbath
Kabbalat Shabbat	The ceremony or prayers welcoming the Jewish Sabbath
Kehillah	Community
Kibbutz/kibbutzim	A type of communal settlement/settlements
Kiddush	Sanctification of wine
Knesset	Israeli parliament
Latkes	Potato pancakes
Lulavim	Sukkot ritual fronds
Matan Torah	Giving of the Torah

Merkaz Habayit	Housekeeping play area
Merkaz Rofeh	Doctor's play area
Midrash	Rabbinic commentary on or interpretation of the Hebrew Bible
Mishna	The first major written collection of the Jewish oral traditions
Mitzvah/Mitzvot	Directive/s found in the written and oral Torah
Mizrachi	From North Africa and Middle Eastern Jewry
Mizrachi stream	The political religious Zionist movement that was established in 1902
Moshav	Settlement with individually owned farms or businesses which shares some communal aspects
Moshava	Privatized farming community established in the pre-Israeli state
Omer	Wheat harvest on Passover
Parshat hashavuah	Weekly Torah reading
Passover Seder	Ritual Passover dinner
Pirkei Avot	Compilation of the ethical teachings and maxims from Rabbinic Jewish tradition
Purim	A Jewish holiday recorded in the book of Esther
Rosh Hashanah	Jewish New Year
Seder plate	A special plate containing symbolic foods eaten or displayed at the Passover dinner known as a Seder
Sephardi/c	Jews who trace their roots back to the Iberian Peninsula, North Africa, and the Middle East
Shabbat	Sabbath
Shalom Sesame	Israeli version of *Sesame Street*
Shavuot	Jewish festival occuring seven weeks after Passover
Shechina	The Divine Presence
Shirei kodesh	Religious songs
Shofar	A ram's horn blown of the Jewish New Year and Day of Atonement
Shul	Synagogue
Sifriyat Pijama	Pajama Library
Sigd	A holiday of Ethiopian Jews
Simchat Torah	A biblical holiday celebrating for the annual completion of reading the Torah scroll
Sukkah	A hut built for usage during the holiday of Sukkot
Sukkot	A biblical holiday celebrated by building huts
Talit	Prayer shawl
Talmud/Talmudic	The body of Jewish civil and ceremonial law and legend
Tefila	Prayer
Tikkun Olam	Repairing the world
Tochnit Misgeret	Framework Program
Torah	The holy scroll containing the Five Books of Moses
Tu Bishvat	Jewish Arbor Day

Tzedakah	A righteous or charitable act
Yishuv	Pre-Israeli state
Yom Ha'atzmaut	Israel Independence Day
Yom Kippur	Day of Atonement
Zionist	Belief in the development and protection of Israel

Contributors

Sigal Achituv is Senior Lecturer and Director of the Early Childhood Education Graduate Program at Oranim Academic College of Education, Israel. She is a research fellow at the Center for Jewish and Democratic Education, University of Haifa, Israel. Her studies deal with Israeli early childhood educators' identity concerning changes that are taking place in early childhood education.

Hanan Alexander is Professor of Philosophy of Education at the University of Haifa, Israel where he served as Dean of the Faculty of Education and Head of the Center for Jewish and Democratic Education. Chair of the committee on "Values Education: Guidelines for Measurement and Evaluation" of the Israel Academy of Sciences and Humanities and past President of the Religious Education Association, he is also Koret Visiting Professor of Education and Israel Studies at the University of California, Berkeley, USA.

Shelley T. Alexander is Project Coordinator and a research fellow for early childhood at the Center for Jewish and Democratic Education, University of Haifa, Israel. She was Director of Early Childhood Services at the Jewish Federation of the Greater East Bay, Oakland, California, in the United States.

David L. Brody is the former Academic Dean and Chair of the Early Childhood Department at Efrata Academic College of Education, Jerusalem, Israel. His career spans a lifetime of work with young children, from nursery caregiver and kindergarten teacher, to academic endeavors in the field of teacher education.

Howard Deitcher is Senior Lecturer in the Seymour Fox School of Education, Hebrew University of Jerusalem, Israel. He has written extensively on philosophy for children in Jewish education and is currently leading educational projects in six countries worldwide.

Ilana Dvorin Friedman is a child development consultant, instructor, and researcher. She is the Early Childhood Policy Analyst at the Jewish United Fund/Jewish Federation of Metropolitan Chicago, USA. She teaches at a variety of academic institutions and designs and facilitates professional development opportunities for early childhood professionals.

Roberta Louis Goodman is a researcher and experienced Jewish educator. She brought her expertise to JECEI (Jewish Early Childhood Education Initiative) aimed at creating schools of excellence in Pittsburgh and throughout the United States. She received the National Jewish Book Award as a coeditor of *What We NOW Know about Jewish Education*.

Haggith Gor Ziv is Senior Lecturer at Seminar HaKibbutzim Teachers College, Israel. She teaches courses on critical feminist pedagogy, disability studies, and inclusion. She teaches gender and education in the Gender Studies program at Tel Aviv University, Israel, and early childhood courses in South East Asia and Africa.

Chaya Gorsetman was Co-chair of the Education Department at Stern College, United States. She specialized in supervision of student teachers with a strong emphasis on constructivist theory. She coauthored *Educating in the Divine Image: Gender Issues in Orthodox Jewish Day Schools* (2013), which was awarded the National Jewish Book Award.

Shulamit Hoshen Manzura is Lecturer at Oranim Academic College of Education, Israel, and Efrata Academic College of Education, Israel. Her research studies deal with Israeli early childhood educators' and children's perspectives on rituals and gender, especially in Orthodox and ultra-Orthodox societies.

Sylvia Kamowitz-Hareven is an early childhood specialist with over thirty years of experience working with Israeli parents and educators. From 2009 to 2019 she served as Director of Education for Sifriyat Pijama, accompanying the program from its inception through its first decade of operation, and overseeing national book-based curricula and professional teacher training.

Sharon Kaplan-Berkley is an early childhood education teacher educator at Efrata Academic College of Education, Jerusalem, Israel. Her mentoring approach and coursework are grounded in socio-emotional learning and teaching, culturally responsive teaching, and values education. Her research explores aspects of young children's identity development, educators' professional identity, and digital pedagogy.

Margalit Kavenstock is an academic advisor, curriculum writer, and teachers' mentor, focused on teaching Hebrew language to young learners around the world. Working with Educating for Impact, she assists schools in building curriculum and training Hebrew teachers. She is also the Pedagogic Director of the hybrid program "Ivrit Misaviv La'Olam."

Lyndall Miller, Director of the Jewish Early Childhood Education Leadership Institute (JECELI) at the Jewish Theological Seminary of America, holds a doctorate in Jewish Education and master's degrees in Early Childhood Leadership, Special Education, and Jewish Education. Her work and her research interests focus on Jewish meaning-making by adults and children.

Meir Muller is Associate Professor in Early Childhood Education at the University of South Carolina, Columbia, in the United States, and cofounder of the Cutler Jewish

Day School. His research interests include cultural relevant pedagogy, justice pedagogy, and Jewish education.

Deborah Schein began a career in early childhood education in 1972, receiving her PhD in 2012, and now provides professional development for early childhood educators. She is an editor for *Soul to Soul*, an online journal, has written two books on spirituality, and continues to research the relationship between spiritual development, nature, play, peace, and well-being.

Mila Schwartz is Professor in Language and Education and Head of Research Authority in Oranim Academic College of Education, Israel. Her research interests include studying language policy and models of early language education; linguistic, cognitive, and sociocultural development of early sequential bilinguals/multilinguals; and family language policy.

Michael Shire is a rabbi and educator with a PhD in Jewish Education. Currently Academic Director of Jewish Education at Hebrew College, Massachusetts, United States, he was formerly Vice Principal of Leo Baeck College, London, UK. He is the founder of Torah Godly Play, a spiritual pedagogy for teaching the Jewish Bible.

Shira Ackerman Simchovitch is Director of Early Childhood at the TALI Education Fund, which provides Judaic enrichment in the Israeli school system. She is also a consultant to the JCCA SHEVA Center and has worked in the field of early childhood Jewish education in Israel and the diaspora for over four decades.

Ilene Vogelstein has extensive professional and volunteer experience in the Jewish community. Her primary focus is on early childhood Jewish education. She conducted the first survey on the state of Jewish preschools in America (2002) and is an adjunct faculty at Baltimore Hebrew Institute, Maryland, and Hebrew College, Massachusetts, United States.

Index

activity-based learning 17, 18, 25
administrators 40, 76
Arab 19, 58, 94, 131, 209
   population 23
arts 24, 48, 50, 56, 139–40
Ashkenazi 3, 73, 85, 92
   ritual 95
assessment 23, 53, 56
assimilation/assimilationist 33, 70–1, 72
autonomy/autonomous 25, 38, 131, 155, 157, 163, 168

Berryman, Rev. Jerome 177–80
Bible teaching 58, 115–25, 154, 177, 189
   approach 17
   challenges and Constructivism 108 (*see also* Constructivism)
   curriculum 18, 20, 24–5, 47, 50, 54
   gender 208
   multiculturalism 207 (*see* multiculturalism)
budget 21, 23, 194

ceremonies/celebrations 17, 86, 108, 147–9, 156–7, 207–8
   (*see also* under holidays/festivals)
Chabad 35, 40
change
   citizen/citizenship 48, 53
   independence 288
Civil Rights Movement 34, 71
cognitive (*see under* development)
collaboration/teamwork 163, 185, 194, 199, 201–2
community\communities 22, 25
   Black 75, 77
   engagement with 37, 74, 107
   of learners/practice 53, 60, 78–9, 100
   schools 90, 107, 200–1
   support 84, 87–91
   (*see also* values, community)

Conservative Judaism 56, 181
Constructivism 56, 58, 99–109
   Bible stories 119–20
   Hebrew classrooms 161–73
creativity 169, 177, 181
cultural
   agent 17, 148
   beliefs and practices 24, 56–7, 86, 89, 156–7
   contexts 197, 202
   diversity 92, 131, 150, 155–7
   education 69–79, 129, 172
   language 116
   norms 55, 155–7
   sensitivity 69–79, 92, 95
   values/valuing 115, 162
Culturally Relevant Pedagogy (*see* Pedagogy, Culturally Relevant)
culture 17, 18, 30
   national 117, 129–144
   school\classroom 52, 58, 91, 194, 200–1
curriculum/curricula
   Bible 116–18
   content 20, 24, 38, 40, 47, 49–50, 54, 71
   development 70–1, 77, 88, 116–17
   emergent 32, 143
   gender awareness 92
   Hebrew 208
   holiday 20
   humanistic 17
   Israeli national 15, 18–26, 54, 130,
   Multicultural 69–72, 74–9, 86, 88, 94–5
   resources 40
   United States programs 31, 38, 39–40, 52, 209

database 47–50
day schools 33, 35–7, 59, 76–8, 161–2, 181
democratic 71, 155

development
  affective/emotional 17, 20, 59, 83, 129, 138
  character 132
  cognitive 17, 48, 50, 58–9, 83
  moral 132
  physical/sensorimotor 17, 172
  social 20, 83, 208–9
  spiritual 55, 59, 152, 177–90, 208
developmentally/age appropriate 83, 105, 130–1, 169, 171, 172, 208
Dewey, John 17, 19
dialogue 25, 70, 75, 77, 87, 120, 143, 165, 194, 197, 199–200, 201, 202, 203
diaspora 45, 48, 50, 51, 60, 143, 147, 165
director 22, 30, 34, 35, 38, 40, 52, 116, 195, 200, 201
disability (*see* special education, needs)
discrimination 33, 201, 209
diversity 38, 69, 72, 74–5, 76, 77–8, 84, 86, 89, 92–3, 96, 100, 185, 207
  in books 132
  in Israel 23, 150
  value of 94, 96

educational approaches, 147
  Anthroposophic/Waldorf 21, 151, 152–3, 185
  Constructivist (*see also* Constructivism)
  Gan Zorem 18
  Junkyard 18
  Montessori 16–18, 21, 38, 148, 165, 178–9, 185, 188
  Reggio-inspired 31–2, 38, 185
  play-based 38, 83, 136, 185
educational challenges 29, 33, 35–7, 41, 54, 55, 76, 104, 107–9, 115, 116, 118–22, 173, 201, 204, 207
educational choices 34–5, 38, 57, 123, 124, 168, 179
educational decisions 22, 33–4, 34, 37, 41, 75, 200
educational mission 25, 29–30, 34, 42, 76, 117
educational practice 19, 49, 50, 59–60
  best 30–1, 25–6, 148
  classroom 74–5, 169, 172–3, 177–85
  leadership 203
  racist/anti-racist 72–9
  reading 143–4, 147–9
  school 72, 79, 152–7
  spiritual 185–90
  teacher training 87–96
  values and 73, 109
  (*see also* Jewish practice)
educational reform 20, 21, 71
educational services 20, 21, 41
educational structural underpinnings 45, 47, 49, 51
educational system 47, 59, 70, 71, 184
  Israeli 2, 3, 5, 15–25, 45, 85, 90, 94–5, 120, 121, 123, 135, 147, 155–6
  United States 2, 3, 5, 29–42, 45, 69
educators (*see* teacher/educator)
enrollment
  in Israel 21, 59
  in United States 33, 34, 35–6, 37, 39
environment
  Constructivist 99, 151, 161–3, 204
  family/home 96
  gender 91, 94, 94–5
  inclusive 88, 90, 91, 95
  Jewish 15, 31, 36, 95
  learning 60, 87, 90, 92, 95
  physical 24, 99, 101, 156
  preparing/creating 19–21, 33, 90, 96, 180, 185, 186, 196, 196–7, 208
  social 59, 88, 94, 150
ethnic/ethnicities 25, 58, 74, 78, 83, 89, 93, 94, 99, 100, 101, 135, 138, 139, 142
  customs/ritual/practices 19, 90
  identity 42, 149
European 17, 56, 77, 88
evaluation 47, 50, 51, 52, 143–4, 153
  evaluators 4, 79, 106, 169, 208
  program 54, 55–7, 60, 144
experiential learning 105, 106, 136, 204

facilitators 79, 173
faith 115, 120, 143, 154, 180, 181–2
  faith based schools 34, 72, 103
  faith development school 179, 180
family 23, 52, 53, 54, 89, 157, 162, 189
  activities 5, 23, 41, 52, 96, 115–16, 136, 139, 142, 143–4, 148, 149
  attitudes and beliefs 50, 142
  connection/engagement 3, 52, 57, 77
  customs/culture 93, 95, 96, 130, 137, 142, 144, 149

education 3, 50, 57, 58, 136, 137
identity 3, 42, 55, 89, 93, 142
influence 57, 89, 93, 95, 96, 209
non-Jewish 3, 55
outreach 39, 41–2
pedagogical considerations 50, 52–3, 56–7
federal (United States)
law 32, 35, 39
feminist approach 59, 92, 95–6, 100, 123–4
pedagogy 54, 85–6, 89, 92, 124
movement/revolution 16, 89
finances 42
difficulties 19
support/responsiblity 19, 136, 137
folk tale 132, 133, 135
Fowler, James 179–80
free choice 17, 18, 121
Freud, Sigmund 17, 18
Fröbel, Friedrich 16, 17, 148
funding 33, 34, 35, 42

Gan Zorem 18
gender 50, 56, 58, 60, 71, 84
awareness 59, 87–96, 162
Bible teaching, (*see* Bible Teaching)
equality/inequality 87, 88, 90, 95–6, 99–100
difference 157
identity 59, 60, 84, 87, 89, 99
issue 56, 60, 87, 89
roles 59, 89, 91, 92, 93, 95, 99, 157
separation 16, 17, 23, 24, 157
Godly Play 177–85
grandparents 38, 39, 93
guidance 19, 21, 39, 137, 163, 168
guidelines 20, 23, 31, 54, 70, 130, 136

Haas, Malka 18
Haredi/ultra-Orthodox 54, 55, 57, 150, 162
curriculum 117, 156
holiday and ceremonies 157
schools 16, 17, 19, 21, 144
teachers 23, 56, 58
Hebrew
calendar (*see* Jewish, calendar)
culture/values 16–17, 54, 169
curriculum 19, 25, 40, 50, 51–2
literacy 25, 143

literature 18, 20, 137, 144, 157
revival 16
second language 18, 19, 50, 52, 57, 60, 168–73
teaching 50, 54, 57
Hebrew Child 17, 18
hegemony 87, 90–1, 150, 207
hermeneutics 115, 124
history
Black 71, 77
early childhood Jewish education 15–22, 29–32
Jewish 18, 26, 135
Holocaust 47, 52, 55, 150
holidays/festivals 17, 24, 38, 86–7, 106, 132 (*see also* ceremonies and celebrations)
activities/experiences 39, 74, 105, 152, 154
ceremonies/celebrations 17, 18, 23, 86–9, 108, 147–57, 207–8
curriculum 19, 22, 29, 31, 51–2, 56, 60, 76, 92, 108
cycle 15, 18, 19, 24, 25, 149
Hanukkah 19, 31, 88, 105, 108, 147, 150, 155
Holocaust Day 52, 55, 150
Israeli Independence Day/Yom Ha'atzmaut 31, 38, 55, 107
Jerusalem Day 150
Literature 17, 135, 151
national 15, 148, 150, 151, 156
Passover 70, 73, 79, 88, 95, 99, 104–5, 107, 108, 117, 149, 150, 155
processions 147–9, 152–3
Purim 88, 104–5, 117, 150
Remembrance Day for Fallen Soldiers and Victims of Terror 55
ritual 17, 31, 32, 86–7, 89, 108, 147–57
Rosh Hashanah 31, 107, 150, 189
services/prayers 39, 55, 90, 95, 108, 148, 188
Shabbat (*see under* Sabbath/Shabbat)
Shavuot 107, 148–55
Sigd 150
Simchat Torah 151
stories 54, 92, 95, 104–6, 152
Sukkot 32, 107, 154, 189
teaching 17, 20, 38, 47, 54, 157

Tu Bishvat 39, 108, 147
home-based 22, 37, 130
homeschooling 32, 56, 57,

identity 17, 54, 78, 84, 86, 89, 93–4, 122, 136
   children 23, 34, 50, 73, 122, 177, 181
   cultural/ethnic 55–8, 59, 87, 89, 122, 134, 143, 207
   educational 120, 122
   family 55
   gender 57, 93–4
   Jewish 53, 66, 47, 50, 53, 55, 58, 73, 86, 89, 93, 129–31, 155, 196
   national 16, 129–44, 148
   professional 93, 96, 196
   religious 118, 120, 122, 207–8
   teacher/educator (*see under* teacher/educator, identity)
ideology
   institutional 152, 208
   teacher/educator 122
immigrant 18, 20, 70, 84, 131–2, 136, 137, 143, 148, 153, 209
inclusivity/inclusion 48, 59–60, 69, 77–8, 86, 88, 90–1, 95–6, 118, 137
independent schools 19, 21, 35, 37, 52, 131, 144
indoctrination (*see also* religious coercion) 132
infants/toddlers 20, 25, 29, 36–7, 52–3, 57, 78, 104
Input-Interaction-Output Hypothesis 161, 164
inquiry 30, 102, 177
instruction 16, 22, 25, 33, 35, 78, 104–5, 151, 163, 171–2
intellectual development (*see* cognitive development)
intervention 24, 94, 130, 137, 143
Israel Compulsory Education Law 16, 18, 20, 148
Israel
   culture 96, 124, 130, 134, 137, 143, 147, 149, 156–7, 162, 165
   history 15–21, 26, 46, 56, 92, 130, 135
   Land of Israel 117, 162
   Ministry of Education 3, 6, 19–22, 24–5, 117, 130–1, 137, 143, 152

society's attitudes/norms 23, 55, 117, 148–52, 157, 207
state education 15–26, 46, 83, 88, 116–7, 144, 149–57
state religious education 15–26, 46, 54, 58, 83, 88, 90, 116, 119–10, 155–7
teaching about and engagement with 38–9, 47, 49, 54–6, 162

Jewish
   blessing 25, 31, 38, 90–1, 151, 152–4, 189, 210
   calendar 15, 31, 47, 50, 54–5, 166, 188
   community 30, 37, 39, 55, 57, 89, 162, 177, 200–1, 203
   culture 17, 26, 72–3, 84, 95, 117, 124, 156, 188
   custom 73, 86, 95, 106, 135, 151, 153, 154, 155
   history 16–21, 26, 29–32, 56, 131, 135, 152
   identity 36, 41, 48, 53, 73, 86, 89, 94, 131, 144, 155
      children's 34, 58, 59, 92, 147–8
      (*see also* teacher, identity)
   learning 38, 39, 197–9, 203–4
   life 24, 26, 30, 34, 37, 42, 45, 92, 143, 195–6, 200, 203, 209
   literacy 25, 129–31
   literature 17, 18, 20, 45–60, 79, 108, 116–17, 129–44, 151, 197, 199, 208`
   liturgy 150, 177, 181, 209
   people 26, 38, 73, 75, 95, 104, 116, 117, 152, 157
   practice 20, 23–25, 31, 50, 55, 73, 83, 86, 89, 91, 95, 108, 131, 150–1, 155–7, 177, 181, 185, 188
   observance and ritual 25, 209
   prayer 25, 31, 48, 55, 90, 95, 188, 210
   ritual 30, 48, 86–7, 89, 132, 207
   studies 25, 35, 166, 197
   symbols 38, 54, 70, 88, 95, 117, 148, 151–2, 155, 157, 177, 179–81, 184, 185
   texts 16, 24, 25, 36, 115–19, 133, 137, 150, 179, 196–9, 202, 204, 209
   tradition (*see* Tradition, Jewish)
Jewish Community Center (JCC) 35, 37, 39, 40, 52

JCC Association of North American (JCCA) 37, 39, 40, 195
Jewish Early Childhood Education Initiative (JECEI) 31, 36, 39, 40, 52, 53, 57
Jewish Early Childhood Education Leadership Institute (JECELI) 31, 40

kibbutz 16, 21, 84, 148–9
  education 18, 21, 107, 124, 148–9, 151, 154–5,
kindergarten 16, 18, 23, 29, 35–6, 40, 46, 58–9, 87, 120, 123–4, 148–9, 161–2, 166–7
  prekindergarten 35–7, 166–7
knowledge 99–109
  Jewish 24–6, 35–6, 104–5, 117–8, 134, 178, 197–8, 203
  logico-mathematical, 101, 107
    physical 101, 104–5, 107
  social 96, 101–2, 104–5, 107–8

language
  acquisition/development 129, 140, 143, 161–75
  religious 23, 50, 177, 179–85, 189
language conducive strategies 161, 164, 168–9, 172
learning
  environment 15, 190, 83, 86, 88, 90–5, 105, 172
  Jewish 38–9, 196–202, 204
  materials/ tools 109, 125, 171
  by play/activity 17, 24–5, 83, 186
  process 99, 106, 109, 163–4, 168
leader/leadership 18–9, 84, 147, 173, 193–204
  capacities 18–19, 86, 194–204
  community 34, 41, 46
  development 39, 47, 51–2, 88, 198–9, 201, 203–4
  lay 34, 41, 46, 201
  non-Jewish 196, 202, 203
  school 70, 76, 78, 194, 196, 203
  shared 194, 202
  vision 194, 201,
legend 45, 104, 129, 132–3, 134–6, 148, 207
legislation 20, 22, 32–3, 35–6
Levine, Gideon 18, 20

licensing 19, 39–40
literature education 20, 47, 50, 54, 78, 78–9, 122
  Sifriyat Pijama 129–44

meaning making 179, 181, 184, 199
media 15, 48, 50–1, 56, 59, 134, 144
melting pot 6, 69–71, 73, 79
mentoring 9, 40, 84, 89–91, 194, 198–9, 202, 204
Mizrachi
  ethnicity 75, 84–5, 92, 94–5
  Political stream 149
model/modelling 102, 121, 164, 169, 171–3
Montessori, Maria 16–17, 148, 178–9
  approach 17–18, 21, 38, 165, 179, 185
moral/ethics education 48, 69, 84, 180, 183, 185, 187
  issues 109–10, 116, 118–9, 121–2, 132, 139
motivation 168–9, 171
  teacher 172, 208
multiculturalism 69–79, 84, 96, 132, 207–8, 209
  pedagogy (see pedagogy, multiculturalism)
  and teaching Bible 115–16, 120–2, 124
multimodality 169, 171–2
music 17, 48, 56, 58, 89, 172
  song, 17, 38, 56, 73, 88–90, 95, 106, 151–2, 153–4

National Association for the Education of Young Children (NAEYC), 30, 83
nature/natural world 32, 151, 154–5, 179, 185–9, 197, 208, 217
network 21, 30, 34, 39, 196
norms
  community/cultural 55, 118, 194

Orthodox Judaism 23, 29, 33, 59, 84, 92, 124, 132
  education 35, 40, 56, 58, 75, 90, 104, 123, 165
"other" the, 54, 88, 90, 120–2, 124, 180
outreach 20, 32, 39, 41, 57

Palestinian 56
Paradigm Project 141

parents, 41, 50–3, 56–7, 59, 84, 88, 93, 108, 162
   attitudes 48, 56, 76, 132
   choices 34, 36–7, 70–1, 93
   empowerment 131, 134, 137
   influence 56, 59, 189
   involvement/engagement 34, 37–9, 48, 50, 57–8, 75, 130, 137–44, 154–5, 165, 177
   needs 98
   parenting 39, 136, 143
   performances/ceremonies 108, 149, 157
pedagogy 18, 24–5, 38, 48–50, 54–60, 84, 197, 202
   Constructivist (*see* Constructivism) 20, 106–9, 119–20, 208, 209–10
   Critical Feminist (*see also* Feminist Approach, Pedagogy) 55, 85–6, 96
   Culturally Relevant 71, 74
   Culturally Responsive Teaching 84, 86
   European Kindergarten Movement 16
   multicultural 69–79, 208–9
   spirituality 55, 177–90
   teaching holidays 54–5
   teaching identity 55
Piaget, Jean 21, 34, 41, 97, 111, 113–14, 118, 124–5, 200
PJ Library®, 25, 39, 53–4, 57, 130
play 48, 91, 94, 131, 179, 208
   area 38, 93–4, 122
   based 38, 83, 136, 185
   drama 119, 148,
   free/open ended 17–18, 22, 24, 167, 185–6, 188–9
   learning through play 17, 19, 167, 169
   socio-dramatic 22, 93–4, 173
Pestalozzi, Johann Heinrich 16, 148
pluralism/pluralistic 42, 57, 71, 88, 96, 165
policy 45, 49, 52, 60,
   makers/making 19, 41, 45–7, 53, 150, 173
pre-k 32, 34, 40, 166
   universal 35–6
professional development
   Hebrew teachers 161
   in Israel 21, 24–5
   leadership, 199, 201, 204

literature 47, 50, 53–4
multicultural 74–5, 78
progressive education 16, 19–20, 71, 85, 149, 165

quality
   Hebrew teaching 161–4
   indicators of 24–5, 34, 52–3, 59, 143, 203
   literature 108, 131–3, 135, 140, 208
   standards 36, 39–40, 47, 53–4

reflective practitioner/reflection 46, 75–6, 83–4, 173, 184, 194, 196, 200, 202–3
Reform Judaism 2, 34, 37, 195
religiosity 24, 179, 181, 184
religious education 4, 32–4, 69, 124, 177, 180–1
   autoethnographic 87
   Christian 120
   ethnographic 58, 167
   funding 33–5
   future 178, 189, 203–4, 207–9
   Israeli Jewish 85, 117, 150 (*see also* state religious education and state education)
research
   literature 45–60, 103–4, 151
   narrative 57
   neuroimaging 171
   qualitative 47, 143, 167, 194
   quantitative 47
ritual 86–7, 89, 95, 150, 179 (*see also* Jewish ritual)
   high ritual/low ritual 155
   school 38, 147–57, 207
   for spiritual development 179–81, 184, 185

Sabbath/Shabbat 25, 30, 31, 38–9, 148–51, 188
   celebrations 18, 38, 90–1, 108, 148, 154
   literature 47, 54
   ritual 17, 135, 151, 157
sacred text 16, 24, 89, 121, 179–81, 197
Sacks, Lord Rabbi Jonathan 99, 109
scaffolding 163–4, 169, 180
second language learning 161–73 (*see also* language acquisition)
secular 18, 25, 34, 40, 58, 86, 155

culture 17, 87, 124, 131, 135, 149, 156
education 83, 91, 132, 177, 208
holiday 150
Israelis 132, 155–6
kibbutz 18, 149
schools 18–20, 34, 36, 39, 40, 149, 151–5
secularization 33, 149
student 118, 121–2
teachers 23, 24, 50, 84, 118, 122
sensory experience 32, 86, 100, 101, 172, 181, 208
Sephardi 21, 73, 75
separation of church and state 32–3
Sifriyat Pijama 25, 53, 54, 129–44
    Book selection 131–3
    evaluation of 53, 137–43
    impact 140–1
    shared reading and conversations 129–31, 136–8, 143–4
social critical consciousness 84, 88
social development (*see* development, social)
social justice 76, 84, 87, 201–2
    advocacy 194, 204, 207
    in books 132, 133
    focus 84, 87, 88, 94
    and inequity 69, 71–2, 74–5, 77–9, 132–3, 208
song (*see* music)
special education 48, 92
    Special Education Law 20
    special needs 24, 25, 48, 50, 56, 59, 60, 107, 133
spiritual moments 178, 185–9
spirituality 177–90
    and ritual 55, 177, 179, 180, 181, 184–5
    and values 48–9, 50, 54, 55
standards 21, 29–31, 39–40, 47, 53
storytelling 54, 104–6, 115–25, 129, 154, 177–9, 181–4
    sacred 95, 177–81, 184–5
    (*see also* Holiday, stories and PJ Library®)
supervision 19–22, 157
synagogue(s) 31, 32, 35, 39, 107, 117, 151–2, 154, 188
    Conservative 53, 84, 181
    Orthodox 149
symbols 155, 179–81, 184 (*see also* Jewish, symbols)

TALI schools 21, 25
teacher/educator
    attitude and beliefs 48, 50, 55–9, 76, 83, 87, 92, 116–25, 154, 156, 196, 208, 209
    benefits 24, 36
    certification 23–4
    education/training 15, 18–26, 35, 38, 40–1, 83–96, 118, 137, 162, 173
    identity 47, 54, 55, 56, 57, 58, 88–96, 118–24, 196, 198, 202, 207
    non-Jewish 203, 209
    recruitment and retention 35–6, 47
    salaries 24, 36, 201
    shortage of 40–1, 162
    supervision 19–24, 157
technology 24, 87, 136, 144
Temple in Jerusalem 148, 152, 153, 154
Torah 25, 31, 38, 45, 107, 109, 117, 123, 143
    Matan Torah 148–9, 151–5
Torah Godly Play 177–90
Total Physical Response 171
tradition 89, 120, 134, 184
    approach 103, 119, 157, 207–8
    blessing 151, 153–4, 188–9
    family 23, 134, 137
    holiday 19, 70, 74, 95, 105, 147
    Jewish 18, 20, 54, 72, 83, 109, 115–16, 118, 120, 130, 132, 134–5, 149, 150–1, 155, 181, 189, 193, 197, 198–9, 202, 208, 209
    new 157, 208
    Oral 134, 154
    sources/texts 17, 132, 193

Ultra-Orthodox (*see under* Orthodox Judaism and Haredi)
Union for Reform Judaism (URJ) 34, 37, 40
United States public school 3, 33–5, 73
Universal Education, 20, 35–6

values 121, 123, 124, 201
    community 106–7, 143
    cultural 86, 115, 162, 207
    curriculum content 48, 50, 54, 55
    democratic 155
    educational 70, 86, 119, 129–44
    humanistic 116
    Israeli 23, 130–44, 162

Jewish 20, 25, 31, 36, 38, 48, 72, 74, 92, 96, 106, 108, 130–44, 189, 198, 200, 201–2
liberal 124, 155, 207
national 46, 116–17, 121, 149, 155
personal/family 90–1, 93, 116, 120, 129–44, 208
religious 84, 115–16, 119, 120, 124, 150, 155, 156
teaching 36, 38, 55, 87, 88, 107, 108–9, 116–17, 119–21, 149, 207, 208
Zionist 50, 120
violence/terror 52, 56, 77, 150
vision 30, 34

leadership 104, 200–2
school 76–7, 207
voucher 33, 36
Vygotsky, Lev 20, 99–100, 162–3, 171

Waldorf (*see* educational Approaches)

Yishuv/pre-independence 15–18, 148, 151
pre-state 56, 116

Zionism/Zionist 16, 19, 50, 55–6, 84
movement 17, 148–9
religious 120, 149, 150, 155
(*see also* values, Zionist)

www.ingramcontent.com/pod-product-compliance
Lightning Source LLC
Chambersburg PA
CBHW062214300426
44115CB00012BA/2057